Access 97 One Step at a Time

Access 97
One Step at a Time

Julia Kelly

IDG Books Worldwide, Inc.

An International Data Group Company

FOSTER CITY, CA · CHICAGO, IL · INDIANAPOLIS, IN · NEW YORK, NY

Access 97 One Step at a Time

Published by
IDG Books Worldwide, Inc.
An International Data Group Company
919 E. Hillsdale Blvd., Suite 400
Foster City, CA 94404
www.idgbooks.com (IDG Books Worldwide Web site)

Library of Congress Catalog Card No.: 97-70943

ISBN: 0-7645-8027-2

Printed in the United States of America

10 9 8 7 6 5 4

1P/RT/RR/ZX/FC

Distributed in the United States by IDG Books Worldwide, Inc.

Distributed by Macmillan Canada for Canada; by Transworld Publishers Limited in the United Kingdom; by IDG Norge Books for Norway; by IDG Sweden Books for Sweden; by Woodslane Pty. Ltd. for Australia; by Woodslane Enterprises Ltd. for New Zealand; by Longman Singapore Publishers Ltd. for Singapore, Malaysia, Thailand, and Indonesia; by Simron Pty. Ltd. for South Africa; by Toppan Company Ltd. for Japan; by Distribuidora Cuspide for Argentina; by Livraria Cultura for Brazil; by Ediciencia S.A. for Ecuador; by Addison-Wesley Publishing Company for Korea; by Ediciones ZETA S.C.R. Ltda. for Peru; by WS Computer Publishing Corporation, Inc., for the Philippines; by Unalis Corporation for Taiwan; by Contemporanea de Ediciones for Venezuela; by Computer Book & Magazine Store for Puerto Rico; by Express Computer Distributors for the Caribbean and West Indies. Authorized Sales Agent: Anthony Rudkin Associates for the Middle East and North Africa.

For general information on IDG Books Worldwide's books in the U.S., please call our Consumer Customer Service department at 800-762-2974. For reseller information, including discounts and premium sales, please call our Reseller Customer Service department at 800-434-3422.

For information on where to purchase IDG Books Worldwide's books outside the U.S., please contact our International Sales department at 415-655-3200 or fax 415-655-3295.

For information on foreign language translations, please contact our Foreign & Subsidiary Rights department at 415-655-3021 or fax 415-655-3281.

For sales inquiries and special prices for bulk quantities, please contact our Sales department at 415-655-3200 or write to the address above.

For information on using IDG Books Worldwide's books in the classroom or for ordering examination copies, please contact our Educational Sales department at 800-434-2086 or fax 817-251-8174.

For press review copies, author interviews, or other publicity information, please contact our Public Relations department at 415-655-3000 or fax 415-655-3299.

For authorization to photocopy items for corporate, personal, or educational use, please contact Copyright Clearance Center, 222 Rosewood Drive, Danvers, MA 01923, or fax 508-750-4470.

 is a trademark under exclusive license to IDG Books Worldwide, Inc., from International Data Group, Inc.

ABOUT IDG BOOKS WORLDWIDE

Welcome to the world of IDG Books Worldwide.

IDG Books Worldwide, Inc., is a subsidiary of International Data Group, the world's largest publisher of computer-related information and the leading global provider of information services on information technology. IDG was founded more than 25 years ago and now employs more than 8,500 people worldwide. IDG publishes more than 275 computer publications in over 75 countries (see listing below). More than 60 million people read one or more IDG publications each month.

Launched in 1990, IDG Books Worldwide is today the #1 publisher of best-selling computer books in the United States. We are proud to have received eight awards from the Computer Press Association in recognition of editorial excellence and three from *Computer Currents'* First Annual Readers' Choice Awards. Our best-selling ...For Dummies® series has more than 30 million copies in print with translations in 30 languages. IDG Books Worldwide, through a joint venture with IDG's Hi-Tech Beijing, became the first U.S. publisher to publish a computer book in the People's Republic of China. In record time, IDG Books Worldwide has become the first choice for millions of readers around the world who want to learn how to better manage their businesses.

Our mission is simple: Every one of our books is designed to bring extra value and skill-building instructions to the reader. Our books are written by experts who understand and care about our readers. The knowledge base of our editorial staff comes from years of experience in publishing, education, and journalism — experience we use to produce books for the '90s. In short, we care about books, so we attract the best people. We devote special attention to details such as audience, interior design, use of icons, and illustrations. And because we use an efficient process of authoring, editing, and desktop publishing our books electronically, we can spend more time ensuring superior content and spend less time on the technicalities of making books.

You can count on our commitment to deliver high-quality books at competitive prices on topics you want to read about. At IDG Books Worldwide, we continue in the IDG tradition of delivering quality for more than 25 years. You'll find no better book on a subject than one from IDG Books Worldwide.

John Kilcullen
CEO
IDG Books Worldwide, Inc.

Steven Berkowitz
President and Publisher
IDG Books Worldwide, Inc.

Eighth Annual Computer Press Awards ≥1992

Ninth Annual Computer Press Awards ≥1993

Tenth Annual Computer Press Awards ≥1994

Eleventh Annual Computer Press Awards ≥1995

IDG Books Worldwide, Inc., is a subsidiary of International Data Group, the world's largest publisher of computer-related information and the leading global provider of information services on information technology. International Data Group publishes over 275 computer publications in over 75 countries. Sixty million people read one or more International Data Group publications each month. International Data Group's publications include: **ARGENTINA:** Buyer's Guide, Computerworld Argentina, PC World Argentina; **AUSTRALIA:** Australian Macworld, Australian PC World, Australian Reseller News, Computerworld, IT Casebook, Network World, Publish, Webmaster; **AUSTRIA:** Computerwelt Österreich, Networks Austria, PC Tip Austria; **BANGLADESH:** PC World Bangladesh; **BELARUS:** PC World Belarus; **BELGIUM:** Data News; **BRAZIL:** Annuário de Informática, Computerworld, Connections, Macworld, PC Player, PC World, Publish, Reseller News, Supergamepower; **BULGARIA:** Computerworld Bulgaria, Network World Bulgaria, PC & MacWorld Bulgaria; **CANADA:** CIO Canada, Client/Server World, ComputerWorld Canada, InfoWorld Canada, NetworkWorld Canada, WebWorld; **CHILE:** Computerworld Chile, PC World Chile; **COLOMBIA:** Computerworld Colombia, PC World Colombia; **COSTA RICA:** PC World Centro America; **THE CZECH AND SLOVAK REPUBLICS:** Computerworld Czechoslovakia, Macworld Czech Republic, PC World Czechoslovakia; **DENMARK:** Communications World Danmark, Computerworld Danmark, Macworld Danmark, PC World Danmark, Techworld Denmark; **DOMINICAN REPUBLIC:** PC World Republica Dominicana; **ECUADOR:** PC World Ecuador; **EGYPT:** Computerworld Middle East, PC World Middle East; **EL SALVADOR:** PC World Centro America; **FINLAND:** MikroPC, Tietoverkko, Tietoviikko; **FRANCE:** Distributique, Hebdo, Info PC, Le Monde Informatique, Macworld, Reseaux & Telecoms, WebMaster France; **GERMANY:** Computer Partner, Computerwoche, Computerwoche Extra, Computerwoche FOCUS, Global Online, Macwelt, PC Welt; **GREECE:** Amiga Computing, GamePro Greece, Multimedia World; **GUATEMALA:** PC World Centro America; **HONDURAS:** PC World Centro America; **HONG KONG:** Computerworld Hong Kong, PC World Hong Kong, Publish in Asia; **HUNGARY:** ABCD CD-ROM, Computerworld Szamitastechnika, Internetto online Magazine, PC World Hungary, PC-X Magazin Hungary; **ICELAND:** Tolvuheimur PC World Island; **INDIA:** Information Communications World, Information Systems Computerworld, PC World India, Publish in Asia; **INDONESIA:** InfoKomputer PC World, Komputek Computerworld, Publish in Asia; **IRELAND:** ComputerScope, PC Live!; **ISRAEL:** Macworld Israel, People & Computers/Computerworld; **ITALY:** Computerworld Italia, Macworld Italia, Networking Italia, PC World Italia; **JAPAN:** DTP World, Macworld Japan, Nikkei Personal Computing, OS/2 World Japan, SunWorld Japan, Windows NT World, Windows World Japan; **KENYA:** PC World East African; **KOREA:** Hi-Tech Information, Macworld Korea, PC World Korea; **MACEDONIA:** PC World Macedonia; **MALAYSIA:** Computerworld Malaysia, PC World Malaysia, Publish in Asia; **MALTA:** PC World Malta; **MEXICO:** Computerworld Mexico, PC World Mexico; **MYANMAR:** PC World Myanmar; **NETHERLANDS:** Computer! Totaal, LAN Internetworking Magazine, LAN World Buyers Guide, Macworld Netherlands, Net, WebWereld; **NEW ZEALAND:** Absolute Beginners Guide and Plain & Simple Series, Computer Buyer, Computer Industry Directory, Computerworld New Zealand, MTB, Network World, PC World New Zealand; **NICARAGUA:** PC World Centro America; **NORWAY:** Computerworld Norge, CW Rapport, Datamagasinet, Financial Rapport, Kursguide Norge, Macworld Norge, Multimediaworld Norge, PC World Ekspress Norge, PC World Nettverk, PC World Norge, PC World ProduktGuide Norge; **PAKISTAN:** Computerworld Pakistan; **PANAMA:** PC World Panama; **PEOPLE'S REPUBLIC OF CHINA:** China Computer Users, China Computerworld, China InfoWorld, China Telecom World Weekly, Computer & Communication, Electronic Design China, Electronics Today, Electronics Weekly, Game Software, PC World China, Popular Computer Week, Software Weekly, Software World, Telecom World; **PERU:** Computerworld Peru, PC World Profesional Peru, PC World SoHo Peru; **PHILIPPINES:** Click!, Computerworld Philippines, PC World Philippines, Publish in Asia; **POLAND:** Computerworld Poland, Computerworld Special Report Poland, Cyber, Macworld Poland, Networld Poland, PC World Komputer; **PORTUGAL:** Cerebro/PC World, Computerworld/Correio Informático, Dealer World Portugal, Mac*In/PC*In Portugal, Multimedia World; **PUERTO RICO:** PC World Puerto Rico; **ROMANIA:** Computerworld Romania, PC World Romania, Telecom Romania; **RUSSIA:** Computerworld Russia, Mir PK, Publish, Seti; **SINGAPORE:** Computerworld Singapore, PC World Singapore, Publish in Asia; **SLOVENIA:** Monitor; **SOUTH AFRICA:** Computing SA, Network World SA, Software World SA; **SPAIN:** Communicaciones World España, Computerworld España, Dealer World España, Macworld España, PC World España; **SRI LANKA:** Infolink PC World; **SWEDEN:** CAP&Design, Computer Sweden, Corporate Computing Sweden, Internetworld Sweden, it.branschen, Macworld Sweden, MaxiData Sweden, MikroDatorn, Natverk & Kommunikation, PC World Sweden, PCaktiv, Windows World Sweden; **SWITZERLAND:** Computerworld Schweiz, Macworld Schweiz, PCtip; **TAIWAN:** Computerworld Taiwan, Macworld Taiwan, NEW ViSiON/Publish, PC World Taiwan, Windows World Taiwan; **THAILAND:** Publish in Asia, Thai Computerworld; **TURKEY:** Computerworld Turkiye, Macworld Turkiye, Network World Turkiye, PC World Turkiye; **UKRAINE:** Computerworld Kiev, Multimedia World Ukraine, PC World Ukraine; **UNITED KINGDOM:** Acorn User UK, Amiga Action UK, Amiga Computing UK, Apple Talk UK, Computing, Macworld, Parents and Computers UK, PC Advisor, PC Home, PSX Pro, The WEB; **UNITED STATES:** Cable in the Classroom, CIO Magazine, Computerworld, DOS World, Federal Computer Week, GamePro Magazine, InfoWorld, I-Way, Macworld, Network World, PC Games, PC World, Publish, Video Event, THE WEB Magazine, and WebMaster; online webzines: JavaWorld, NetscapeWorld, and SunWorld Online; **URUGUAY:** InfoWorld Uruguay; **VENEZUELA:** Computerworld Venezuela, PC World Venezuela; and **VIETNAM:** PC World Vietnam.   3/24/97

CREDITS

Acquisitions Editor
John Osborn

Development Editor
Tracy Thomsic

Technical Editors
Marilyn Kyd
Maryann Brown

Copy Editors
Henry Abrecht
Carolyn Welch

Production Coordinator
Susan Parini

Book Designer
Seventeenth Street Studios

Graphics and Production Specialists
Renée Dunn
Kurt Krames
Shannon Miller
Maureen Moore
Trevor Wilson
Elsie Yim

Quality Control Specialists
Mick Arellano
Mark Schumann

Illustrator
David Puckett

Proofreader
Jennifer K. Overmyer

Indexer
Rebecca Plunkett

ABOUT THE AUTHOR

Julia Kelly is a respected writer and Access developer who has authored several computer-specific books, including *Microsoft Access for Windows 95 Step by Step*, *Microsoft Excel for Windows 97 Step by Step*, *Mastering Excel 5*, and *Discover Outlook 97*.

Julia is a former biotechnology laboratory scientist and United States Air Force pilot (she became the first female member of the Caterpillar Club after being ejected from a disabled aircraft and returned to earth via parachute). She now lives in Idaho.

WELCOME TO ONE STEP AT A TIME!

The book you are holding is very special. It's just the tool you need for learning software quickly and easily. More than a book, it offers a *unique learning experience*. Along with our text, the dynamic *One Step at a Time On-Demand* software included on the bonus CD-ROM in this book coaches you through the tutorials at *your own pace*. You'll never feel lost!

See examples of how to accomplish specific tasks. Listen to clear explanations of how to solve your problems.

Use the *One Step at a Time On-Demand* software in three ways:

- **Demo mode** shows you how to perform a task in movie-style fashion — in sound and color! Just sit back and watch the *One Step* software demonstrate the correct sequence of steps on-screen. Seeing is understanding!

- **Teacher mode** simulates the software environment so you can practice completing a task without worrying about making a mistake. The *One Step* software guides you every step of the way. Trying is learning!

- **Concurrent mode** allows you to work in the actual software environment while still getting assistance from the friendly *One Step* helper. Doing is succeeding!

Our goal is for you to learn the features of a software application by guiding you painlessly through valuable and helpful tutorials. Our *One Step at a Time On-Demand* software — combined with the step-by-step tutorials in our One Step at a Time series — will make your learning experience fast-paced and fun.

See it. Try it. Do it.

PREFACE

Welcome to *Access 97 One Step at a Time*. This book is part of a unique new series from IDG Books Worldwide, Inc. Our goal with this series is to help you with every step of learning the many features of Access 97.

This book has been designed to facilitate learning in the following ways:

- Your lessons are paced to present small, manageable chunks of information, so you never feel you're in over your head; you always feel prepared for each step you're asked to take.

- You learn Access 97 by doing; every lesson is packed with hands-on examples and procedures.

- Many figures accompanying the steps contain corresponding numbered callouts, so you can see the results of your actions.

- You are told at the start of each lesson what resources you need to master the lesson and how much time to set aside to complete it.

- A CD-ROM with practice files accompanies this book, so you can begin working in a typical database right from the first page.

Whom Is This Book For?

Access 97 One Step at a Time is for people who have a basic knowledge of computers and may or may not have used Access before. I assume you have rudimentary computer skills, such as turning on a computer, using a mouse and keyboard, and the like; however, I have provided detailed steps for each procedure I cover, so even readers with minimal knowledge will be comfortable with these lessons.

If you have used previous versions of Microsoft Access, but want to get up to speed with Access 97 quickly, this book is for you, too. You can read only those sections that relate to the portion of Access you want to brush up on, or you can start from Lesson 1 and proceed in a linear fashion through the entire book. I recommend the latter course if you consider yourself a rank beginner.

Special Elements to Help You Learn

In designing this series, we at IDG Books thought long and hard about how people learn. We came up with some features that are structured to make you feel in control of your learning, yet challenged in a way that keeps you interested. Every lesson has a consistent structure, so you can quickly become comfortable using all the following elements:

- **Stopwatch** Because the best way to learn is to complete each lesson without interruption, we've provided a Stopwatch symbol at the beginning of each lesson. This stopwatch tells you approximately how much time to set aside to work through the lesson.

- **Goals** The goals of each lesson are stated at the beginning, so you can anticipate what skills you will gain.

- **Get Ready** This section explains what you will need to complete the steps in the lessons and shows you an illustration of the parts of the database you will create in the process.

- **Visual Bonus** This is a one- or two-page collection of illustrations with callouts that help you understand a process, procedure, or element of an Access database more clearly.

- **Skills Challenge** Every lesson ends with a long exercise that incorporates all the skills you've learned in the individual exercises. The Fitness Challenge is a little less explicit about the steps to take, so you're challenged to remember some of the details you've learned. This exercise reinforces your learning and significantly improves your retention.

- **Bonus Questions** Sprinkled throughout the Fitness Challenge section are Bonus Questions. If you want to push yourself a little harder, you can answer these questions and check Appendix C to see if you got them right.

- **Troubleshooting** This section appears near the end of each Lesson and contains a table of troubleshooting questions and answers that address common mistakes or confusions that new users of Access often encounter.

- **Wrap Up** This section provides you with an overview of the skills you learned, as well as a suggested practice project you might try to get more experience with these skills.

Appendix B contains suggestions of real-world projects that give you further practice with Access 97. Projects, such as creating a client database, help you take that important step of applying what you've learned to your real-life work.

Finally, there are two elements you'll see sprinkled throughout the book, **Notes** and **Tips**. Notes provide some background or detail that helps you understand the feature being discussed. Tips offer time-saving recommendations, reassurances, or solutions to common problems.

How This Book Is Organized

Access 97 One Step at a Time has an easy-to-follow structure.

The Jump Start section, which precedes Chapter 1, introduces you to the principles and concepts behind databases. It gives you an overview of what a relational database does and how interrelated database objects work together to give you ready access to your data in any form you choose.

- **Part I** provides an overview of Access 97 to give you a feel for "the lay of the land" in a database environment. Lesson 1 is a look at the parts of a database and how they work together. Lesson 2 shows you how to create an Access 97 template database quickly using a wizard. You can begin using your own database before you even begin Part 2!

- **Part II** begins using the Fruitsweets database. The Lessons here focus on tables and queries and the most basic database procedures. Lesson 3 covers getting data into an existing table and exporting it to another program for further manipulation. In Lesson 4 you'll learn how to find specific records in a table by searching, sorting, and filtering, and how to print a table of data directly without first creating a report. Lesson 5 teaches you how to create new tables and define relationships between them, and Lesson 6 introduces queries, which are the heart of a relational database.

- **Part III** goes beyond the basic procedures, delving into forms and reports, which are convenient and attractive interfaces between your database and other users. Lesson 7 introduces you to forms and custom form design, and Lesson 8 shows you how to fine-tune your forms. Lesson 9 introduces you to reports and custom report design. If you want to skip Parts I and II and start at Lesson 7, copy the file FSPart3.mdb from the book's CD-ROM to your hard drive and use that database to do the lessons in Part III. The lessons build on one another throughout each part and throughout the book.

- **Part IV** guides you through creating an application out of the Fruitsweets database, with custom features and automated performance so that even a nonproficient user can use the Fruitsweets database. Lesson 10 is a brief introduction to macros—what they are and how you can use them to automate database procedures. In Lesson 11 you'll create a switchboard, and in Lesson 12 you'll create custom toolbars and menus. Finally, in Lesson 13, you'll polish your forms and learn how to publish information from your database on the Web. If you want to skip Parts I, II, and III and start at Lesson 10, copy the file `FSPart4.mdb` from the CD-ROM to your hard drive and use that database to do the lessons in Part IV.

- Finally, you'll find four appendixes: What's on the CD-ROM, Practice Projects and Database Design, Answers to Bonus Questions, and Installing Access 97. You'll also find a glossary and, of course, the CD-ROM with practice files.

Now that you know what's in store for you, you're ready to begin learning Access 97. Remember, go at your own pace, and have fun!

Conventions Used in This Book

These terms and conventions are used throughout the book to make your lessons easy to read:

Term or convention	Meaning
Click	Using the mouse, point to the specified item and click the left mouse button once.
Double-click	Using the mouse, point to the specified item and click the left mouse button twice in rapid succession.
Right-click	Using the mouse, point to the specified item and click the *right* mouse button once.
Drag	Move the mouse pointer over the specified item. Then press the left mouse button and move the mouse pointer while holding down the left mouse button. Release the mouse button to "drop" the item into a new location.

Term or convention	Meaning
Select	Highlight text by dragging over the specified words or characters. Highlight an item in a list by clicking it.
File ➢ Open	On the File menu, select the Open command. All menu command selections follow this format.
Enter, Tab, Shift, Ctrl	The Enter, Tab, Shift, and Ctrl keys on your keyboard.
Illustrations	All illustrations in the book occur just after the relevant step or comment in the text. There is no need to search for figure numbers; the visual reinforcement you need is always right where you need it.
Boldface text	In numbered steps, the actual text you type is in **boldface**.

What's in the Practice Database?

The practice database is a typical database for a mail-order business, in this case a fictitious outfit called Fruitsweets. Fruitsweets packages different kinds of fruits into a variety of giftpaks that customers can order and have shipped to themselves or to friends.

In these lessons, you manage the Fruitsweets database. Others in the company have access to the database, to enter data and perform other simple procedures, but you are the designated Access 97 "expert" for Fruitsweets.

You'll create a new folder named "Access One Step at a Time" on your hard drive and then copy the beginning database, named `Fruitsweets.mdb`, and the accessory files (some Microsoft Excel and bitmap files) into the new folder. The book and practice files are designed so you only need to use the `Fruitsweets.mdb` database file, and you'll continue using the same database as you work through each lesson in the book.

- If you begin the book in Lesson 1 and work straight through the entire book, you can work in the same Fruitsweets database for each lesson. In each lesson, you'll build new parts of the database that you'll use in later lessons, so the Fruitsweets database will grow as you work through the book.

- If you want to begin working in Part III instead, you can copy the file FSPart3.mdb into your Access One Step at a Time folder and start working in that database, beginning with Lesson 7. The FSPart3.mdb database contains everything completed up to the end of Part 2.

- If you want to begin working in Part IV, you can copy the file FSPart4.mdb into your Access One Step at a Time folder and start working in that database, beginning with Lesson 10. The FSPart4.mdb database contains everything completed up to the end of Part III.

- If you want to take a look at what the database will look like when you finish the book, open the FSFinal.mdb database.

That's it! Sit back, relax, and enjoy your sessions with your own *Access 97 One Step at a Time*.

ACKNOWLEDGMENTS

I am grateful for the efforts of everyone who helped with this book—especially my delightful uber-editor (and fellow member of the Irregardlessly Disorientated and Derivatized Words fan club), Tracy Thomsic; my agent, Chris Van Buren (of Waterside Productions, Inc.), who finds me books to write and then motivates me to write them; Marilyn Kyd and Mary Ann Brown, my patient technical editors, who made the book so much better by pointing out the things that didn't make sense; hard-working copy editors Henry Abrecht and Carolyn Welch, for tying up loose ends and tracking down inconsistencies; John Osborn, Jr., the acquisitions editor who gave me this book to write; Marla Timmons, Armelle O'Neal, Leanda Lelani Keahi Bevans, Beth Biggs, and Kurt Hampe, for plying me with entertaining e-mail which always brightened up my day, even during Ice Storm '96; and everyone behind the scenes at IDG Books whose efforts were invaluable in bringing *Access 97 One Step at a Time* to bookstores everywhere.

Special thanks to Tom McCaffrey, Marilyn Russell, and everyone at Real Help Communications, Inc. (http://www.realhelpcom.com) for creating the several thousand sound files required for the CD-ROMs in this series, under very aggressive deadlines.

Thank you, everyone.
Julia Kelly

CONTENTS AT A GLANCE

CONTENTS

Jump Start

GOALS

In this section, you'll learn the following:

15 MINUTES

- Definitions of the terms *record, field,* and *relational database*

- What *related tables* are

- Why databases use related tables

- How you can use relationships between tables to retrieve just the data you want

Get ready

GET READY

You're about to learn how to use Microsoft Access 97, a full-featured relational database program. Of course, you'll learn how to enter data and extract it in an existing database, but you'll also learn a great deal more. You'll create new database objects, such as tables, forms, and reports and then customize them to make an existing database more useful. You'll also create new databases and automate some database procedures to make your database easier to use for someone unfamiliar with Access.

Before you start to click and drag and enter and create items in a database, it's helpful to understand just what a database is—since it's nothing like a Word document or a PowerPoint presentation, and it's only slightly similar to an Excel workbook. Because I like to know where I'm going before I start a journey, I'm going to make sure you do, too. This Jump Start introduces the principles and concepts behind a relational database. If you're already familiar with Access or other relational databases, this will be old news to you, so you should feel free to skip right to Lesson 1. If you're new to databases, this Jump Start will give you a better idea of what a relational database is and how it works.

For this Jump Start, you don't need to turn on your computer yet.

UNDERSTANDING DATABASES

A *database* is a list of information, organized into rows (called *records*) and columns (called *fields*). A database can be as simple as a single list of phone numbers: a column for names, a column for numbers, and many rows of name–number combinations. In database terminology, the columns are the Name and Number *fields*, and each name–number combination is a *record*. The accompanying illustration shows a simple database.

Of course, a database as simple as a phone list doesn't require an actual database program such as Access. You can keep a single list in a spreadsheet file, such as Microsoft Excel, or even in a text-based file, such as Microsoft Word. The advantage and power of a *relational* database become apparent when you have two or more lists of data that are about different subjects, and the lists are *related* to each other.

Understanding databases

For example, suppose you're a school attendance secretary in charge of the lists of student contact information (addresses and phone numbers) and enrollment information (which students are in which classes). Each list of information pertains to a specific subject, student contact information or class enrollment, but the two types of lists are related by the students' names. You could keep all the information in a single list (called a *flat-file database*) in a spreadsheet program such as Excel, but you'd have to repeat all the student information for every class each student is enrolled in, which is repetitious and inefficient as you can see in the accompanying illustration.

In a relational database, each student's information is recorded only once, in the Student Information list. Each student's record in the Student Information list is assigned an identification (ID) number, and those ID numbers are used to identify the students in the Class Enrollment lists. Each Class Enrollment list contains only information about which students are in that class. All lists are concise and efficient, and none of the information is repeated.

The lists, or *tables*, are related to each other by the student ID numbers. You can use this relationship to retrieve related information from two different tables. For example, you can create a report showing the phone numbers of all students in a specific class, as shown in the accompanying illustration.

This example illustrates a basic characteristic of relational databases. But Microsoft Access 97 can do a lot more, such as create forms for easy data entry, validate data entry to ensure that only the correct type of data is entered, customize the look of printed reports, calculate totals, move data into a spreadsheet program for more advanced mathematical calculations, and automate procedures by using macros. You'll learn how to do all these things in this book.

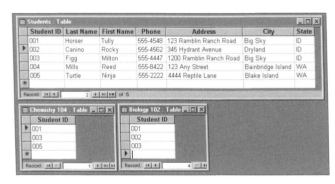

NOTE

If you have an existing database created in a previous version of Access, you can convert it to Access 97 by simply opening it in Access 97 and clicking Yes when Access asks if you want to convert it. But you can't convert it back to the previous version, so if there's a chance you might need to use a database in its original version, copy it and convert the copy to Access 97.

Wrap up

WRAP UP

You ran through several key concepts and principles of relational databases, including the following:

- Records and fields
- Related tables
- Efficient data storage
- Retrieval of data from multiple tables

In the process, you got an overview of the relational database landscape and an understanding of what makes relational databases tick—why a relational database is constructed the way it is and how that makes data storage more efficient.

In the following lessons, you'll work with the many objects in a database, such as tables, forms, reports, and queries. You'll learn how to create new objects and how to modify those objects to be customized and more functional.

An Overview of Access

This part provides an overview of Access 97 to give you a feel for "the lay of the land" in a database environment, and includes the following lessons:

- Lesson 1: Getting Acquainted and Getting Started—this lesson is a look at the parts of a database and how they work together.

- Lesson 2: A Quick Tour of Access—this lesson is a guided tour through the quick creation of one of Access 97's template databases using a wizard, to show you how quickly you can create and use a brand new database. After you complete Lesson 2, you can create and use a database for your own information before you do any more lessons in the book!

To work the lessons in this part, use the practice database file named `Fruitsweets.mdb` This is the database file you'll use throughout the book lessons; later lessons in the book will build further on the objects you create in this file in the early lessons.

Getting Acquainted and Getting Started

20 MINUTES

GOALS

In this lesson, you'll master the following skills and concepts:

- Starting Access
- Opening the practice database
- Looking at tables
- Looking at forms
- Looking at queries
- Looking at reports
- Getting help from the Office Assistant
- Closing the database and exiting Access

Starting Access

GET READY

To complete this lesson's exercise, you must have installed Microsoft Access 97 and the practice database from the One Step at a Time CD-ROM that accompanies this book. (See Appendix A, What's on the CD-ROM, for help with installing the practice database, and see Appendix D, Installing Access 97, for help installing Access.)

   When you finish these exercises, you'll know how to start Access, open a database, close a database, and exit Access. You'll also be familiar with the essential parts of a database, including tables, forms, queries, and reports.

TRY OUT THE

INTERACTIVE TUTORIALS

ON YOUR CD!

STARTING UP

Windows 95 provides several ways to start Access, or any other program, but we'll use the simplest in this exercise.

▶ Starting Access

Most computers are configured to load Windows when you first turn on the computer, so you'll start there.

1 Turn on your computer and let Windows load.

2 On the Windows taskbar, click the Start button.

3 Point to Programs.

4 Click Microsoft Access.

NOTE

When you installed Microsoft Office, it may have installed itself to a different folder, such as the Microsoft Office folder. If you don't see Microsoft Access on the Programs list, click the Start button; then point to Programs; then point to Microsoft Office; then click Microsoft Access.

Opening the practice database

The Access window opens, and the Microsoft Access dialog box appears, as shown in the accompanying figure.

 NOTE *If you have the Office Assistant installed, you may see the Office Assistant's welcome message first. Click the Start Access option button, and the Microsoft Access dialog box appears.*

Opening the practice database

If you just finished Exercise 1, the Microsoft Access dialog box is displayed in the Access window, and you can make a selection now.

 TIP *If you haven't installed the practice database provided in the back of this book, do so now. The installation instructions are simple. They can be found in Appendix A, What's on the CD-ROM.*

1 Be sure the Open An Existing Database option button is selected.

2 Click OK.

The Open dialog box appears, as shown in the accompanying figure, usually opened to your Personal or My Documents folder, depending on how Microsoft Office installed itself.

 NOTE *If you've been working in another database and already have Access open, you'll need to use a different method to open the practice database. On the toolbar, click Open Database, and the Open dialog box will appear.*

3 In the Open dialog box, click the Look In Favorites button.

Starts the Database Wizard

Opens a new, empty database

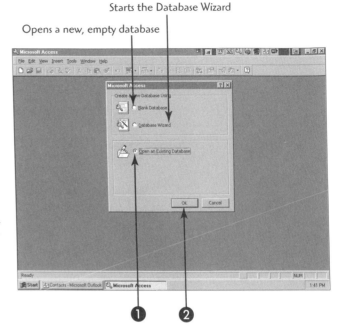

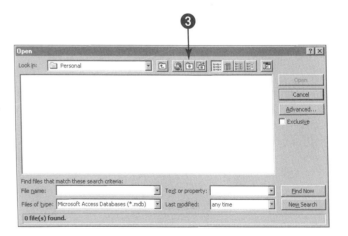

Opening the practice database

4 Double-click the Access One Step at a Time folder.

The Open dialog box shows the list of databases in the Access One Step at a Time folder, which is where your database, `Fruitsweets.mdb`, was installed.

5 Double-click the `Fruitsweets.mdb` file.

NOTE *The beginning database is called* `Fruitsweets.mdb`. *There are other databases on the CD-ROM—* `FSPart3.mdb`, `FSPart4.mdb`, *and* `FSFinal.mdb`—*which you can copy onto your hard drive and use if you want to jump into the book at Part II, Part III, or Part IV, or if you want to see the finished database (FSFinal.mdb). If you work through this book from the beginning, continue to use the file* `Fruitsweets.mdb` *in all of your lessons.*

The Fruitsweets database window appears on the screen, as shown in the accompanying figure.

Now that the practice database is open, let's take a look at what's in it.

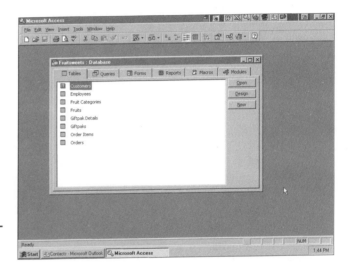

THE PARTS OF A DATABASE

The database window is the central location for all the database parts.

The parts of a database all work together: data is stored in *tables* and can be entered in those tables directly or by using *forms*; tables can be related to one another, and specific data can be retrieved from one or more tables by using *queries*; forms and *reports* can be based on queries, which allow both forms and reports to display data from two or more tables.

VISUAL BONUS

Database Parts

This Visual Bonus shows you the parts of a database and how they all work together.

A database is a container for tables, queries, forms, and reports.

Use tables to store data efficiently (this table stores data about the fruits that Fruitsweets uses).

Click the Tables tab and double-click the table name to open it.

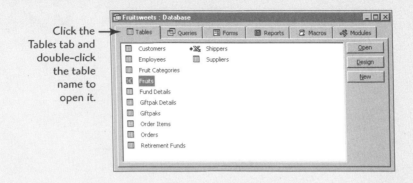

Records

Total number of records

Selected record

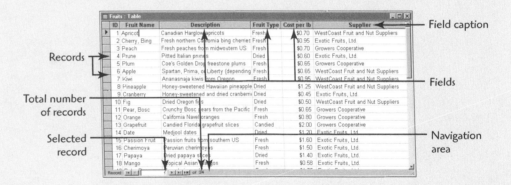

Field caption

Fields

Navigation area

continued

1

Getting Acquainted and Getting Started

Opening the practice database

Title bar → 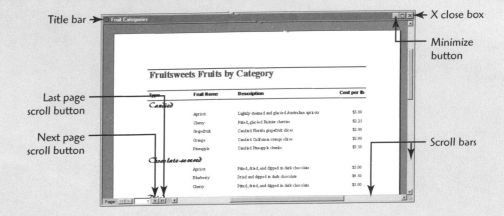 ← X close box

Minimize button

Last page scroll button

Next page scroll button

Scroll bars

Use reports to present data in an easy-to-read format.

Label

First record scroll button

Use forms to enter data into tables.

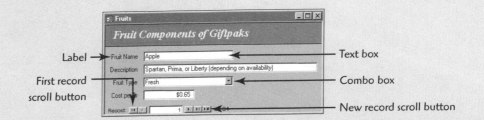

Text box

Combo box

New record scroll button

Sorted field

Records

Use queries to compile selected data from tables; then build forms and reports from queries.

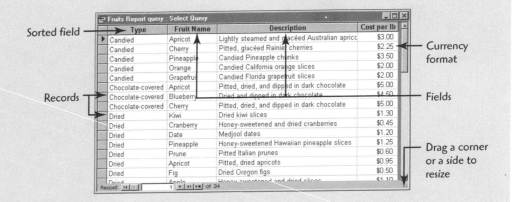

Currency format

Fields

Drag a corner or a side to resize

Looking at tables

A table is the basic data container—all the data stored in an Access database is stored in tables. *Data* (information) consists of *records* (rows) and *fields* (columns). A field is a category of information, such as Name or Street Address, and a record is the set of fields for a specific item (for example, all the information about a customer). Each table contains information about a specific topic, such as a Customers table for customer names and addresses or an Orders table to record orders from various customers.

In the following exercise, you'll open a table in the Fruitsweets database and take a tour through common table elements.

1 In the database window, verify that the Tables tab is displayed; if it's not, double-click the Tables tab to display it.

2 Double-click the Fruits table.

The Fruits table opens in Datasheet view, as shown in the accompanying figure.

3 In the ID field, click in the gray box to the left of the number 5.

Record number 5 is selected.

4 In the navigation area, click the Last Record scroll button.

The last record in the table is selected.

NOTE *The navigation area tells you which record is selected and how many records are in the table.*

5 Click the New Record scroll button.

A new record is selected and ready for entering data.

6 Click the First Record scroll button.

The first record in the table is selected.

7 On the toolbar, click the View button.

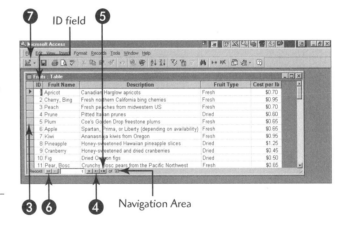

ID field

Navigation Area

Getting Acquainted and Getting Started

1

Looking at forms

The table switches to Design view, as shown in the accompanying figure.

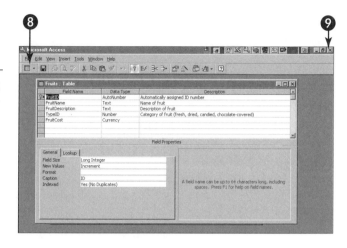

Each time you select a different view, the View button face changes to show another view you can select. For example, when Datasheet view is displayed, the View button shows the Design view face, which you can click to display Design view.

8 Click the View button again.

The table switches back to Datasheet view.

9 Click the table's X close box.

The Fruits table closes.

The accompanying illustration shows some Datasheet view elements you'll want to be familiar with. The toolbar that appears is specific to the view that's displayed—a table in Datasheet view has a different toolbar than a table in Design view. The toolbar buttons aren't identified because they identify themselves—you'll see a ToolTip (button name) whenever you hold the mouse pointer over a button.

You'll learn more about creating and using tables in Lesson 5.

Looking at forms

A form is a convenient way to enter or find data in tables. Although you can enter data directly in a table, it's often easier to enter data in a form. This method is especially useful if someone unfamiliar with Access is entering data in the database. Another advantage of using a form is that you can show and enter data in several different tables if the form is based on a query.

In the following exercise, you'll open a form and get acquainted with common form elements. The form you'll open (Fruits) is based on the table you opened in the previous exercise, so the field names will look familiar. You can use this form to enter data in the Fruits table.

View button   Current record

Selected   Scroll   Total records in table

1 In the database window, click the Forms tab.

2 Double-click the Fruits form.

The Fruits form opens in Form view, and the first field is selected, as shown in the accompanying figure.

3 Press the Tab key.

The next field in the form is selected.

4 Press the Tab key three more times.

Each field is selected in turn; then the next record appears in the form.

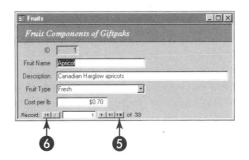

TIP

To back up to a previous field, press Shift + Tab.

5 In the navigation area, click the New Record button.

A new record is opened for data entry.

6 In the navigation area, click the First Record button.

The first record in the Fruits table is displayed.

7 On the toolbar, click the View button. [icon]

The form switches to Design view, and the Form Design toolbar replaces the Form View toolbar.

8 Drag the lower right corner of the form window down and to the right until you can see the entire form, as shown in the accompanying figure.

9 On the toolbar, click the View button. [icon]

The form switches to Form view.

10 Select Window.

11 Select Size To Fit Form.

The form window is resized to fit the form.

Controls Toolbox

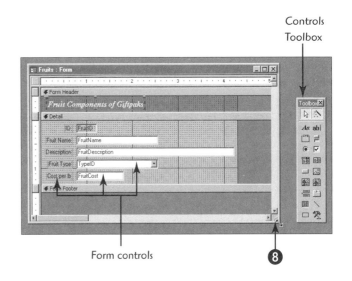

Form controls

Getting Acquainted and Getting Started

1

Looking at queries

⑫ Click the form's X close box to close the form.

In the accompanying figure you'll see some common elements of forms in Form view. You'll learn more about creating and using forms in Lesson 7.

Looking at queries

Tables can be related to one another, which is the reason for using a relational database such as Access (instead of a spreadsheet or a text list). For example, Customers and Orders tables can be related to each other by assigning an identification (ID) number to each customer in the Customers table and then entering the customer's ID number for each order in the Orders table. This ability to relate tables prevents the storage of redundant information because you don't have to enter the customer name, address, phone number, and so forth for each order—you enter only the customer ID number. When you want to find the customer information for a specific order, you use a query to look it up.

A query retrieves specific data from a table or from two or more related tables. A query can retrieve records and/or fields that meet specific criteria you set (such as records for only dried fruits or all orders placed in June). The result of a query is called a *dynaset* and consists of just the information you designed the query to retrieve. A query's dynaset can be presented in a table format, in a form, or in a report.

In the following exercise, you'll open a query that displays records from the Fruits table, which you saw earlier, and a related table, Fruit Categories.

❶ In the database window, click the Queries tab.

❷ Double-click the Fruits Report query.

The query opens in Datasheet view, as shown in the accompanying figure. It looks just like a table, but the title bar tells you this is a query.

❸ On the toolbar, click the View button. 📊 ▾

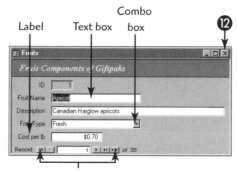

Combo
Label   Text box   box   ⑫

Record navigation area

The query switches to Design view, as shown in the accompanying figure.

The query design view shows the tables the query is based on and the fields from those tables that are displayed in the query's dynaset.

4 Click the query's X close box to close the query.

You'll learn more about creating and using queries in Lesson 6.

Looking at reports

A report is an organized presentation of data from a table or a query that's designed to be printed. Reports can calculate and show subtotals and totals, and they can have any number of formatting and graphic elements that make the report easier to read. Reports can be generated from a single table or from a query of two or more tables.

In the following exercise, you'll open and cruise through a report that's based on the query you opened in Exercise 5.

1 In the Database window, click the Reports tab.

2 Double-click the Fruits by Category report.

The Fruits by Category report opens in Print Preview, as shown in the accompanying figure.

What you see is how the printed report will appear. Because the report is based on a query that draws data from two related tables, the report can display data from both tables (Type from the Fruit Categories table; and Name, Description, and Cost from the Fruits table).

TIP

The report title may be truncated; you'll learn to fix this in Lesson 9.

3 Move the mouse pointer over the report until it becomes a zoom pointer, which looks like a magnifying glass.

Related tables

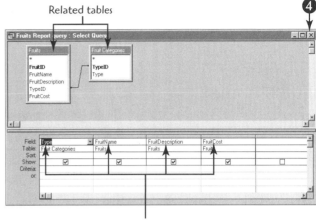

Fields shown in query

Zoom

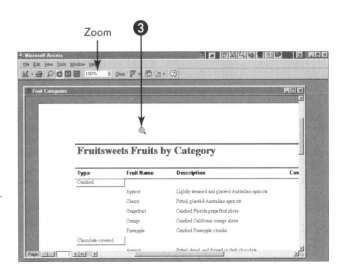

Looking at reports

4 Click the zoom pointer on the report.

The magnification changes, so you can see the full printed page.

> **TIP**
>
> *To see the report at an intermediate magnification (for example, 75 percent) click the down arrow in the toolbar Zoom box and select a different number, or type a number not shown on the list.*

5 On the toolbar, click the Two Pages button. 🔲

The report's two pages are displayed, as shown in the accompanying figure.

6 Click the zoom pointer on one of the pages.

The window zooms in for a close-up view of the area you clicked.

7 On the toolbar, click the View button. 🖉▾

The report switches to Design view, as shown in the accompanying figure.

> **TIP**
>
> *This might look confusing now, but you'll understand it after you finish Lesson 9.*

8 On the toolbar, click the View button. 🔍▾

The report switches back to Print Preview.

9 Click the report's X close box to close the report.

You'll learn to create and customize reports in Lesson 9.

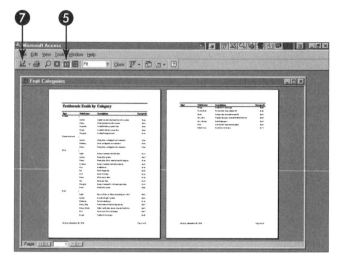

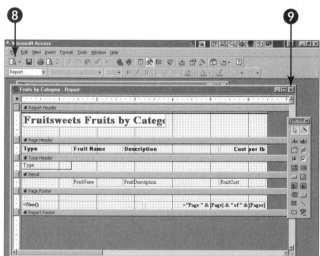

GETTING HELP

Occasionally, you'll need a little help remembering how to perform an operation, or you'll want to learn how to do something new and more advanced. You can look up your question in the Access Help files (on the Help menu, click Contents And Index), or you can ask the Office Assistant to help you.

To demonstrate the Office Assistant's expertise, let's look for help with tables.

Getting help from the Office Assistant

❶ On the toolbar, click Office Assistant. 🔲

The Office Assistant appears on your screen, probably dancing or gyrating in an attempt to seem friendly.

❷ Click in the Type Your Question Here box.

❸ Type **table**.

❹ Click Search.

The word "table" covers a broad range of subject matter, so the Office Assistant displays a list of topics that might interest you.

❺ Click the Tables: What They Are And How They Work option button.

A Help file appears, as shown in the accompanying figure. This one contains three parts (see the numbers in the upper left corner).

❻ Click the items you want to know about.

❼ When you finish reading this Help file, close it by clicking its X close box.

If you leave the Office Assistant on your screen, it'll keep trying to help you. Sometimes this is welcome, but it can be annoying.

❽ To banish the Office Assistant temporarily, click its X close box.

TIP To change the Office Assistant character, right-click the Office Assistant title bar; then click Choose Assistant. Follow the instructions in the Office Assistant dialog box to select a new assistant (I like the Mother Earth character best).

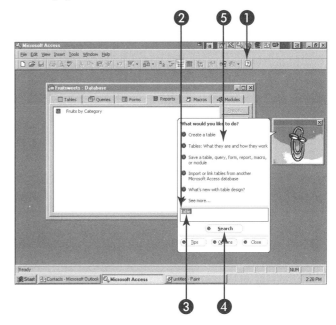

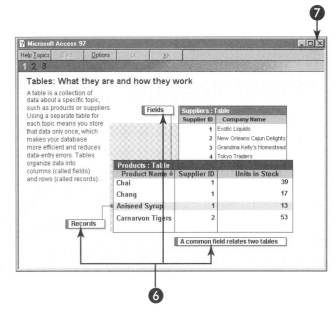

Closing the database

CLOSING ACCESS

When you finish working in a specific database, you need to close it; and when you're finished with Access, you'll need to close it, too.

Closing the database and exiting Access

1 To close the Fruitsweets database, on the File menu, click Close.

2 To exit Access, on the File menu, click Exit.

> **TIP**
> *You can also close the database and Access by clicking their respective X close boxes.*

SKILLS CHALLENGE: SPRINTING THROUGH THE PARTS OF A DATABASE

In this Skills Challenge, you'll run through the parts of a database just like you did in the previous exercises, but without any extra help along the way.

1 Start Access.

2 Open the Fruitsweets database.

3 Open the Giftpaks table.

 Do you remember how to open a new record?

 How can you switch to Design view?

4 Close the Giftpaks table.

5 Open the Giftpaks form.

 Do you remember how to size a form window to fit the form?

TRY OUT THE
INTERACTIVE TUTORIALS
ON YOUR CD!

6 Close the Giftpaks form.

7 Open the Fruits Report query.

 4 *How can you tell if this datasheet view is a table or a query?*

 5 *How can you find out what table or tables a query is based on?*

8 Close the query.

9 Open the Fruits By Category report.

 6 *How can you see the entire page?*

10 Close the report.

11 Close the Fruitsweets database.

TROUBLESHOOTING

You've learned your way around the parts of a database — tables, forms, queries, and reports. The following solutions might answer some questions that came up during this lesson.

Problem	Solution
I double-clicked a table (or form or query or report) to open it, and instead of opening, the name got highlighted with a box around it.	You need to speed up your double-click. If you double-click too slowly, Access thinks you're clicking twice (not a double-click) and highlights the name for renaming. Until you get the hang of double-clicking quickly, click once on the name and then click the Open button.

continued

Wrap up

WRAP UP

Problem	Solution
I can't see the navigation area at the bottom of my table.	Your table is probably just too low in your Access window. You can maximize the table (click the Maximize button or double-click the table's title bar) or drag the table upward by dragging its title bar.
I can't abide that Office Assistant. How can I make it go away?	You can hide it (right-click its title bar; then click Hide Assistant), or you can remove it (click the Start button; then point to Settings and click Control Panel; then double-click Add/Remove Programs; then select Microsoft Office 97, click the Add/Remove button, and follow the instructions to remove the Office Assistant).

WRAP UP

Before you finish, let's go over some of the things you learned in this lesson:

- You learned how to start Access.

- You learned how to open a database.

- You got familiar with the parts of a database, including tables, forms, queries, and reports.

- You learned how to get help from the Office Assistant.

- You learned how to close a database and exit Access.

For more practice, open the database again and cruise around in it at your leisure.

In the next lesson, you'll see how easy it is to create your own database by letting Access Wizards do the work for you.

A Quick Tour of Access

20 MINUTES

GOALS

In this lesson, you'll master the following skills and concepts:

- Creating a database
- Entering data
- Printing a report
- Deleting a database

Creating a database

GET READY

This lesson won't use any practice files because you'll be learning how to create a new database from scratch. All you need to do to begin this lesson is turn on your computer and start Windows.

TRY OUT THE

INTERACTIVE TUTORIALS

ON YOUR CD!

USING A WIZARD TO CREATE A DATABASE

The purpose of this lesson is to show you how quickly you can create and start using your own database. The Database Wizard builds it for you and works rapidly, but it also does the work behind the scenes. The advantage is that you can start using Access immediately. The disadvantage is that you don't know how it's constructed, so personalizing it can be difficult until you understand how the database is put together.

Nevertheless, it's exciting to be able to start using Access 97 right away instead of spending hours learning how to put it together first, so here goes. You'll create an address book database, and you'll instruct the wizard to include sample data in the database so you can see it in action and have a report to print after the database is built.

Creating a database

You'll begin by starting Access, but instead of opening the Fruitsweets database, you'll start the Database Wizard.

1 Click the Start button.

2 Point to Programs and click Microsoft Access.

3 In the Microsoft Access dialog box, click the Database Wizard option button.

4 Click OK.

The New dialog box appears, as shown in the accompanying figure.

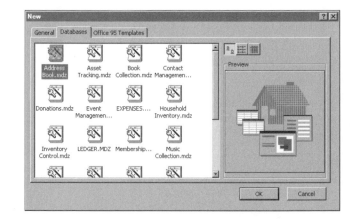

24   ACCESS 97 ONE STEP AT A TIME

TIP

You can also start the Database Wizard by selecting File ➢ New Database.

5 Click the Databases tab (if it's not already selected).

6 Double-click `Address Book.mdz`.

The File New Database dialog box appears, as shown in the accompanying figure, so you can name and save the new database. The filename should already be selected. If it's not, drag across the filename to select it.

7 Type **My Address Book**.

8 Click the Create button.

The Database Wizard starts, and an informational dialog box appears.

9 Click Next.

The second wizard dialog box appears and shows you what tables and fields will be included in the database, as shown in the accompanying figure. (The Address Book database has only one table.)

10 Click the Yes, Include Sample Data check box.

11 Click Next.

The third wizard dialog box appears. Here you can choose a background pattern for windows in your database, as shown in the accompanying figure.

12 Select Standard.

13 Click Next.

TIP

You can select a different pattern if you prefer. I selected the Standard pattern because it looks clearest in these book illustrations.

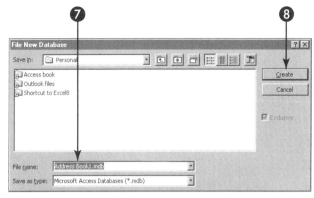

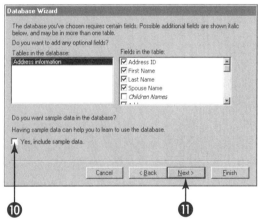

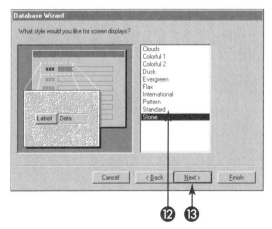

Entering data

The fourth wizard dialog box appears. Here you can choose a default style for printed reports, as shown in the accompanying figure.

NOTE *Your wizard might default to a different style, depending on what style was selected the last time this wizard was run.*

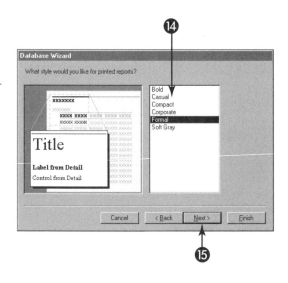

⑭ Select Casual.

⑮ Click Next.

⑯ The fifth wizard dialog box appears. Here you can give your new database a title. The default title Address Book suffices.

⑰ Click Next.

The sixth and last wizard dialog box appears.

⑱ Click Finish.

The wizard goes to work and uses your choices to create your new address book database.

When the database is complete, a form called the Main Switchboard appears, as shown in the accompanying figure.

NOTE *The Switchboard is just a form that uses VBA procedures (or macros) to automate the selection of different procedures. You can use the switchboard if you like it, but if you don't, you can close it or delete it from the database without causing any problems. For the remainder of this lesson, however, you'll use the switchboard and see how an automated database works for you.*

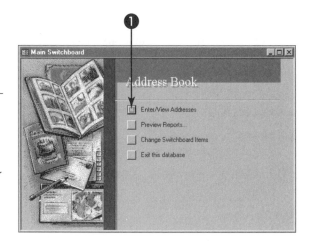

▶ *Entering data*

In this exercise, you'll enter a new record (a name and e-mail address) in your address book. The Switchboard should still be displayed on your screen.

❶ On the Switchboard, click the Enter/View Addresses button.

Entering data

The Addresses form appears, and the first record of sample data is displayed.

② Click the New Record scroll button.

The form opens a new record, ready for you to enter data.

NOTE

In a new record, the Address ID box reads "Autonumber". You can't select it or type in it because consecutive ID numbers are automatically entered for each new record. This ensures that each ID number is unique.

③ The flashing insertion point should be in the First Name box. Type **Hilton**.

④ Press Tab.

⑤ Type the Last Name **Drake**.

⑥ Press Tab.

⑦ At the bottom of the form, click the Page 2 button.

A second form opens for entering more address book information, as shown in the accompanying figure. The flashing insertion point should be in the Email Address box.

⑧ Type **hd@bigdog.com**.

⑨ Press Enter.

⑩ Click the Preview Fact Sheet button.

A one-page report showing the data you entered for Hilton Drake appears, as shown in the accompanying figure.

⑪ Click the X close box on the report window to close it.

⑫ Click the X close box on the Addresses form to close it.

The Switchboard appears.

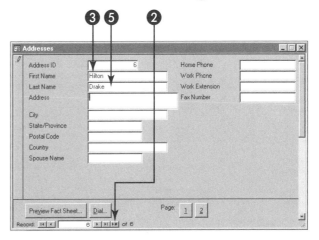

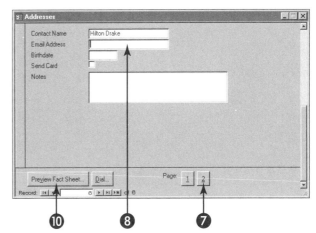

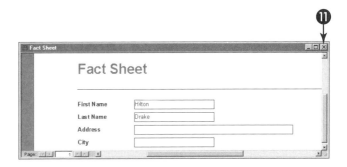

2

A Quick Tour of Access

PART I: AN OVERVIEW OF ACCESS **27**

Printing a report

Printing a report

Next, you'll print a report from the data in your new database.

1 On the Switchboard, click the Preview Reports button.

Another Switchboard form opens, as shown in the accompanying figure, with options for four wizard-created reports.

2 Click the Preview The Addresses By Last Name Report button.

A report showing the names and addresses of all the entries in the database displays and is ready to print, as shown in the accompanying figure.

3 On the toolbar, click Print.

The one-page report is sent to your printer.

4 Click the X close box in the report window to close the report.

5 On the Reports Switchboard, click the Return To Main Switchboard button.

6 On the Switchboard, click the Exit This Database button.

Deleting a database

In this exercise, you'll delete the new database. If you want to continue using the Address Book database for your personal address list, just use the New Database Wizard to recreate it.

1 Click File.

2 Click Exit (to close Access).

TIP *You don't need to close Access to delete a database; instead, you can minimize Access. Your objective is to see the My Computer icon on your desktop.*

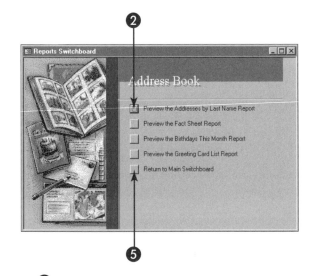

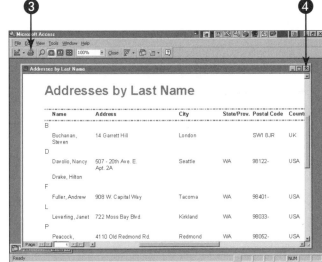

3 On your desktop, double-click the My Computer icon.

The My Computer window appears, as shown in the accompanying figure.

4 Double-click the hard drive icon.

5 Navigate through your folders to the folder where the new database, My Address Book, is saved.

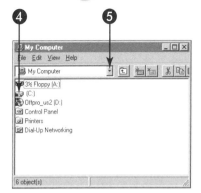

TIP

By default, Access usually saves new databases in the Personal folder. Unless you specified a different folder when you created the database, you'll find the new database in the Personal folder in the Windows folder. (Some systems default to a different folder, such as the My Documents folder.)

6 Click the `My Address Book.mdb` file.

7 Click File, then click Delete.

The address book database is deleted. It's been sent to the Recycle Bin, so you can recover it if you want to. To remove it from your computer and free up the space on your hard drive, you'll need to delete it from the Recycle Bin.

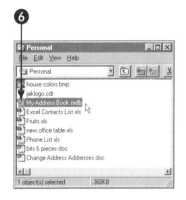

As you saw, the New Database Wizard can create a fully functional, automated database for you quickly, which can be a great time-saver. It's not, however, a substitute for learning to construct a database from scratch because you don't know how the wizard-created database works. Throughout the rest of this book, you'll learn what goes on behind the scenes. By the time you finish all the lessons, there won't be any mystery about a new database.

Skills challenge

SKILLS CHALLENGE: CREATING ANOTHER NEW DATABASE

In this Skills Challenge, you'll create another new database. This time it'll be a book collection database, which has more than one table. Once again, you'll add a record and print a report.

1 Start Access 97.

2 Start the New Database Wizard.

 Do you remember how to start the New Database Wizard if Access is already open?

3 Create a new Book Collection database, selecting your choices from the options offered by the wizard.

 How many tables are included in the Book Collection database?

4 On the Switchboard, click the Enter/View Books button, and enter the following data in a new record:

Title   **Discover Outlook 97**

Topic   **Technical**

(Click the arrow and select Technical from the drop-down list.)

TIP

*If you created this database without including sample data, the Topic field will be empty. You'll have to double-click the field and type **Technical**. At that point, Technical will be added to the field and you'll be able to select it for all future technical book entries.*

Publisher Name   **IDG Books**

Author   **Julia Kelly**

TRY OUT THE

INTERACTIVE TUTORIALS

ON YOUR CD!

(Double-click the Author box, and enter the author name in the Authors form.)

 3 *What is the purpose of the AutoNumber data type in the Author ID field?*

5 Close the Authors form.

TIP

You've added the name to the Author field. In the future, you can simply select the name from the drop-down list to enter other books by the same author.

6 In the Books form, click the arrow in the Author box and select the author name from the list.

7 Close the Books form.

8 On the Switchboard, click the Preview Reports button.

9 Preview and print the Titles by Author report.

10 Close the database and delete it.

 4 *Do you remember how to delete a database from your computer's hard drive?*

TROUBLESHOOTING

You've learned how to create a fully functional new database rapidly by using the New Database Wizard. The following solutions might answer some questions that came up during this lesson.

Troubleshooting

Problem	Solution
I included sample data when the wizard built my database. How do I get rid of the sample data?	To get rid of the sample data, you must open the tables the data is entered in, select the records, and delete them. You'll learn more about records and tables in Lesson 5.
How do I delete the Switchboard from the database?	First close the Switchboard; then click the Forms tab in the database window, click the form named Switchboard, and press Delete. You'll learn more about forms in Lessons 7 and 8.
How do I save my entries?	You don't have to save your entries; entered data is automatically saved.
I deleted my database. How can I recover it?	If it's still in the Recycle Bin, open the Recycle Bin window and drag the database out onto the desktop or into another folder window. If you emptied the Recycle Bin, you can't recover the database.
I noticed a misspelling in my report when I looked at it in Print Preview, but I can't select the error to correct it. How do I correct the error?	Errors must be corrected in the table in which they are stored. Close the report; then open the table the data is stored in and correct the misspelling; then close the table and open the report. You'll find the error corrected.

WRAP UP

Before you finish, let's go over some of the things you learned in this lesson:

- You learned how to create a new database using the Database Wizard.
- You learned how to enter data in a form.
- You learned how to preview and print a report.
- You learned how to delete a database.

For more practice, create another new database with the wizard, and delete it when you're finished to free up hard drive space.

In the next lesson, you'll learn a number of different ways for getting data into a database. You'll also learn how to export this data to a Microsoft Excel file to calculate numbers using Excel's number-crunching power.

Data Basics

Part II focuses on tables and queries and the most basic database procedures. It includes the following lessons:

- Lesson 3: Getting Data In and Out — this lesson covers getting data into an existing table and exporting it to another program for further manipulation.

- Lesson 4: Retrieving Data — here you'll learn to find specific records in a table by searching, sorting, and filtering, and how to print a table of data directly without first creating a report.

- Lesson 5: Setting Up Tables — this lesson teaches you how to create new tables and define relationships between them.

- Lesson 6: Querying Your Tables — this lesson opens up the subject of queries, which are the heart of a relational database.

In this Part, you begin to do real work in the `Fruitsweets.mdb` database file. The objects you create in this part will be used again in Parts III and IV for further work.

Getting Data In and Out

GOALS

In this lesson, you'll master the following skills and concepts:

25 MINUTES

- Entering data using a form
- Changing row height in Datasheet view
- Entering data directly in a table
- Editing data in a table
- Importing data from another file
- Combining two tables
- Linking to a table in a different file
- Exporting data to an Excel file

Entering data using a form

GET READY

To complete this lesson, you'll need to start Access 97 and open the Fruitsweets database. Refer to Lesson 1 if you need help.

When you finish these exercises, you'll have mastered the skills required to get data into your database by several different means: you'll have added new data to the Fruitsweets database by entering new records, by importing data from another file, and by linking to a table in a different file.

TRY OUT THE

INTERACTIVE TUTORIALS

ON YOUR CD!

ENTERING DATA

You already know that all data in a database is stored in tables. There are several ways to get data into those tables, including entering it record by record, importing an entire table of data at once, and linking to a table in another file. The last way enables you to use the data in a file without creating a new table in your database. You'll learn all these procedures in this lesson, beginning with entering data record by record.

You can enter data by using a form, as you did in Lesson 2, or you can enter data directly into a table. The advantages of using a form are that data entry can be simpler, especially for a user who is unfamiliar with your database, and a single form can be used to enter data into two or more tables. The advantages of entering data directly in a table are that it can be faster, and you can see many records at once.

In the following exercises, you'll enter information about new products into the Giftpaks table, first by using the Giftpaks form and then by opening the Giftpaks table and entering data directly.

Entering data using a form

The operations manager sent you a note, as shown in the accompanying figure, about a new giftpak the company has decided to add to its product line. You'll need to enter the information about the new giftpak in the Giftpaks table, and you'll use the Giftpaks form, which is based on the Giftpaks table, to enter it.

> The new product will be called Gourmet's Tin, and it'll be
>
> "Fancy and exotic fruits for the most discriminating tastes . . ."
> weight: 8 lbs
> price: $65

The operations manager also requested that you reduce the price of the Small Fruit Basket giftpak to $10. You can make that change while you have the Giftpaks form open.

1 In the Fruitsweets database, click the Forms tab.

2 Double-click the Giftpaks form.

Another way to open the form is to select the form name and then click the Open button on the Forms tab. This is the way to go if you have trouble with the double-click.

The Giftpaks form opens in Form view, as shown in the accompanying figure, and displays the first record.

3 Click the New Record scroll button at the bottom of the form.

The form opens a new, blank record, and the ID field is selected.

You can also press Enter to move from field to field.

4 In the ID field, type **GT** and press Tab.

5 In the Giftpak Name field, type **Gourmet's Tin** and press Tab.

6 In the Description field, type **Fancy and exotic fruits for the most discriminating taste** and press Tab.

7 In the Price field, type **65** and press Tab.

The 4 lbs option button is selected by default. The Giftpaks form uses an option button group for giftpak weight to reduce the chance of error in data entry. You'll learn how to create option buttons on a form in Lesson 8.

8 Click the 8 lbs option button and press Tab.

The record is entered, and a new record is opened.

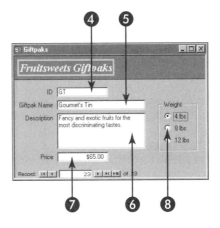

3

Getting Data In and Out

Entering data using a form

NOTE When you move to a different record, the additions and changes you've made are automatically saved.

Now you can edit the Small Fruit Basket record with the price change the operations manager requested.

9 Press the Page Up key until the Small Fruit Basket record is displayed (press six times).

TIP You can also use the Previous Record scroll button to scroll backward through the records.

10 Tab through the fields until Price is selected and type **10**.

11 Press Page Down to move to a new record and save your edit.

The Small Fruit Basket price is edited and saved. Now you'll take a look at the Giftpaks table to see the changed data.

12 Close the Giftpaks form.

13 Click the Tables tab.

14 Double-click the Giftpaks table to open the Giftpaks table, as shown in the accompanying figure.

The table is sorted alphabetically by ID, so you'll find the new record easily by scanning the ID field for "GT." Searching by eye is easy in a short list, but in a longer list of data, you'll need more efficient methods of finding records — methods you'll learn in Lesson 4.

15 Use the vertical scrollbar on the right side of the table to find and check the data you entered and edited.

The only problem is that you can't easily see the entire description entry. This problem will be remedied in the next exercise, where you'll make the rows taller.

15

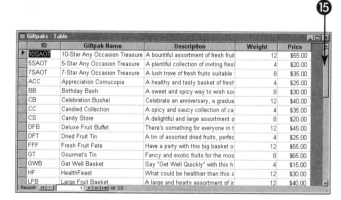

Changing row height in Datasheet view

You can change the layout of the Giftpaks table to make it easier to read the descriptions.

1 Position the pointer on the border between any two record selectors (the gray column on the left side of the table).

The pointer becomes a two-headed arrow, indicating that you can drag the border up or down.

2 Drag the border downward to make the row taller.

> **TIP** *All of the rows in the table will be resized; you can't resize only one row.*

3 Adjust the height of the rows until you can read the entire description for each record.

4 Close the Giftpaks table.

5 A message asks if you want to save changes to the layout; click Yes.

> **TIP** *You can also click File ➢ Close to close the table.*

Here are a few more of the many ways you can change a Datasheet view layout to work better for you. It doesn't matter whether the object in Datasheet view is a table, form, or query—they all work the same way.

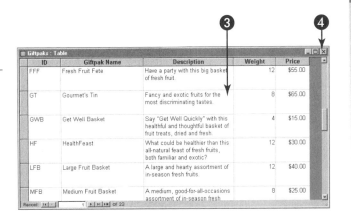

Drag to adjust all row heights

Drag to adjust a single column width or double-click to "best fit" a column width

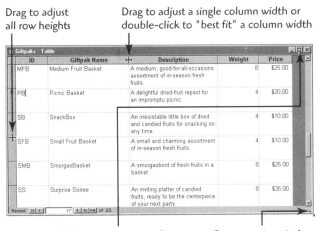

Click to maximize window

Drag to resize window

3

Getting Data In and Out

Entering data directly into a table

Entering data directly into a table

Often it's faster to enter and edit data directly into a table, especially if the database is yours and you understand how it's constructed. The advantages are that you can see all the records at once and can avail yourself of a few tricks for making repetitive data entry faster. The only caveat is that you must be careful to spell entries properly in certain fields, such as the Weight field in the Giftpaks table, and that's where using a form with option buttons comes in handy—you can't misspell the Weight entry because the form enters the data for you.

There are, however, a few techniques for making data entry directly in a table error-proof, and you'll see one of those techniques, a lookup field, in action in the next exercise.

Earlier in this lesson, you added a new giftpak to the Giftpaks table; now you need to add the details of that giftpak to the Giftpak Details table. The details are shown in the accompanying note.

1 On the Tables tab, double-click the Giftpak Details table to open it.

2 Click the New Record scroll button to select a new record.

The insertion point moves to the Giftpak field in a new record at the end of the table.

The right-pointing triangle in the record selector (the gray box at the left) shows which record is currently selected.

TIP *The Giftpak field has a down arrow in it because the field is formatted as a* lookup field, *which saves time and reduces errors by enabling you to select a value from a drop-down list (called a* combo box) *rather than typing the value. The drop-down list is looked up in the Giftpaks table; you'll learn how to create lookup fields in Lesson 5.*

3 In the Giftpak field, click the down arrow.

4 Scroll down and click Gourmet's Tin.

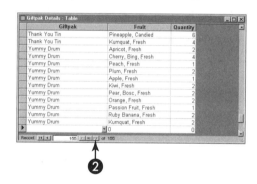

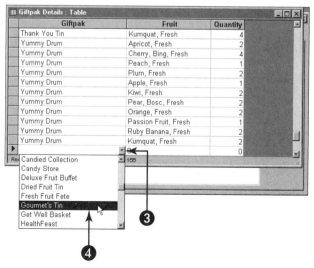

Gourmet's Tin is entered in the Giftpak field. The lookup field looks up giftpak names in the Giftpaks table, where you entered Gourmet's Tin in Exercise 1.

5 Press Tab to move to the Fruit field.

In the record selector column, a pencil icon indicates that the current record is not yet saved. The Fruit field is also a lookup field, which looks up fruit data from a query. You'll learn about queries in Lesson 6.

6 In the Fruit field, click Cherimoya, Fresh and press Tab.

The insertion point moves to the Quantity field.

7 Type **2** and press Tab.

The added record is saved (the pencil icon disappears from the record selector) and a new record is ready for data entry. You still need to add the remaining fruits that go into the new giftpak.

8 In the Giftpak field, type **G** and press Tab.

The first entry in the lookup table that begins with "G" is automatically entered.

> *If you want to enter "Get Well Basket" instead of "Gourmet's Tin", type **ge** and Access will enter the first entry that begins with "ge".*

9 Finish the record by entering **Ruby Banana, Fresh** and a quantity of **3**.

> *You can type **r** to enter Ruby Banana in the Fruit lookup field.*

10 In the next record's Giftpak field, press Ctrl+' and then press Tab.

The keystroke Ctrl+' (apostrophe) copies the entry in the cell above. You can use this technique in any field in any table.

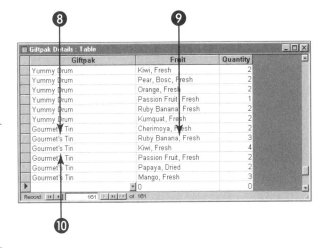

Giftpak	Fruit	Quantity
Yummy Drum	Kiwi, Fresh	2
Yummy Drum	Pear, Bosc, Fresh	2
Yummy Drum	Orange, Fresh	2
Yummy Drum	Passion Fruit, Fresh	1
Yummy Drum	Ruby Banana, Fresh	2
Yummy Drum	Kumquat, Fresh	2
Gourmet's Tin	Cherimoya, Fresh	2
Gourmet's Tin	Ruby Banana, Fresh	3
Gourmet's Tin	Kiwi, Fresh	4
Gourmet's Tin	Passion Fruit, Fresh	2
Gourmet's Tin	Papaya, Dried	2
Gourmet's Tin	Mango, Fresh	3
		0

3

Getting Data In and Out

Editing data in a table

⑪ Finish the entries for the Gourmet's Tin by entering the data in the note from the operations manager at the beginning of this exercise.

⑫ Close the Giftpak Details table.

TIP
To delete a record, click its record selector to select it; then press Delete.

Editing data in a table

The marketing department has asked you to change the wording in the description of the Appreciation Cornucopia. They want the description to read "luscious and lively" instead of "healthy and tasty."

NOTE
If you've used other Microsoft programs such as Word or Excel, you'll find that editing data in Access works the same way. You delete the words or characters you don't want and type in the words or characters you want to include. To replace a word, double-click the word to select it and type the new word in its place.

❶ Open the Giftpaks table.

❷ In the Appreciation Cornucopia record, click in the Description field.

❸ Drag to select the words "healthy and tasty".

❹ Type **luscious and lively**.

❺ Click in a different record to save your changes and then close the Giftpaks table.

TIP
To undo a change, select Edit ➢ Undo Saved Record.

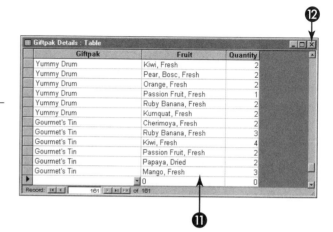

Giftpak	Fruit	Quantity
Yummy Drum	Kiwi, Fresh	2
Yummy Drum	Pear, Bosc, Fresh	2
Yummy Drum	Orange, Fresh	2
Yummy Drum	Passion Fruit, Fresh	1
Yummy Drum	Ruby Banana, Fresh	2
Yummy Drum	Kumquat, Fresh	2
Gourmet's Tin	Cherimoya, Fresh	2
Gourmet's Tin	Ruby Banana, Fresh	3
Gourmet's Tin	Kiwi, Fresh	4
Gourmet's Tin	Passion Fruit, Fresh	2
Gourmet's Tin	Papaya, Dried	2
Gourmet's Tin	Mango, Fresh	3

ACC	Appreciation Cornucopia	A healthy and tasty basket of fresh and candied fruits - a great way to show your appreciation.		4	$25.00

IMPORTING DATA

If you need data that has already been entered in another file, such as a spreadsheet or another database, you can import it directly to your database, saving time and eliminating keystroke errors.

 Importing a list creates a copy of the data in your database without affecting the source file.

Importing data from another file

A co-worker attended a trade show and returned with a list of people who want to be placed on Fruitsweets' catalog mailing list, but the list is in an Excel worksheet, and you need to get it into your database in an efficient manner. You already have a Customers table set up, and you want to add the new names to your existing Customers table.

Although you can import data from a spreadsheet to an existing table (if you set up the spreadsheet exactly like the Access table you're importing to), it's often easier to import the spreadsheet as a new Access table, and then combine the old and new Access tables. In this case, you'll import the Excel list into a new table and then combine the records in the new table with the records in the existing table.

 It doesn't matter if you have Microsoft Excel on your computer—Access can still read the Excel file.

❶ On the File menu, point to Get External Data and click Import.

The Import dialog box appears, as shown in the accompanying figure.

❷ If the Import dialog box did not open to the Access One Step at a Time folder, navigate to that folder now.

❸ At the bottom of the dialog box, in the Files Of Type box, select Microsoft Excel.

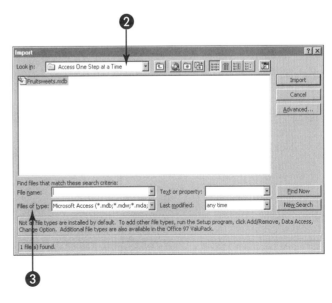

Importing data from another file

The New Mailing List file appears in the dialog box file list.

TIP

To make the procedure go smoothly, the New Mailing List spreadsheet has been set up with column names identical to those in the Access table, and no ID field.

4 Double-click the New Mailing List file.

The Import Spreadsheet Wizard starts, and the first wizard dialog box appears.

5 Click the First Row Contains Column Headings checkbox and click Next.

The second wizard step appears, as shown in the accompanying figure.

6 Leave the In A New Table option button selected and click Next.

The third wizard step appears and enables you to set Data Type and Index definitions; you don't need to make any changes.

7 Click Next.

The fourth wizard step appears, as shown in the accompanying figure, and asks if you want to set a primary key—you don't need a primary key in this table because you're going to append it to a different table.

8 Click the No Primary Key option button and click Next.

The last wizard step appears.

9 Name the new table **New Customers** and click Finish.

A new table is created, and Access tells you it's finished importing the data.

Next you'll combine the records in the new table with the records in your existing table, because you don't need two separate customer lists.

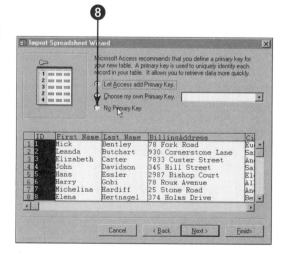

Combining two tables

Now you have two tables of customer data, and you need to combine them. The simplest way to combine two tables is to create a third table; then copy and paste both sets of records into it.

1 On the Tables tab, select Customers, but don't open it.

2 On the toolbar, click Copy.

3 On the toolbar, click Paste.

The Paste Table As dialog box appears, as shown in the accompanying figure.

4 In the Table Name box, type **Combined Customers**.

5 Be sure the Structure And Data option button is selected and click OK.

A new table named Combined Customers is created, and all the fields and records from your Customers table are copied into the new table.

6 Select the New Customers table.

7 On the toolbar, click Copy.

8 On the toolbar, click Paste.

The Paste Table As dialog box appears again.

9 In the Paste Table As dialog box, in the Table Name box, type **Combined Customers**.

10 Select the Append Data To Existing Table option button and click OK.

The new customer records are combined with the old customer records in the new table.

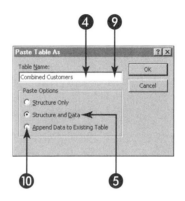

Linking to a table in a different file

TIP *The new table creates consecutive Customer ID numbers because of the field's AutoNumber data type. You'll learn more about data types and AutoNumber in Lesson 5. For now, you should be aware that previous customer ID numbers can be changed in an operation like this one, so if you're combining data of this type, you should make sure any ID numbers pasted into a new table are correct.*

At this point, you can delete the Customers and the New Customers tables (select the table name and press Delete) and rename the Combined Customers table to simply "Customers".

NOTE *You don't have to delete the Customers and New Customers tables. If you want to repeat this lesson, or if a colleague wants to do the same lesson, you might want to leave the Customers table in place in the database.*

LINKING TO DATA

If someone in the company keeps a table of data in another file, and you need access to that data periodically, you can *link* to that table instead of importing it. Linking enables you to use the data in the other file without making a copy of it in your database. The advantage is that you always have access to current data, whereas a copy of the table imported to your file is not updated when the original file is updated.

Linking to a table in a different file

At Fruitsweets, the shipping department watches shipping costs from various companies and selects the best-cost air, ground, and overnight delivery services. They keep the list of currently used delivery services in a Microsoft Excel file, and the list can change without warning.

Linking to a table in a different file

You need access to the most current list of delivery services when you fill in order forms, and the best way to have current data is to link to the shipping department's Excel list.

In this exercise, you'll create a link in your database to the Shippers file.

1 On the File menu, point to Get External Data, then click Link Tables.

The Link dialog box appears.

2 If the Link dialog box did not open to the Access One Step at a Time folder, navigate to that folder now.

3 In the Files Of Type box, click Microsoft Excel.

The Excel files in the Access One Step at a Time folder appear in the file list.

4 Double-click the Shippers file.

The Link Spreadsheet Wizard starts, as shown in the accompanying figure.

5 Click the First Row Contains Column Headings checkbox.

6 Click Next.

The second wizard step appears, and it shows that the linked table is Sheet1 in the Excel file.

7 Click Finish.

The wizard creates a link to the Excel file in your Tables tab and tells you that it's finished.

A linked table is identifiable by its special icon. In this case, the icon shows a link to an Excel file, but it needs a more descriptive name than "Sheet1".

8 In the database window, click the linked table name (click only once).

The name is selected.

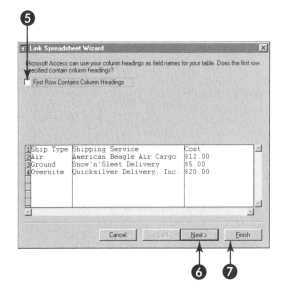

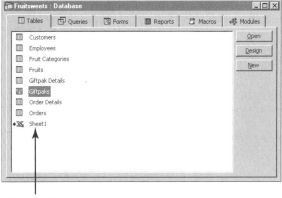

Linked table

Exporting data to an Excel file

9 Type **Shippers**.

10 Press Enter.

The linked table is renamed. Now is a good time to take a look at the new linked table

 NOTE *You don't need to have Excel in your computer to open the new linked Shippers table; Access can still read the data in the Excel file.*

11 Double-click the Shippers table.

The linked table opens as an Access table that contains the current Excel file data. When the data in the Excel file is changed, the data in your linked table changes, too, because the linked table is not an actual table of data in your database, but merely a link to the Excel file.

12 Close the Shippers table.

EXPORTING DATA

Access is appropriate for storing large numbers of records and tables of related data, but Excel is more appropriate for manipulating numbers, comparing "what if" scenarios, and performing extensive calculations. It's easy to store your data in Access and work with it in Excel by exporting a copy of the Access records to an Excel file.

Exporting data to an Excel file

Jerome in Marketing wants to use Excel to create some giftpak price change scenarios; you'll export the giftpak data to an Excel file so it'll be ready for him to use.

1 On the Tables tab, click the Giftpaks table to select it (but don't open it).

2 Click File ➤ Save As/Export.

The Save As dialog box appears.

③ Be sure the To An External File Or Database option button is selected.

④ Click OK.

The Save Table 'Giftpaks' In dialog box appears, as shown in the accompanying figure.

⑤ In the Save As Type box, select Microsoft Excel 97.

The File Name changes to Giftpaks.xls, an Excel file with the same name as the Access table.

⑥ Click Export.

An Excel spreadsheet is created with the Giftpaks table information. You can tell Jerome he can find the spreadsheet where you saved it, in your Access One Step at a Time folder.

SKILLS CHALLENGE: ADDING AND EDITING MORE DATA

In this Skills Challenge, you'll edit data, add a new record, and change a datasheet layout.

You received the following note and need to make the appropriate changes in the Fruitsweets database.

① Open the Fruits table.

② Add the new fruit specified in the note to the Fruits table.

 ❶ *Do you remember what keystroke copies data from the cell above?*

 ❷ *Do you remember what a drop-down list is called?*

③ Make the Fruit Type column narrower to "best-fit" the entries.

④ Close and save the Fruits table.

⑤ Open the Employees table.

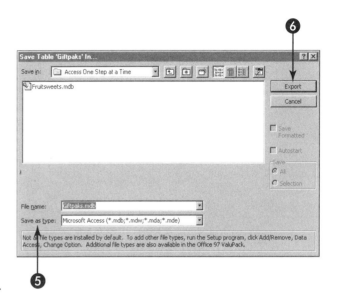

Database updates:

Nora Sparrow got married last weekend, and she's Nora McGinty now … also, please add Kumquat to the fruit line; it's a fresh Nagami Kumquat grown in Oregon, cost is $3 per pound …

Thanks!

3

Getting Data In and Out

Troubleshooting

Change Nora Sparrow's last name to McGinty (her married name).

 3 *How can you tell which record is currently selected?*

 4 *Do you remember how to save changes to a record?*

6 Close the Employees table.

5 *Do you remember how to delete a record?*

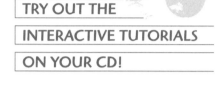
TRY OUT THE
INTERACTIVE TUTORIALS
ON YOUR CD!

TROUBLESHOOTING

You've learned how to get data into and out of a database by adding and editing records, importing a table, linking to a table in another file, and exporting to a spreadsheet. The following solutions might answer some questions that came up during this lesson.

Problem	Solution
I tried importing a list from Word, but it doesn't work.	You cannot import data from word-processing files such as Microsoft Word; you can, however, import data from most spreadsheet files, other databases, and text files.
I imported a table from Excel to an existing table in my database, but all the data came out in the wrong columns.	Be sure the columns in the file you are importing are in the same order as the columns in your existing table.
Importing data takes a really long time.	There might be a great many errors occurring during the import process; press Ctrl+Break to cancel the import.

Problem	Solution
I imported a list of addresses, and the zip codes lost their leading zeroes.	The import process might have assigned a number *data type*, or format, to your zip code field instead of the text data type it should have. Be sure the data type (in Excel, it's called format) is set correctly in the source field before you import. You'll learn how to change the data type in an Access table in Lesson 5.
When I try to add a new record to a table, I get the following error message: "The changes you requested to the table were not successful because they would create duplicate values in the index, primary key, or relationship...."	The problem is that the field you are entering data in is defined as Indexed: Yes (No Duplicates) and won't accept duplicate values. If it is supposed to accept duplicate values (like in the Giftpak Details table), open the table in Design view, and on the General tab, change the Indexed setting to Yes (Duplicates OK) or to No.
I tried to combine two identical tables, but I got an error saying "You tried to assign the Null value to a variable that isn't a Variant data type."	You are probably trying to combine a field that has no values in one table with a field that requires values in the other table (for example, an ID field without any values and an ID field with AutoNumber). Delete the field with no values so that Access doesn't try to import "Null" values.

WRAP UP

Before you finish, let's go over some of the things you learned in this lesson:

- You learned how to enter data in a table.

- You learned how to edit records in a table.

- You used lookup fields to enter data, and you learned other techniques for making data entry more efficient.

Wrap up

- You learned how to import a table of data from an Excel file.

- You learned how to link to a table of data in another file.

- You learned how to export data to a spreadsheet for further mathematical manipulation.

For more practice, try exporting the Employees table to a spreadsheet file; try importing or linking to other spreadsheet files you may have on your computer.

In the next lesson, you'll learn how to find specific records by sorting, searching, and filtering. You'll also print data directly from a table or query.

Retrieving Data

GOALS

In this lesson, you'll master the following skills and concepts:

20 MINUTES

- Sorting records by a text field

- Sorting records by a number field

- Searching for a record

- Filtering related records

- Filtering records with one criterion OR another

- Printing from a datasheet

Sorting records by a text field

To complete this lesson, you'll need to start Access 97 and open the Fruitsweets database (refer to Lesson 1 if you need help opening the Fruitsweets database).

When you finish these exercises, you'll have mastered the skills required to find specific records and groups of records by sorting, searching, and filtering. You'll also be able to print a Datasheet view of information.

TRY OUT THE

INTERACTIVE TUTORIALS

ON YOUR CD!

SORTING RECORDS

Sorting is a time-tested and essential method of organizing data, and Access makes it easy to sort data in any of your tables or queries. You can sort datasheets by a specific field to make the data easier to use for different purposes. You can also sort data in a Form view so you can scroll through individual records more efficiently.

Sorting records by a text field

Hans in Operations wants to know how many fruits are in each Fruit Type category. The quickest way to find out is to open the Fruits table, sort the records so they're grouped by Fruit Type, and take a look.

1 In the database window, verify that the Tables tab is selected. If it is not, click it.

2 Double-click the Fruits table.

The Fruits table opens, as shown in the accompanying figure.

The table is currently sorted by ID number.

3 Click in any cell in the Fruit Type field.

4 On the toolbar, click Sort Ascending.

The records in the table are sorted in ascending alphabetical order (A–Z) based on Fruit Type, as shown in the accompanying figure.

ID	Fruit Name	Description	Fruit Type	Cost per lb
1	Apricot	Canadian Harglow apricots	Fresh	$0.70
2	Cherry, Bing	Fresh northern California bing cherries	Fresh	$0.95
3	Peach	Fresh peaches from midwestern US	Fresh	$0.70
4	Prune	Pitted Italian prunes	Dried	$0.60
5	Plum	Coe's Golden Drop freestone plums	Fresh	$0.65
6	Apple	Spartan, Prima, or Liberty (depending on availability)	Fresh	$0.65
7	Kiwi	Ananasnaja kiwis from Oregon	Fresh	$0.95
8	Pineapple	Honey-sweetened Hawaiian pineapple slices	Dried	$1.25
9	Cranberry	Honey-sweetened and dried cranberries	Dried	$0.45
10	Fig	Dried Oregon figs	Dried	$0.50
11	Pear, Bosc	Crunchy Bosc pears from the Pacific Northwest	Fresh	$0.65
12	Orange	California Navel oranges	Fresh	$0.80
13	Grapefruit	Candied Florida grapefruit slices	Candied	$2.00
14	Date	Medjool dates	Dried	$1.20
15	Passion Fruit	Passion fruits from southern US	Fresh	$1.60
16	Cherimoya	Peruvian cherimoyas	Fresh	$1.50
17	Papaya	Dried papaya slices	Dried	$1.40

Record: 1 of 34

ID	Fruit Name	Description	Fruit Type	Cost per lb
33	Apricot	Lightly steamed and glacéed Australian apricots	Candied	$3.00
29	Cherry	Pitted, glacéed Rainier cherries	Candied	$2.25
28	Pineapple	Candied Pineapple chunks	Candied	$3.50
27	Orange	Candied California orange slices	Candied	$2.00
13	Grapefruit	Candied Florida grapefruit slices	Candied	$2.00
32	Apricot	Pitted, dried, and dipped in dark chocolate	Chocolate-covered	$5.00
31	Blueberry	Dried and dipped in dark chocolate	Chocolate-covered	$4.50
30	Cherry	Pitted, dried, and dipped in dark chocolate	Chocolate-covered	$5.00
23	Kiwi	Dried kiwi slices	Dried	$1.30
9	Cranberry	Honey-sweetened and dried cranberries	Dried	$0.45
14	Date	Medjool dates	Dried	$1.20
8	Pineapple	Honey-sweetened Hawaiian pineapple slices	Dried	$1.25
4	Prune	Pitted Italian prunes	Dried	$0.60
20	Apricot	Pitted, dried apricots	Dried	$0.95
10	Fig	Dried Oregon figs	Dried	$0.50
22	Apple	Honey-sweetened and dried slices	Dried	$1.10
17	Papaya	Dried papaya slices	Dried	$1.40

Record: 1 of 34

Searching for a record

You can count the fruits in each category and send Hans an e-mail message with the answer.

Sorting records by a number field

Now Hans wants to know what the highest- and lowest-cost fruits are. The table is currently sorted by Fruit Type, but you want to see fruits sorted by cost, from highest to lowest.

1 Click in any cell in the Cost per lb field.

2 On the toolbar, click Sort Descending. ⬇

The records in the table are sorted in descending numeric order (10–1) based on cost per pound, as shown in the accompanying figure.

You can look at the first record to see the highest-cost fruit (two fruits are each $5.00 per pound), and you can look at the last record to see the lowest-cost fruit ($.45 per pound).

3 Close the Fruits table.

4 When asked if you want to save changes to the table, click No.

SEARCHING FOR SPECIFIC RECORDS

You can search for a specific record in either Datasheet view or Form view; in this exercise, you'll search in Form view. The search procedure is the same, whether you search in Form view or Datasheet view, or in a form, table, or query.

Searching for a record

Frederick in Shipping called you with a request—some goo dripped on a package, obscuring the address. He needs to write a new address label, but he needs a complete address. From what little he can read on the current label, he can tell you the customer's last name is "Stri"-something.

Filtering to find groups of records

① Click Forms tab; then double-click Customers form.

② Click in the Last Name field (the text box that shows the last name).

③ On the toolbar, click Find. 🔍

The Find In Field dialog box appears, as shown in the accompanying figure.

④ In the Find What box, type **Stri**.

⑤ Click the down arrow in the Match box.

TIP

To search for a whole last name, select Whole Field in the Match box.

⑥ In the Match box drop-down list, click Any Part Of Field.

The dialog box should resemble the accompanying figure.

⑦ Click the Find First button.

The form displays a customer address for Ethan Striker, as shown in the accompanying figure.

⑧ To be sure this is the customer you're looking for, click the Find Next button.

A message appears telling you there are no other records with "Stri" as part of the last name. You've found the record you're looking for, and you can call Frederick in Shipping with the address he needs.

⑨ On the Find In Field dialog box, click Close.

⑩ Close the Customers form.

④
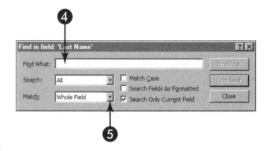
⑤

⑦ ⑧
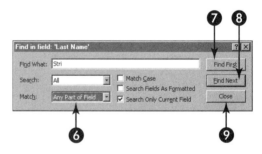
⑥ ⑨

⑩

FILTERING TO FIND GROUPS OF RECORDS

To find a group of records that shares common *criteria*, or field entries, use a filter. Because a filter is looking for a set of records, you must perform a filter on a Datasheet view. You can filter tables, queries, or forms.

Filtering related records

Hans in Operations wants to review the dried fruits Fruitsweets uses in its giftpaks. You'll filter the Fruits form in Datasheet view, using the dried fruit type as a criterion.

1 On the Forms tab, double-click the Fruits form.

The Fruits form opens (the form is sorted alphabetically by Fruit Name).

2 On the toolbar, click the down arrow on the View button. ☑ ▾

3 Select Datasheet View.

The Fruits form switches to Datasheet view, as shown in the accompanying figure.

4 Drag the lower right corner of the datasheet window to make the window larger.

NOTE *The Fruits form datasheet is similar to the Fruits table because the form gets its data from the table; but the form displays only four of the fields in the table, and the Form datasheet displays the same fields that are displayed on the form.*

The Fruit Type field contains the criterion "Dried" that you want to filter on. You'll use the "filter by selection" method of filtering, which is the quickest way.

TIP *You can use the Find button to locate a dried fruit type.*

5 Click in any Fruit Type cell that contains the entry "Dried".

6 On the toolbar, click Filter By Selection. ☑

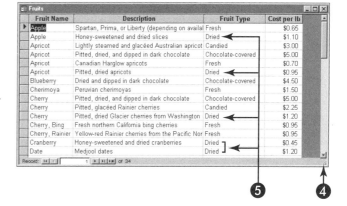

4

Retrieving Data

Filtering records with one criterion

All the records for dried fruit types are displayed in the datasheet, and all other records are hidden.

The navigation area at the bottom of the datasheet window tells you the data are filtered, as shown in the accompanying figure.

TIP *To run a filter that shows all fruit records* except *dried, you can right-click a Fruit Type cell that contains the entry "Dried" and then click Filter Excluding Selection on the shortcut menu.*

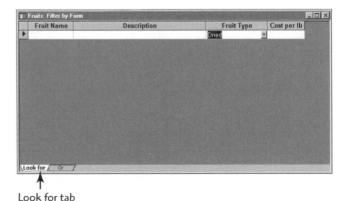

Filtering records with one criterion OR another

Hans called with a changed request: he wants a printed list of both chocolate-covered and candied fruits.

To produce this list, you'll create an "OR" filter, which is a filter that looks for records that meet one criterion OR another—in this case, records that have a fruit type of chocolate-covered OR candied.

TIP *When a filter is applied, the Apply Filter button becomes the Remove Filter button. When the filter is removed, the button becomes Apply Filter again.*

1 On the toolbar, click Remove Filter. ▽

The previous filter is removed, and all the Fruits records are displayed.

2 On the toolbar, click Filter By Form. 🖼

The datasheet is replaced by a Filter By Form window, shown in the accompanying illustration. Access remembers previous filter criteria, so the Dried criterion appears in the Fruit Type field.

You'll use the tabbed sheets in the Filter By Form window to select your filter criteria.

Look for tab

3 On the toolbar, click Clear Grid. ☒

All previous filter criteria for the datasheet are removed.

4 Click the Look For tab at the bottom of the Form window.

5 In the Fruit Type field, click the down arrow.

6 Select Chocolate-covered.

7 At the bottom of the Filter By Form Window, click the Or tab.

The Or sheet is identical to the Look For sheet.

8 In the Fruit Type field, click the down arrow and select Candied.

Your window should resemble the accompanying figure.

Another Or sheet has been automatically added to the window in case you'd like to add more OR criteria to your filter.

9 On the toolbar, click Apply Filter. ▽

The OR filter is applied, and your datasheet shows the records for fruits that have a chocolate-covered or candied fruit type, as shown in the accompanying illustration.

Table 4-1 lists several ways to use filters to get the records you want from a datasheet.

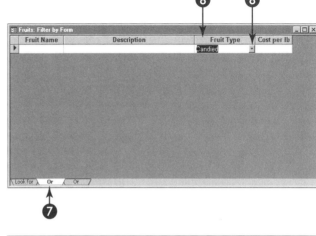

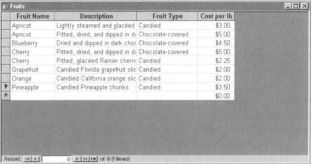

TABLE 4-1 FILTER TIPS

To	Do this
Filter on a single word (for example, the word "honey" in the Description field)	Select the entire word; then click Filter By Selection on the toolbar.
Filter on part of a word (for example, "pit" in the Description field)	Select the characters you want to filter on; then click Filter By Selection on the toolbar.

continued

TABLE 4-1 *(continued)*

To	Do this
Filter on two or more fields—an AND filter (for example, an AND filter consisting of 'California' in the Description field and 'Fresh' in the Fruit Type field)	Select the words or characters in one field; then click Filter By Selection. In the filtered list, select the second criterion you want to filter on; then click Filter By Selection again. Repeat this process to add more AND criteria.
Filter on a word that appears only at the beginning of an entry (for example "Dried", as in "Dried Oregon figs")	Select the word at the beginning of an entry; then click Filter By Selection. Only records beginning with the selected word will be shown in the filtered list.
Filter on a word that appears anywhere in an entry (for example, "Oregon", as in "Dried Oregon figs")	Select the word in the middle of an entry; then click Filter By Selection. All records containing the selected word anywhere in the entry will be shown in the filtered list.
Filter on a word that appears only at the end of an entry (for example, "Oregon", as in "Ananasnaji kiwis from Oregon")	Select the word at the end of an entry; then click Filter By Selection. Only records ending in the selected word will be shown in the filtered list.

TIP

To delete all records that share specific criteria (for example, to delete all records for Candied or Chocolate-covered fruit types), filter the table to show only the records you want to delete; then drag across the record selectors for all the displayed records to select them; then press Delete.

Hans wants a printout of this list. In the next exercise, you'll set up the datasheet and print it.

PRINTING TABLES

You'll learn how to create and print reports for an elegant presentation in Lesson 8. But sometimes (as in this case) you don't need an elegant presentation, just a quick printout of data.

Printing from a datasheet

The filtered Fruits datasheet is still open from the previous exercise. This is the information Hans wants, so you'll print it for him.

1 On the toolbar, click Print Preview. 🔍

A preview of the printed datasheet appears, as shown in the accompanying figure.

2 Move the zoom pointer over the data area and click.

The preview page zooms in to magnify the data—the fruit descriptions are truncated because the column is too narrow.

3 On the toolbar, click the Close button.

The preview page closes, and the datasheet reappears.

4 Move the pointer over the border between the column headings for Description and Fruit Type and double-click.

The Description column widens to best-fit the entries.

5 On the toolbar, click Print Preview. 🔍

The datasheet preview appears, still zoomed in, and the Description column is wide enough to display all the entries.

6 Click the zoom pointer on the preview page.

The preview page zooms out.

7 On the toolbar, click Print. 🖨

The datasheet with the records Hans needs is printed.

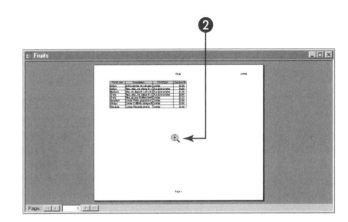

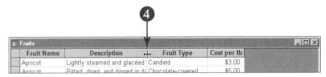

8 On the toolbar, click the Close button.

The preview page closes and the datasheet reappears.

9 Close the Fruits form.

The Fruits form closes, and the filter is automatically removed.

NOTE *Access remembers the last filter or sort you applied to a datasheet, even after you remove it, so the next time you open the Fruits form datasheet, you can reapply the last filter (chocolate-covered or candied fruit types) simply by clicking Apply Filter on the toolbar.*

SKILLS CHALLENGE: FILTERING, SORTING, AND PRINTING A TABLE

In this Skills Challenge, you'll filter, sort, and print the Customers table.

The Marketing division wants to design a special promotion on Northwest-grown fruits. Their target audience is for Fruitsweets' customers in Oregon and Washington, and they want a list of just the customers in those two states.

In this Skills Challenge, you'll filter the Washington and Oregon addresses, sort the filtered records by last name, and print the filtered, sorted datasheet.

TRY OUT THE

INTERACTIVE TUTORIALS

ON YOUR CD!

1 Open the Customers table.

 Which toolbar button can you click to search for a specific record?

2 Filter to display records with addresses in Washington (WA) or Oregon (OR).

3 Sort the filtered records by Last Name, in ascending order.

 Which toolbar button sorts records from Z–A or 10–1?

4 Check Print Preview to be sure you can read all the entries in every column.

 Do you remember how to raise row heights (from Lesson 3)?

Your datasheet should resemble the accompanying illustration.

 How can you get a close-up view of the page preview?

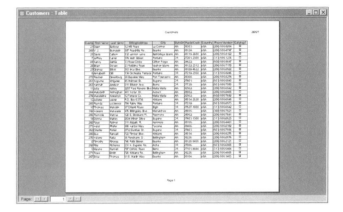

5 Print the page.

6 Close Print Preview.

7 Remove the filter.

8 Close the Customers table. When asked if you want to save changes, click No. If you click Yes, the table will save your filter and sort schemes.

5 *Do you remember how to reapply this filter the next time you open the Customers table?*

TROUBLESHOOTING

You've learned how to search for a record and how to sort, filter, and print a datasheet. The following solutions might answer some questions that came up during this lesson.

Wrap up

Problem	Solution
Every time I open a certain table, I have to sort it. How can I make the table retain the sort order I want?	Open the table, perform the sort you want, and then save the table; the table will retain whatever sort order you save it with.
Records are missing from my table.	Check the Navigation area at the bottom of the table window. If it reads (Filtered), click the Remove Filter button on the toolbar.
I created the wrong filter. How do I fix my mistake?	Click the Remove Filter button; then create the correct filter.
I saved my table with a filter applied. How do I remove the filter?	Open the table and click Remove Filter on the toolbar.

WRAP UP

Before you finish, let's go over some of the things you learned in this lesson:

- You learned how to search for single records based on an entry, or partial entry, in a field.

- You learned how to sort a datasheet view.

- You used filters to display records that share specific criteria.

- You printed a datasheet view of information.

For more practice, try filtering the Customers table for records that have postal codes beginning with "98" and then sorting them by city name in descending order.

In the next lesson, Lesson 5, you'll learn how to create a new table, define the fields in tables, and create relationships between tables. The last skill will enable you to create queries of related tables in Lesson 6.

Setting Up Tables

GOALS

In this lesson, you'll master the following skills and concepts:

- Creating a table using the Table Wizard
- Understanding field definitions
- Adding data to a new table
- Adding a lookup field to a table
- Testing the lookup field
- Exploring table relationships
- Recognizing a many-to-many relationship
- Creating a junction table
- Creating a junction table relationship

40 MINUTES

GET READY

To complete this lesson, you'll need to start Access 97 and open the Fruitsweets database (refer to Lesson 1 if you need help).

When you finish these exercises, you'll have mastered the skills required to create new tables in a database, define table fields and change field definitions, and relate tables to one another so you can use them to create queries.

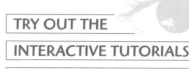

TRY OUT THE

INTERACTIVE TUTORIALS

ON YOUR CD!

ADDING TABLES TO A DATABASE

You learned in previous lessons that tables are the containers for data within a database, and that each table contains records that pertain to a single topic, such as fruits or giftpaks or customers. What makes a database work are the relationships between separate tables, so that information stored in separate tables can be combined in a useful way to give you the answers you need.

In this lesson, you'll learn several procedures: creating new tables, making those tables work for you by defining their fields properly, and creating relationships between tables. *Relationships*, the connections between separate tables, are the heart of queries, which you'll learn how to create and use in Lesson 6.

NOTE

As you go through this lesson, take special note of the difference between field names and field captions, and the idiosyncrasies of the AutoNumber data type, because these issues can be somewhat confusing and can cause stress and frustration later if you don't understand them.

Adding tables to a database

All About Tables

This Visual Bonus illustrates the table elements and concepts you'll learn about during this lesson.

The Relationships window.

Primary key field (bold)

One-to-many relationship

Nonrelated tables

Junction table (joins Giftpaks to Fruits)

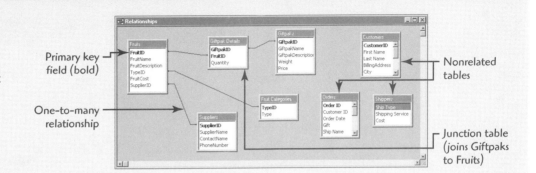

Row selection column

Primary key

Field names (the "official" Access name)

AutoNumber data type

Field attributes for selected field (FruitID)

The Fruits table in Design view.

Field descriptions

Data types

Field caption (the user-friendly column in Datasheet view)

Brief help about selected item

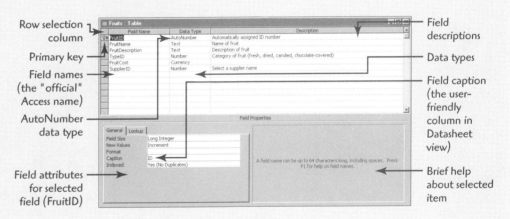

continued

5

Setting Up Tables

Creating a new table

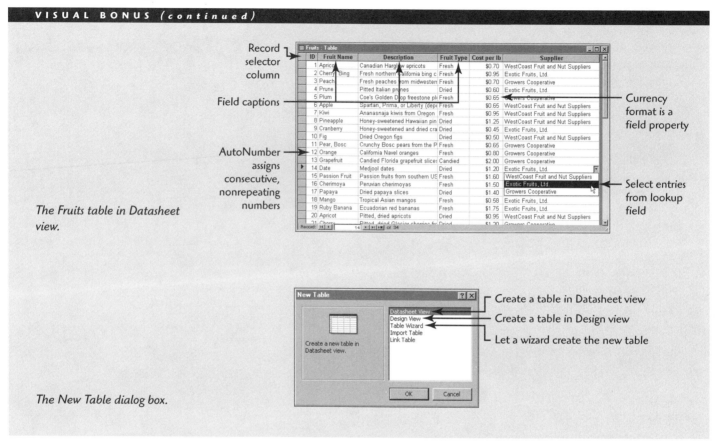

Record selector column

Field captions

AutoNumber assigns consecutive, nonrepeating numbers

Currency format is a field property

Select entries from lookup field

The Fruits table in Datasheet view.

Create a table in Datasheet view

Create a table in Design view

Let a wizard create the new table

The New Table dialog box.

CREATING A NEW TABLE

You can create a new table for a database quickly by using the Table Wizard. Like the Database Wizard you used in Lesson 2, the Table Wizard will ask you a series of questions and then use your answers to construct a new table.

▶ Creating a table using the Table Wizard

The Table Wizard makes table creation quick and easy, but, like the Database Wizard, it does its work behind the scenes, so although you can use the new table right away, you'll still need to understand how it was constructed if you want to use it in relationships with other tables. Nevertheless, the Table Wizard is a good introduction to new table creation.

Fruitsweets' buyer wants to easily be able to look up the supplier for each fruit that Fruitsweets buys. The supplier information should include the contact name and phone number for each supplier.

In this exercise, you'll use the Table Wizard to create the new table; in later exercises, you'll investigate the table's construction and connect it to the Fruits table, so the buyer can look up the contact person for a specific fruit.

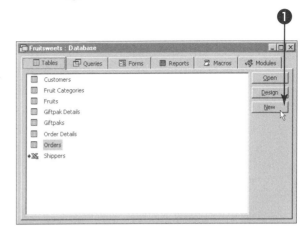

❶ On the Tables tab, click the New button.

The New Table dialog box appears.

❷ In the New Table dialog box, double-click Table Wizard.

The Table Wizard starts, and the first wizard step appears, as shown in the accompanying figure.

❸ Be sure the Business option button (below the Sample Tables list) is selected.

The Sample Tables list shows business-oriented tables.

❹ In the Sample Tables list, scroll down to select Suppliers.

The Sample Fields list shows typical fields for a Suppliers table; you can use as many of the sample fields as you need.

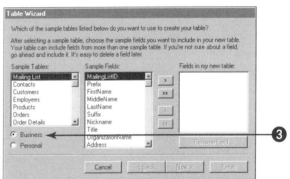

❺ In the Sample Fields list, double-click SupplierID.

The SupplierID field is added to the Fields In My New Table list.

❻ Double-click SupplierName, ContactName, and PhoneNumber to add them to the list of fields in your new table.

Your wizard step should look like the accompanying figure.

❼ Click Next.

The second wizard step appears. Suppliers, the table name Access suggests, is fine, and you can let Access create a primary key in that table. You'll learn about primary keys a little later in this lesson.

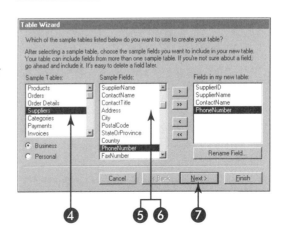

8 Click Next.

The third wizard step appears and asks if you want the wizard to set up any relationships between your new table and existing tables in the Fruitsweets database. You'll create a relationship with the Fruits table in a later exercise, so don't tell the wizard to create any relationships for you now.

9 Click Next.

The fourth wizard step appears; leave the Enter Data Directly Into the Table option selected.

10 Click Finish.

The Table Wizard creates your new Suppliers table, as shown in the accompanying figure.

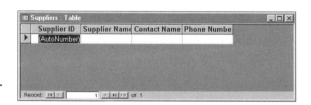

UNDERSTANDING FIELDS

The Table Wizard created a new table for you, but because it did all the work behind the scenes, you need to do a little detective work to understand how the table is set up.

The best way to begin is to explore field definitions, which include data types, data formats and input masks, indexes, captions, and primary keys.

Understanding field definitions

In this exercise, you'll look at the attributes of the fields the Table Wizard set up for you. It's important to understand at least the rudiments of field attributes because they will affect a table's relationships with other tables, as well as data entry.

NOTE *A field's attributes include all kinds of characteristics and properties, such as the type of data and maximum entry size the field will accept, the format in which values in the field are displayed, the field name (by which Access identifies the field), and the field caption (the column heading displayed in the table).*

1 On the toolbar, click View.

The table switches to Design view (drag the lower right corner of the window to make it larger, if you need to).

NOTE *The key icon to the left of SupplierID indicates that SupplierID is the primary key for the table. Primary key is explained in Table 5-1.*

2 Click anywhere in the SupplierID row.

The Data Type for SupplierID is AutoNumber, which means Access supplies a new consecutive ID number for each record in the table. This ensures that each record is uniquely identified.

The Description column is for notes to yourself.

TIP *Any comments you type under Description will be displayed in the database status bar when you enter data in that field.*

3 In the SupplierID row, under Description, type **Access assigns this number**.

4 In the PhoneNumber row, click in the Data Type column.

The General tab in the lower portion of the dialog box displays more information about the PhoneNumber field.

5 In the General tab, click in the Field Size box.

Information about the Field Size attribute is shown in the box on the right side of the General tab. In this case, an entry in the PhoneNumber field cannot be more than 30 characters long.

TIP *You can change the size limitation by typing a different number in the Field Size box.*

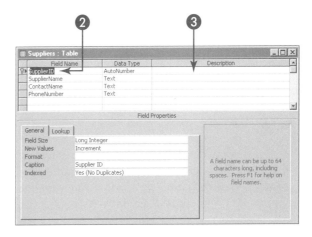

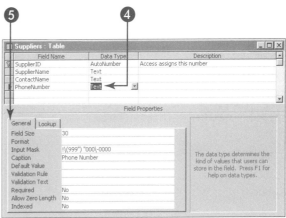

5

Setting Up Tables

Understanding field definitions

Input Mask is a formatting pattern for entries in the PhoneNumber field. The mask helps ensure that complete, valid phone numbers are entered.

Caption is the heading that will be displayed for this field on tables and forms. A caption with spaces in it is more user-friendly than the underlying field names, which have no spaces. A caption does not have to match its field name identically, but it's easier to keep your database understandable if the captions are similar to their field names. (Remember, *captions* are not the same as *names*. Access recognizes and works with the field *name*, while the user sees the field *caption* in the table.)

The Table Wizard created all the field names with no spaces in them, which is a good practice. Although you can include spaces in any Access names (tables, fields, forms, and so on) without problems, if you ever decide to convert this database into an SQL-type database, such as Oracle or SQL Server, the names with spaces will be unusable and will have to be changed throughout the database.

The Required attribute decides whether a *null* value (no data entry) is allowed in this field. "No" means a user does not have to enter a phone number; "Yes" means a phone number must be entered before the database saves this record.

You'll find more information about attributes in Table 5-1.

❻ On the toolbar, click View ▦ ▾. When asked to save the table, click Yes.

The table switches to Datasheet view.

TABLE 5-1 FIELD ATTRIBUTES

Attribute	Stuff to know about it
Primary Key	A field that uniquely identifies each record. There can be two or more primary keys in a table, which work together. You'll see primary keys at work later in this lesson, when you create a junction table. There can't be two identical entries in a table's primary key field(s). Primary key fields are identified by the key icon to the left of the field in Design view.
Indexed	An index is an underlying Access feature that maintains a presorted order of data in the field. It speeds up searching and sorting but can also slow down work in the database. It's usually necessary only for the primary key field.
Data type	Sets the kind of value that can be stored in the field (text, number, yes/no, date/time, and so on).
Data format	How the entered value is displayed (as currency, percentage, scientific notation, and so on).
Input Mask	A pattern for data entered in the field (good for phone numbers, postal codes, dates, and social security numbers).
Caption	How the name of the field is displayed on forms, tables, and reports.

The accompanying illustration summarizes several important elements in a table's Design view.

Adding data to a new table

At this point, you'll add data to the new Suppliers table so you can see the results of the field attributes the wizard set.

The buyer at Fruitsweets wants to be able to look up the supplier of each individual fruit the company uses in its giftpaks, so you'll first add Fruitsweets' three fruit suppliers to the new Suppliers table; then, in a later exercise, you'll connect the Suppliers table to the Fruits table, so the needed data can be looked up easily.

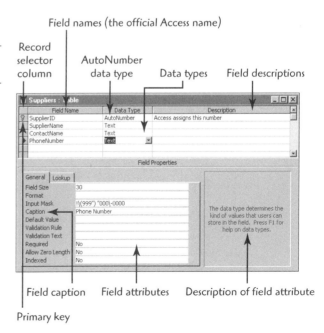

Field names (the official Access name)

Record selector column

AutoNumber data type

Data types

Field descriptions

Field caption   Field attributes   Description of field attribute

Primary key

5

Setting Up Tables

Adding a lookup field to a table

The Suppliers table should still be open, in Datasheet view. The Supplier ID field for the new record is selected, and your description "Access assigns this number" is on the status bar.

1 Press Tab to move the insertion point to the Supplier Name field.

2 Type **WestCoast Fruit and Nut Suppliers**.

3 Press Tab.

The entry is wider than the column, so you can't read all of it.

4 Move the pointer over the border between the column headings for Supplier Name and Contact Name.

5 When the pointer becomes a two-headed arrow, double-click.

The Supplier Name column widens to fit the entry.

6 Enter the Contact Name **Martin Critton**.

7 Enter the Phone Number **415-555-1221**.

You don't need to type any punctuation for the phone number; the Input Mask for the field applies parentheses and dashes automatically.

8 Enter two more records:

Exotic Fruits, Ltd.	**Joanna Paul**	**213-i555-8798**
Growers Cooperative	**Terry Miller**	**818-555-1235**

9 Close the Suppliers table.

10 When asked if you want to save changes to the table, click Yes.

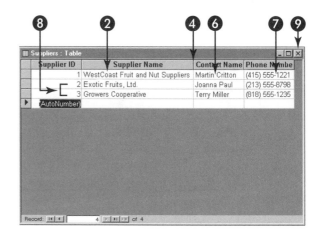

Adding a lookup field to a table

In Lesson 3, you entered fruits in the Giftpak Details table by selecting them from a lookup field. The lookup field looked up its values in the Fruits table and made data entry easy. In this exercise, you'll learn how to add a lookup field to a table.

Adding a lookup field to a table

You'll add a lookup field to the Fruits table, so you can look up supplier names from the Suppliers table. By using a lookup field to enter names instead of typing them in, you speed up data entry and ensure that the supplier names are always spelled correctly.

1 On the Tables tab, click Fruits.

2 Click the Design button.

The Fruits table opens in Design view, as shown in the accompanying figure.

3 In the Field Name column, click in the cell below FruitCost.

4 Type **Supplier**.

5 Press Tab.

Your table window should look like the accompanying illustration.

6 In the Data Type column, click the arrow next to Text.

7 Select Lookup Wizard.

The Lookup Wizard starts, and the first wizard step appears, as shown in the accompanying figure.

You want your lookup field to look up values in the Suppliers table, so leave the first option button selected.

8 Click Next.

The second wizard step appears.

9 In the list of tables, click Suppliers; then click Next.

The third wizard step appears, as shown in the accompanying figure.

10 Double-click SupplierName.

11 Click Next.

The fourth wizard step appears.

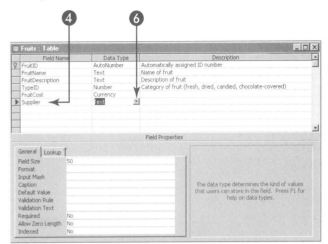

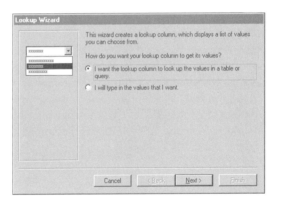

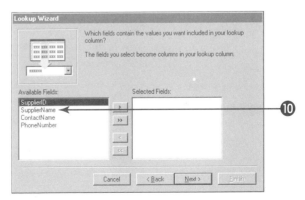

Adding a lookup field to a table

⑫ Double-click the border on the right side of the SupplierName column heading, as shown in the accompanying figure.

The column widens to display all the entries in the column.

⑬ Click Next.

The fifth wizard step appears and asks if Supplier is a good name for your lookup field. It is.

⑭ Click Finish.

⑮ In the message box asking you to save the table, click Yes.

⑯ Press Tab.

⑰ In the Description column, type **Select a supplier name**.

Your table window should look similar to the accompanying illustration.

Even though you've selected supplier *names* from the lookup field, the Fruits table has actually, secretly, stored the corresponding SupplierID from the Suppliers table; therefore, the Data Type the wizard has entered for the lookup field is Number and the Field Size (in the General tab) is Long Integer. The Number, Long Integer data type matches the AutoNumber data type in the Suppliers table, a match that allows the two tables to be related.

NOTE

It's important that entries stored in the lookup field have a data type that matches the SupplierID field being looked up. This allows the table relationship to work. This is explained further in the exercise "Exploring Table Relationships."

⑱ Close the Fruits table.

⑲ When asked if you want to save changes to the table, click Yes.

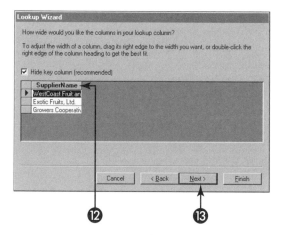

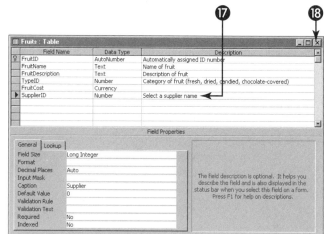

Testing the lookup field

In this exercise, you'll test the lookup field you just created, by entering supplier names for some fruits in the Fruits table.

1 On the Tables tab, double-click Fruits.

The Fruits table opens, as shown in the accompanying figure.

2 Click in the Supplier field for the first record.

3 Click the down arrow and select WestCoast Fruit and Nut Suppliers.

WestCoast Fruit and Nut Suppliers is entered in the record.

TIP

If the entry is truncated, make the column wider by dragging or double-clicking the right border of the Supplier column header.

4 Enter **Exotic Fruits, Ltd.** for the second record and **Growers Cooperative** for the third record.

NOTE

All the fields you added to your lookup column will appear in the finished lookup list (the drop-down list), although only the first, or leftmost, field will appear in the table column after you select an entry. For example, if you add SupplierName and then ContactName to your lookup column in the previous exercise, both will appear in the drop-down list when you are selecting an entry, but only the SupplierName entry will remain in the table column. If this is confusing, try repeating the last two exercises again and add both fields—it may help you to understand lookup fields better.

Your new lookup field makes data entry easy and accurate.

TIP

To make a lookup list (the drop-down list) appear in alphabetical order, open the lookup source table and sort the column that's being looked up, then save the table.

5

Setting Up Tables

5 Close the Fruits table.

6 If you widened the Supplier column, click Yes to save changes.

UNDERSTANDING TABLE RELATIONSHIPS

In the previous exercise, the Lookup Wizard created a *relationship* between the Fruits table and the new Suppliers table that allows you to look up entries in the Suppliers table and store them in the Fruits table.

A relationship simply connects two tables. By using a relationship, you can use a query to look up data from two or more tables (hence the name, "relational database"). For example, by creating a relationship between the Fruits and Suppliers tables, you can create a report that displays the contact name and phone number for each candied fruit that Fruitsweets purchases. You use the relationship to connect related data in different tables.

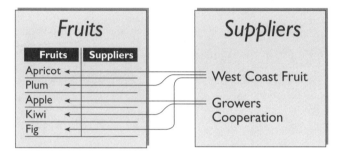

Supplier entries in the Fruits table ...

... are looked up in the Suppliers table.

AUTONUMBER AND DATA TYPE MATCHING

An important concept in table relationships is that of *matching data types*: for two tables to be related, the specific fields that are joined must have matching data types, which may or may not be the same. Because of the idiosyncrasies of the AutoNumber data type, the matching data types issue gets confusing when one data type is an AutoNumber data type.

AutoNumber is simply a Number data type, with Long Integer size, that's special because it automatically assigns consecutive, nonrepeating numbers to the field. AutoNumber is a good choice for an ID field or a primary key field because it guarantees that each record will be uniquely identified (no number assigned by AutoNumber will ever be repeated in those fields). When a wizard assigns a primary key for you, it will always add a new field with an AutoNumber data type to your table.

Because AutoNumber assigns its own numbers to a field, you can't join two AutoNumber fields in a relationship. If you could, each would attempt to assign numbers, and they'd be in eternal conflict. So here's the trick: when you join two fields in a relationship, they must have matching (not necessarily the *same*) data types, and the only data type that matches an AutoNumber data type is a Number data type with size Long Integer.

There are three types of relationships: *one-to-one*, *one-to-many*, and *many-to-many*.

One-to-one relationships, in which each record in one table has only one matching record in the related table, are uncommon because one-to-one data are usually kept in a single table. One reason you might want to use a one-to-one relationship between two tables is to record publicly available information about employees (name, department, supervisor) in one table and private employee information (address, home phone, salary) in another, less-accessible table.

One-to-many relationships are the most common. A good example is the Suppliers-Fruits relationship: each fruit will have only one supplier, but each supplier may supply many fruits.

Many-to-many relationships are also quite common. Each of the tables can have many entries in the other table. Many-to-many relationships are a bit more complex, so we'll reserve discussion of them until later in this lesson. Before you tackle the more complex concept of many-to-many relationships, you need to learn about one-to-many relationships.

In a one-to-many relationship, the table on the "one" side of the relationship is called the *primary* table. In the accompanying drawing, the Suppliers table is the primary table. The table on the "many" side, Fruits, is called the *related* table.

Exploring table relationships

Table relationships are created, deleted, and easily visualized by opening the Relationships window.

In this exercise, you'll practice creating and deleting relationships between tables.

1 On the toolbar, click Relationships.

TIP

If your Relationships window is not completely blank, click the Clear Layout button ⊠ in the toolbar to clear it.

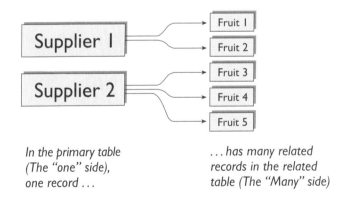

In the primary table (The "one" side), one record . . .

. . . has many related records in the related table (The "Many" side)

Exploring table relationships

② Right-click a blank area in the Relationships window.

③ Click Show Table.

The Relationships window is open, and the Show Table dialog box appears, as shown in the accompanying figure.

④ In the Show Table dialog box, double-click Fruits.

⑤ Double-click Suppliers.

The Fruits and Suppliers tables appear in the Relationships window. The "tables" in the Relationships window are lists of the fields in each table.

These two tables have a one-to-many relationship (one supplier to many fruits) that was created by the Lookup Wizard in Exercise 4. The relationship is shown by the line in between the two tables, as shown in the accompanying illustration. The line connects the Supplier ID fields in each table.

⑥ In the Show Table dialog box, click Close to close the dialog box.

If you can't see all of the fields in a table, drag the bottom border of the table downward to display them.

⑦ Right-click the relationship line (sometimes called a *join line*).

⑧ Click Delete on the shortcut menu.

⑨ In the message box that appears, click Yes.

The line disappears; the tables are no longer related.

Now you'll recreate the relationship.

⑩ Drag the Supplier ID field from the Suppliers table.

⑪ Drop it on the Supplier ID field in the Fruits table, as shown in the accompanying figure.

The Relationships dialog box appears; make sure the two fields are correct.

⑫ In the Relationships dialog box, click Create.

The tables are related once again, as shown by the relationship line between them.

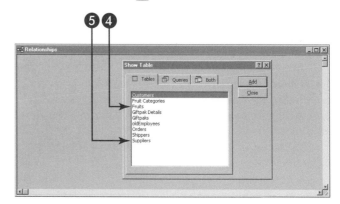

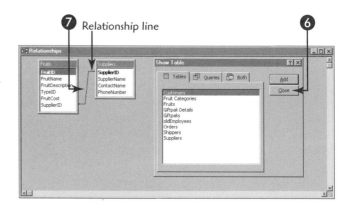

Relationship line

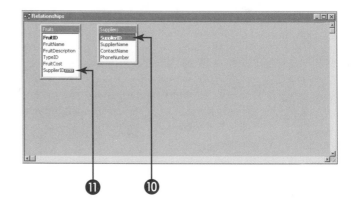

A many-to-many relationship

Recognizing a many-to-many relationship

Many-to-many relationships are fairly common and require a third table, called a *junction* table, to join them. The Giftpaks table and the Fruits table are a good example of a many-to-many relationship: each giftpak contains many different fruits, and each fruit is used in many different giftpaks.

Tables with a many-to-many relationship can't be directly related to one another. Instead, the many-to-many relationship is broken down into a pair of one-to-many relationships by placing a junction table between the two; then each of the "many" tables has a one-to-many relationship with the junction table. You can look up related information between the two "many" tables when they are related to each other through the junction table.

In this exercise, you'll learn to recognize many-to-many relationships in the Relationships window.

1 On the toolbar, click Clear Layout. ☒

2 In the message box that appears, click Yes.

The Relationships window is cleared.

3 Right-click in the Relationships window.

4 Click Show Table.

The Show Table dialog box appears.

5 Double-click Fruits, Giftpak Details, and Giftpaks.

6 Close the Show Table dialog box.

The three tables and the relationships among them are displayed in the Relationships window, as shown in the accompanying figure.

TIP

To see all of the fields in a table, drag the bottom border of the table downward.

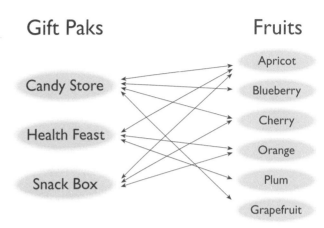

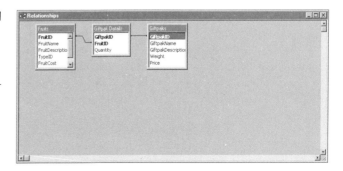

5

Setting Up Tables

A many-to-many relationship

The Giftpak Details table is called a *junction* table because it exists to join the Fruits table to the Giftpaks table. The junction table contains the primary keys of both of the tables you want to relate. It also contains a Quantity field that tells how many of a specific fruit are in a specific giftpak.

Each fruit appears several times in the Giftpak Details table, as does each Giftpak, but each record in the table contains a unique fruit/giftpak combination. The two primary keys in the Giftpak Details table work together to identify each record uniquely.

By using a junction table to join the Fruits and Giftpaks tables, you can find out which giftpaks contain a specific fruit, or which fruits are contained in a specific giftpak. You can see which giftpaks contain fresh peaches, for example, by opening the Giftpak Details table and running a filter for fresh peaches in the Fruit column (see Lesson 4 to remember how to filter). More importantly, you can answer questions such as "What is the cost of ingredients for the Gourmet's Tin giftpak?" and "How much does each giftpak that contains apples weigh?" You'll learn how to ask and answer questions like these by using queries in Lesson 6.

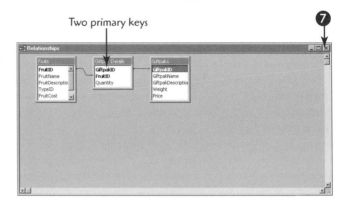

Two primary keys

7 Close the Relationships window by clicking its X close box.

8 When asked if you want to save the layout, click Yes.

CREATING A MANY-TO-MANY RELATIONSHIP

Earlier in this lesson, you created the Suppliers table by using the Table Wizard, which creates a table quickly but leaves you in the dark about the table's construction. Afterward you opened the table and investigated the fields, their data types, sizes, and so forth.

This time you'll create a table from scratch by starting with a blank table datasheet; you'll add fields and define them yourself.

To create a complete record of each order, you'll want to relate the Orders table (which contains customer, shipping, and payment information) to the Giftpaks table (which contains giftpak names and prices). When you're finished, each record will consist of the customer's name, the shipping address, and the number of giftpaks ordered. The Orders table and the Giftpaks table have a many-to-many relationship—a specific giftpak can be included in many different orders, and an order can include many different giftpaks.

To relate these two tables, you'll need to build a junction table that contains an Order ID field and a Giftpak ID field. You'll also need a quantity field, to keep track of how many of each giftpak are included in each order.

Creating a junction table

You'll create your junction table in Datasheet view. You'll add fields and set data types for the table by entering field names and a few records into the blank datasheet. Access will set data types for the fields according to the sample data you enter, and after you save the table, you'll check (and tweak) the settings Access makes. But before you can create the table, you need to plan what you'll include.

The junction table must include an Order ID field that matches the Order ID field in the Orders table, a Giftpak ID field that matches the Giftpak ID field in the Giftpaks table, and a Quantity field that contains integers (whole numbers).

If you open the Orders table in Design view, you'll see that the Order ID field is an AutoNumber data type, which always has a Long Integer size; so, to match, the Order ID field in the junction table must be a Number data type with a Long Integer size.

NOTE *The related fields in two tables must have matching data types (both Text, for example), but "matching" does not necessarily mean "the same." A common problem occurs when an ID field is related between two tables (as in the Orders–Giftpaks relationship), because the ID field in the primary table is often an AutoNumber data type, which is a Long Integer size. The matching related field cannot be AutoNumber because of the idiosyncrasies of the AutoNumber data type; instead, it must be a Number data type with a Long Integer size.*

If you open the Giftpaks table in Design view, you'll see that the Giftpak ID field is a Text data type; so, to match, the Giftpak field in the junction table must also have a Text data type.

Order #1	Order #2	Order #3
▪ Snack Box ▪ Health Feast	▪ Snack Box ▪ Candy Store	▪ Candy Store ▪ Health Feast ▪ Smorgas Basket

5

Setting Up Tables

Creating a junction table

Now that you've determined what the field data types must be, you can build the junction table.

1 On the Tables tab, click the New button.

The New Table dialog box appears.

2 In the New Table dialog box, double-click Datasheet view.

A blank-table datasheet with 20 columns and 30 rows appears, as shown in the accompanying figure.

3 Double-click the Field1 column header.

4 Type **OrderID**.

5 Press Enter.

The first field is named OrderID. A field name can be up to 64 characters long, including spaces and punctuation; it cannot include periods (.), exclamation points (!), grave accents (`), or brackets ([]).

6 Name the second field **GiftpakID**.

7 Name the third field **Quantity**.

8 Enter the following sample record (you can delete this record later):

OrderID: **1**

GiftpakID: **SnackBox**

Quantity: **1**

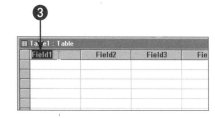

NOTE *Typing in mock, or sample, data is an important step in creating a new table in Datasheet view. Access uses the mock data to determine what data type to set for each field.*

9 Save the record by clicking in another record.

Your table should look like the accompanying illustration.

10 On the toolbar, click Save. 💾

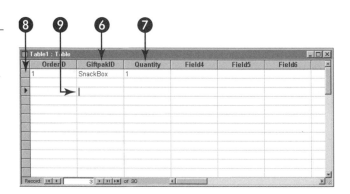

11 In the Save As dialog box, type **Order Items**.

12 Click OK.

13 In the message box that asks if you want to create a primary key now, click No.

The table is saved, and the extra columns and records are removed, as shown in the accompanying figure.

14 On the toolbar, click the View button. 📈 ·

The table switches to Design view, as shown in the accompanying illustration.

15 In the OrderID row, check the data type and field size.

The data type is Number and the field size is Long Integer, so the field matches the OrderID field in the Orders table, and a relationship can be created (remember, AutoNumber matches Number, Long Integer). The GiftpakID data type is Text, which matches the GiftpakID field in the Giftpaks table.

16 Drag in the record selector column to select both the OrderID and the GiftpakID rows as shown in the accompanying figure.

17 On the toolbar, click Primary Key. 🔑

Both fields are set as primary keys; together they uniquely identify each record in the table.

18 On the toolbar, click View to switch to Datasheet view.

19 When asked to save the table, click Yes.

20 Select the record you entered earlier (click in the record selector column).

21 Press Delete.

22 When asked to confirm the deletion, click Yes.

The record is deleted. Remember, you entered this sample data to give Access clues to the data types in each field, but you don't want to save it.

23 Close the Order Items table.

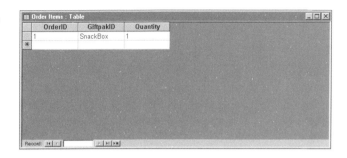

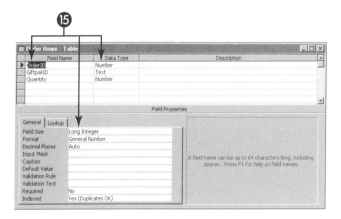

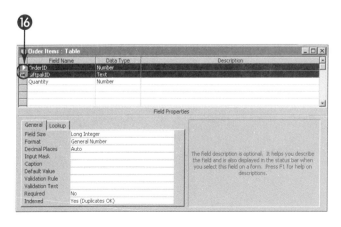

Creating a junction table relationship

Creating a junction table relationship

You've created a junction table to relate the Orders table to the Giftpaks table. All that remains is to create the relationships between the three tables.

1 On the toolbar, click Relationships. [icon]

The Relationships window opens.

2 On the toolbar, click Clear Layout. [X]

3 Click Yes to confirm clearing the window.

4 Right-click the Relationships window and click Show Table.

5 Add the Orders table, the Order Items table, and the Giftpaks table to the Relationships window.

6 Close the Show Table dialog box.

Your window should look like the accompanying illustration.

You'll create a one-to-many relationship between the Giftpaks table and the Order Items table (Giftpaks is the primary, or "one," table); and you'll create a one-to-many relationship between the Orders table and the Order Items table (Orders is the primary, or "one," table).

7 Drag the GiftpakID field from the Giftpaks table.

8 Drop it on the GiftpakID field in the Order Items table.

The Relationships dialog box appears. It should look like the accompanying illustration.

9 The correct fields are selected. Click Create.

The relationship line is drawn between the two GiftpakID fields.

10 Create a relationship between the OrderID fields (drag from the Orders table to the Order Items table).

The relationships should look like the accompanying illustration.

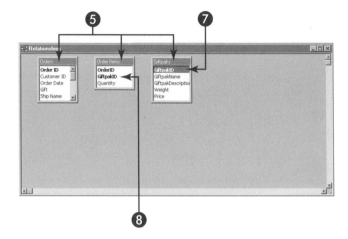

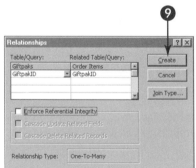

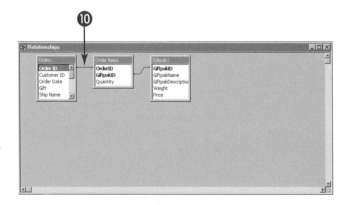

CREATING TABLES IN DESIGN VIEW

So far in this lesson you've learned new and easy ways to create tables: by using the Table Wizard and by creating a table in Datasheet view. But sometimes it's easier to create a new table the old way, by building it in Design view.

You've seen the table Design view window often enough in this lesson to understand it, so creating a new table in

Design view is a simple procedure. Click the New button on the Tables tab; then double-click Design View. In the Design view window, type Field Names; then set the data types and field properties for each field; then name the table and save it.

NOTE *Saving the layout in the Relationships window saves only the appearance of the window, not the relationships.*

⑪ Close the Relationships window.

⑫ Click Yes to save your layout.

SKILLS CHALLENGE: CREATING NEW TABLES AND A MANY-TO-MANY RELATIONSHIP

Fruitsweets offers its employees a retirement plan consisting of three investment funds. The employees decide how to divide their retirement contributions among those three funds — 100 percent to a single fund, one-third to each fund, 50 percent to each of two funds, or whatever they choose. You want to keep track of the investment funds that each employee contributes to and how much they contribute. This requires two new tables: a table to store the investment fund names from which the employees choose and a second table that matches employee names with their contributions to each fund.

In this Skills Challenge, you'll create a new table to store investment fund names and their Internet Web site addresses; then you'll relate the new table to the Employees table, so you can look up the funds to which each employee contributes.

TRY OUT THE

INTERACTIVE TUTORIALS

ON YOUR CD!

Skills challenge

In Access 97, you can store *hyperlinks* (jumps to Web site addresses or other files on your hard drive or network) in tables and then display them in forms, just like any other data. When the hyperlink is clicked, the file or Web site it points to is opened.

An Internet hyperlink begins with "http://", followed by the Internet Web site address, and will be blue and underlined when Access recognizes it as a hyperlink. The hyperlinks you enter in the following Skills Challenge are Internet hyperlinks (but they're phony URLs, so don't expect them to open real Web pages).

A hyperlink to another file on your hard drive consists of the path to the document, enclosed by # symbols. For example, a hyperlink to the Shippers table, an Excel file in your practice files, would look like this:

#c:\windows\favorites\access one step at a time\shippers.xls#

When you type this hyperlink, the entire address is displayed in the hyperlink; but there is a way to display the hyperlink as a shorter, more user-friendly link. Type appropriate text *in front of* the first # symbol. For example, if you type this:

Shippers#c:\windows\favorites\access one step at a time\shippers.xls#

the hyperlink will read Shippers instead of the entire address. Try it!

If you need to change a hyperlink, right-click the hyperlink. On the shortcut menu, point to Hyperlink, then click Edit Hyperlink. Make changes in the Edit Hyperlink dialog box, and click OK.

The Employees table and the new Retirement Funds table will have a many-to-many relationship (an employee can invest in more than one fund, and each fund can be selected by several employees), so you'll need to create a junction table to relate them. The junction table is where employee names will be matched with their investment fund choices. To make it easy to use, you'll create lookup fields for both the employee names and the investment fund names.

This Skills Challenge asks you to perform several procedures you've completed in this lesson, but you won't be led through them step-by-step (if you were, it wouldn't be a challenge!). Instead, the process will be more like a real-life situation, in which you'll be told what the results should be, and you must use what you learned in the lesson to achieve those results.

TIP

You may find it easier to create the new Retirement Funds table in Design view.

1 Create a new table; name it **Retirement Funds** and put three fields into it: **FundID**, **FundName**, and **WebSite**.

2 Make the FundID field an AutoNumber data type, the FundName field a Text data type, and the WebSite a Hyperlink data type.

 Do you remember how to set a primary key in a table?

3 Make FundID the primary key.

 If a field has an AutoNumber data type, what data type and size does its related field have to be?

4 Enter these three fictitious records in the new table:

1   **GetRichQuick Fund**   **http://www.getrich.com**

2   **Bahamas Portfolio**   **http://www.bahport.com**

3   **Stocks'r'Us**   **http://www.stocksrus.com**

NOTE

These are the investment fund names, web site addresses, and IDs; the ID numbers will be entered automatically by the AutoNumber data type in the FundID field.

 Do you remember how to set up a many-to-many relationship?

Skills challenge

5 Create a junction table to join the Employees table to the Retirement Funds table; name it **Fund Details** and include three fields: **EmployeeID**, **FundID**, and **Percent** (to record the percentage of the employee's retirement contribution that goes into that fund).

6 Be sure the EmployeeID fields in both tables (Employees and Fund Details) have matching data types, and be sure the FundID fields in both tables (Retirement Funds and Fund Details) also have matching data types. The Percent field in the junction table should be a Number data type, so the percentages can be calculated if necessary.

Remember, an AutoNumber field matches a Number field that has a size of Long Integer. The ID fields in the Employees and Retirement Funds tables both have AutoNumber data types, so, to match, the fields they will be joined to in the Fund Details table must have Number, Long Integer data types.

7 Make EmployeeID and FundID the two primary keys in the junction table.

Do you remember how to create a lookup field in a table?

8 In the Fund Details table, make the FundID and EmployeeID fields into lookup fields that look up Employee names and Fund names (the Lookup Wizard will create the relationships between the tables).

When you use the Lookup Wizard to make the EmployeeID field into a lookup field, add both the LastName field and the FirstName field (in that order) to your lookup column, so you can select employee names from a list that shows both last names and first names. (See Exercise 4 to remember how to create a lookup field.)

5 *Do you remember how to change the width of a column in a table?*

9 Enter the following records in the Fund Details table:

Name	Fund	Percent
Mary Santo	**GetRichQuick Fund**	**50**
Mary Santo	**Bahamas Portfolio**	**50**
Jerome Gilbert	**Stocks'r'Us**	**33**
Jerome Gilbert	**GetRichQuick Fund**	**33**
Jerome Gilbert	**Bahamas Portfolio**	**34**

Your table should look like the accompanying illustration.

 6 *When you save the Relationships window, what is saved?*

10 Close the table.

TROUBLESHOOTING

You've learned how to create new tables in two ways: with the Table Wizard and from scratch in Datasheet view. You've also learned how to set and change field definitions in a table and how to relate tables so they can work together. You've learned about the different kinds of relationships, how to determine whether two tables have a one-to-many relationship or a many-to-many relationship, and how to create a junction table to make a many-to-many relationship work. The following Troubleshooting section might answer some questions that came up during this lesson.

Troubleshooting

Problem	Solution
My junction table doesn't work.	Check that the data types for the related fields match. If one field is an AutoNumber data type, be sure the related field is a Number with a Long Integer size.
I can't create a table relationship, even though the fields I'm trying to join have the same AutoNumber data type.	You cannot join an AutoNumber field to another AutoNumber field. The field types must match, which doesn't necessarily mean they are the same. An AutoNumber field always matches a field with a Number, Long Integer data type, so give the field in the primary table (the table on the "one" side of the relationship) an AutoNumber data type, and give the field in the related table (the table on the "many" side of the relationship) a Number, Long Integer data type.
When I created a new table, Access unexpectedly added a new field with an AutoNumber data type!	When you allow Access to create a primary key for you, it does so by adding a new field, usually named ID, with an AutoNumber data type. If you have planned for this, great; otherwise, just answer "No" when asked if you want Access to create the primary key and then switch the new table to Design view and set the primary key yourself.
In a lookup field, how can I differentiate between two employees who have the same last name?	You can create a query, based on the Employees table, with a calculated field that concatenates, or joins, the FirstName and LastName fields into a single field (you'll learn how to do this in Lesson 6); then you create the lookup field to look up names in the new query instead of in the Employees table.

WRAP UP

Before you close the book, let's go over some of the things you learned in this lesson:

- You learned how to create a new table using the Table Wizard.

- You learned how to create a new table in Datasheet view.

- You learned how to set field definitions.

- You learned how to relate tables to one another.

- You learned about the difference between a field name and a field caption.

- You learned about the quirky but important AutoNumber data type and its matching Number, Long Integer data type.

- You learned how to create a lookup field in a table, to make data entry easier and more accurate.

For more practice, try creating a table for employee continuing-education training courses and relating it to the employees table. Create a junction table between the two tables to join them; then create lookup fields in the junction table so you can select employee names and training courses. Keep in mind that each employee can take several courses and that each course can be taken by several employees.

In the next lesson, you'll learn about queries and how you can use them to extract precise information from multiple tables.

Querying Your Tables

GOALS

In this lesson, you'll master the following skills and concepts:

30 MINUTES

- Querying a single table

- Running a query

- Adding criteria to a query

- Sorting a query

- Setting parameters for a query

- Creating a two-table query

- Concatenating (joining) names in one field

- Setting an order date criteria

- Creating a query that consolidates data

- Creating a query that calculates data

- Creating a crosstab query

Get ready

GET READY

To complete this lesson, you'll need to start Access 97 and open the Fruitsweets database (refer to Lesson 1 if you need help).

When you finish these exercises, you'll have mastered the skills required to pull precise answers out of your database by creating queries.

TRY OUT THE

INTERACTIVE TUTORIALS

ON YOUR CD!

HOW QUERIES CAN HELP YOU

A query is a request for specific information, such as "Which giftpaks do our customers in Alaska order the most?" or "How many orders have we shipped to each country?" Queries enable you to focus on the specific data you need for your current task.

By using queries, you can examine your data in any way you can think of. You can choose the tables, fields, and records that contain the information you want to see, summarize, or calculate; you can sort the data to organize it; you can create reports and forms that show just the information you choose (always the most current information); and you can even create charts from the data to present it graphically.

NOTE *In a single table, a query can sift through records for you, similar to a filter, but the advantage of using a query over a filter is that when you filter, you get all the fields associated with those records; when you query, you can select both records and specific fields within those records.*

The result of a query is called a *dynaset* (short for *dynamic set* of records). A dynaset is not stored in the database (and, therefore, does not take up space on your hard disk); instead, it's created each time you run the query and dissolved each time you close the query. This not only saves hard disk space (although if you have a brand new 32-gigabyte hard drive, you won't care about that—yet), it also ensures that your query displays only the most current data. If you're querying data from a table someone else on your network keeps updated, you won't know when data in the table has changed, but a query will always give you data that's current as of the moment you run the query.

USING A WIZARD TO CREATE QUERIES

Although there are several Query Wizards in Access 97, it's often easier to build a query from scratch—and you'll know how the query is constructed if you need to change it in the future. If you need to create a more complicated query, such as one that finds duplicate values or unmatched records, then, by all means, use a query wizard. Later in this lesson, you'll use the Crosstab Query Wizard to create a query that lays out the results in a crosstab format. Meanwhile, you'll focus on the mechanics of simple queries by creating them yourself.

DECIDING WHAT INFORMATION YOU NEED

The first step is to decide what information you want to see; next, you determine what tables the data are stored in.

Perhaps you want to see a list of all customers in Virginia, or a summary totaling the Fruitsweets customers in each state or country. All of this information can be found in the Customers table, and you would create a query of that single table to get the lists you want.

On the other hand, suppose you want to know how many giftpaks were ordered by customers in New York. This information is a combination of data in the Customers table (customers' states), the Orders table (which customers placed which orders), and the Order Items table (how many giftpaks were included in each order).

To gather related information from several tables, the tables must be related, but you don't have to create a permanent relationship in the Relationships window to relate two or more tables for a query. The tables you want to use in a query can be related temporarily when you run the query, as you'll see when you create queries in the following exercises. The only requirement for relating two tables in a query is that they share common data in fields with the same data type and size (just like when you related tables in the Relationships window in Lesson 5).

Querying a single table

CREATING A SIMPLE QUERY

Nora in Marketing wants a list of customer names by state. She doesn't want any extra information, just names and states. You can query this information using the Customers table alone.

▶ Querying a single table

In this exercise, you'll create a query that pulls customer names and states from the Customers table.

1 On the Queries tab, click the New button.

The New Query dialog box appears.

2 In the New Query dialog box, double-click Design View.

A new query window and the Show Table dialog box appear, as shown in the accompanying figure.

3 In the Show Table dialog box, double-click Customers.

4 Close the dialog box.

The Customers table (list of fields) is added to the *table pane* of the query window, as shown in the accompanying figure.

5 In the Customers table, double-click the Last Name field.

The Last Name Field is added to the QBE (Query By Example) grid.

6 Double-click the First Name field and the StateOrProvince field to add them to the grid. (You may have to scroll down in the table to find the StateOrProvince field.)

Your query window should look like the accompanying illustration.

7 On the toolbar, click Save. 🖫

8 Save the query with the name **Customers by State**.

That's it! Now you're ready to run the query.

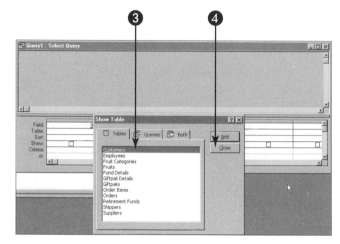

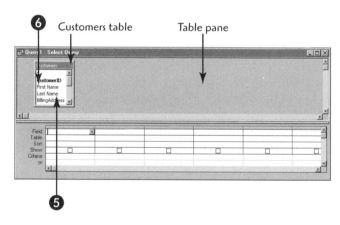

Customers table   Table pane

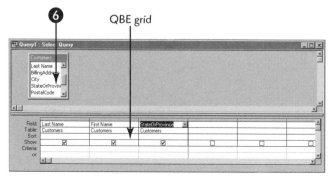

QBE grid

VISUAL BONUS

A Query in Design View

Here is an integrated look at the way a query combines specific fields and records from multiple tables to show only the data you want to see.

The Customers table.

Names are concatenated into a single column in the Customers Order Dates query

Names are concatenated into a single column in the Customers Order Dates query

Customers : Table

Customer	First Name	Last Name	Billing Address	City	StateOrProvin	PostalCode	Country
1	Albert	Dogg	87 Polk St.	San Francisco	CA	94117-1234	USA
2	Michelle	Garfunkel	2743 Bering St.	Anchorage	AK	99508-	USA
3	Marla	Tamons	2817 Milton Dr.	Albuquerque	NM	87110-1200	USA
4	Matthew	Tiburon	3400 - 8th Aven	Albuquerque	NM	87110-1300	USA
5	Wayne	Runnell	707 Oxford Roa	Bend	OR	97101-4444	USA
6	Charles	Black	2453 Baker Stre	Boise	ID	83720-1200	USA
7	Jeffrey	Carter	374 Main Street	Portland	OR	97201-2300	USA
8	Annabeth	Gill	134 Orchestra T	Portland	OR	97219-2350	USA
9	Timothy	Rhodes	746 Polik Street	Seattle	WA	98128-5455	USA
10	Thomas	Malcolm	67 Chianti Road	Elgin	OR	97827-1000	USA
11	Julia	Kelley	2937 Paul Reve	Walla Walla	WA	99362-	USA
12	Juliette	Lester	P.O. Box 6373E	Kirkland	WA	98034-2520	USA
13	Reed	Mills	7264 Bering Str	Anchorage	AK	99508-	USA
14	Donna	Marley	2534 Milton Driv	Eugene	OR	97403-1300	USA
15	Ethan	Striker	234 Suffolk Lan	Boston	MA	02134-2123	USA
16	Rocky	Stallings	P.O. Box 233	Ann Arbor	MI	48104-4562	USA

Record: 1 of 350

Customer Order Date later than November 14, 1996, goes into the Customers Order Dates query

Orders : Table

Order ID	Customer	Order Date	Gift	Ship Last Name	Ship First Name	Ship Street	Ship City
1	23	02-Nov-96	☑	Burchard	Kristi	980 Cornerstone Dr.	Manassas
2	33	02-Nov-96	☑	Carter	Bill	761 Custer St.	San Antonio
3	158	02-Nov-96	☑	Dawousson	Helen	51 Schulz Dr.	Carlisle
4	332	03-Nov-96	☑	Gobi	Colleen	78 Roux Rd.	New Orleans
5	21	03-Nov-96	☑	Hertnagel	Vicky	89 Holms Dr. N.	Baltimore
6	1	03-Nov-96	☑	Kahn	Juliet	1099 Broadway	New York
7	275	04-Nov-96	☐	Bingsley	Hope	454 Bering St.	Anchorage
8	231	04-Nov-96	☐	Lopez	Maria	96 Willamette Loop	Loma Linda
9	348	04-Nov-96	☑	Kelly	Juliette	10 Pepper Dr.	San Jose
10	7	05-Nov-96	☐	Carter	Jeffrey	374 Main Street	Portland
11	148	05-Nov-96	☑	Khout	Kim	42 El Camino Dr.	Charleston
12	154	05-Nov-96	☑	Leland	Earl	2893 Dorothy Dr.	Fairborn
13	80	06-Nov-96	☑	Lester	Richard	1503 Mockingbird Ln	Louisburg
14	229	06-Nov-96	☑	McGinty	Bruce	9308 Dartridge Ave.	San Francisc

Record: 1 of 410

The Orders table.

continued

Running a query

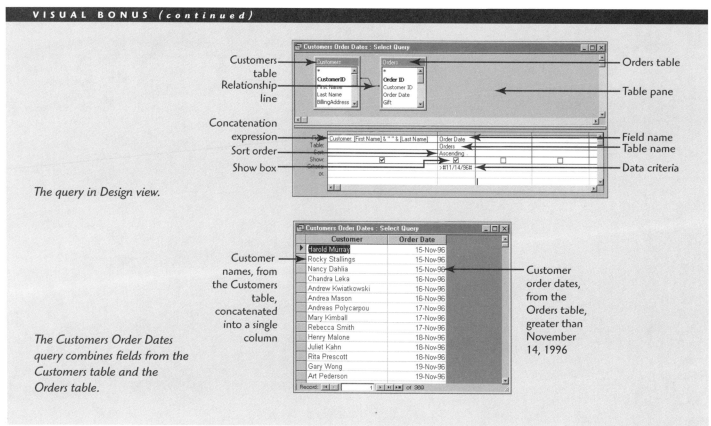

Customers table
Relationship line
Concatenation expression
Sort order
Show box

Orders table
Table pane
Field name
Table name
Data criteria

The query in Design view.

Customer names, from the Customers table, concatenated into a single column

Customer order dates, from the Orders table, greater than November 14, 1996

The Customers Order Dates query combines fields from the Customers table and the Orders table.

Running a query

Now you'll run the query you just created.

1 On the toolbar, click View.

Your query appears as a datasheet, similar to the accompanying illustration.

The records are displayed in the order in which they were entered in the table, but this isn't useful to Nora in Marketing. To make the list more useful, you can sort it.

Adding criteria to a query

2 Click in any Last Name cell.

3 On the toolbar, click Sort Ascending.

The list is sorted by last name, but it might be more useful sorted by state.

4 Click in any StateOrProvince cell.

5 On the toolbar, click Sort Ascending.

The list is sorted by state/province.

6 Click the query window's X close box to close the query.

7 Click Yes to save changes to the query—the sort order will be saved with the query.

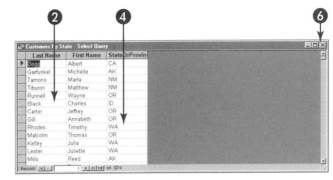

Adding criteria to a query

A *criteria* is a rule, or a filter, that tells Access which records you want to see. For example, you can set a criteria in your query to display only records from specific states in the dynaset, or names beginning with "A", or customers who don't want catalogs.

Nora in Marketing decided that, for now, she wants the names of customers in Arizona and New Mexico only. You can set criteria that limit the records in the dynaset to customers in those two states.

1 On the Queries tab, select the Customers by State query.

2 Click the Design button.

The Customers by State query opens in Design view, as shown in the accompanying figure. You'll set criteria for Arizona (AZ) or New Mexico (NM) in the StateOrProvince field.

3 In the Criteria row of the StateOrProvince column, located in the QBE grid, type **AZ**.

4 In the next cell below (in the Or row), type **NM**.

5 Click in a different cell.

When you click in a different cell, the criteria you typed is surrounded by quotation marks. Your query window should look like the accompanying illustration.

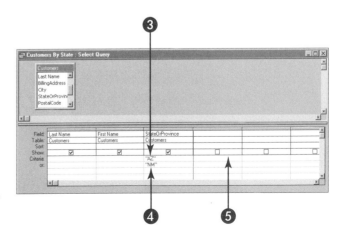

Adding criteria to a query

6 On the toolbar, click View. ▦ ▾

The query switches to Datasheet view, as shown in the accompanying figure.

Records for Arizona and New Mexico customers are displayed in the query datasheet.

The sort you applied earlier is lost when you set new criteria, but you can sort the data again if you want to.

7 Close the query and save your changes.

Table 6-1 shows some commonly used query criteria operators. You can type criteria as shown in the Examples column, and Access will convert your criteria to the proper format (which is a lot easier than trying to remember the formats).

7 ⓻

Customers By State : Select Query		
Last Name	**First Name**	**StateOrProvin**
Tamons	Marla	NM
Tiburon	Matthew	NM
Saraway	Sonya	AZ
Pisa	Terri	AZ
Scott	Marjorie	AZ
Rahman	Farhana	AZ
MacDonald	Alvin	NM
Otis	Paulene	NM
Rodas	Mario	NM
Snyder	Linda	NM
Polycarpou	Andreas	AZ
Gobi	Harry	NM
Rivera	Molly	NM

Record: ◄ ◄ 1 ► ►I ►* of 13

TABLE 6-1 TABLE OF COMMON CRITERIA

Criteria operator	Purpose	Examples
And	Records having one characteristic AND another characteristic	**like *fr* and like *cal*** (in the Fruits Report query, Description field entries that contain the words "Fresh" and "California")
Or	Records having one characteristic OR another characteristic	**apple or kiwi** (in the Fruits Report query, Fruit Name field entries that contain the word "Apple" or the word "Kiwi")
Not	Records that do not have a specified characteristic	**not apple** (any value other than Apple)
&	Concatenates fields into a single column	**[City]&", "&[State]&" "&[Zip]** (concatenates the City, State, and Zip fields, commas, and spaces into an address line such as "Rathdrum, ID 83858")

Criteria operator	Purpose	Examples
Like	Records having the criteria as part of a field's value	**like a*** (entries that start with the letter A); **like *son** (entries that end with "son"); **like [t-v]*** (entries that start with the letters T, U, or V); **like *ba*** (entries that include the letter sequence "ba")
Between . . . And	Records having a value between two values you specify	**between 1/1/98 and 2/1/98** (values from January 2, 1998, through January 31, 1998)
In	Records with a characteristic IN in a list you supply	**in(Dried,Candied)** (a value of Dried or Candied; same result as **Dried OR Candied**)
Is Null	Records having no entry in the field	**is null** in a PhoneNumber field finds records with no phone number entered
Is Not Null	Records having an entry in the field	**is not null** in a PhoneNumber field finds records with a phone number entered
=, <>, >, <	Indicates equal, unequal, greater than, less than	**=42** (entries of 42); **<>3** (entries other than 3); **>1/1/98** (dates after January 1, 1998); **<10.50** (values less than 10.50)
*, /, +, –	Multiplies, divides, adds, subtracts	**[Price]*[Quantity]** (multiply the value in the Price field by the value in the Quantity field); **[Weight]/12** (divide the value in the Weight field by 12)

Sorting a query

NOTE

To get more information about using criteria in your queries, complete the following steps. Select Help ➤ Contents And Index, and click the Contents tab; then double-click Working With Queries; then double-click Using Criteria And Expressions To Retrieve Data; and then double-click Using Criteria to Perform Specific Tasks With Queries.

Sorting a query

If you set a sort order in the query design, the query will sort properly no matter how you change the criteria.

You can sort a query on more than one field. For example, you can sort your Customers-by-State query by State and then by Last Name within each State.

❶ Open the Customers by State query in Design view.

❷ In the QBE grid, click the Sort cell in the StateOrProvince field.

❸ Click the down arrow.

❹ Select Ascending.

The query will be sorted by state/province, but you also want to sort it by last name.

Access performs multiple sorts from left to right. The StateOrProvince field must be moved to the left of the Last Name field in Design view, so the query will sort by state/province and then by last name within each state/province.

❺ In the gray bar at the top of the StateOrProvince field, click when the pointer becomes a down-pointing arrow.

The StateOrProvince field is selected.

❻ Point to the bar at the top of the selected field.

❼ Drag it to the left end of the QBE grid and drop it on the left side of the Last Name field, as shown in the accompanying figure.

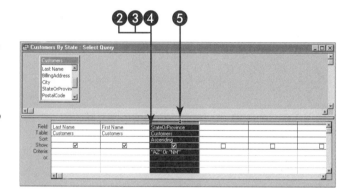

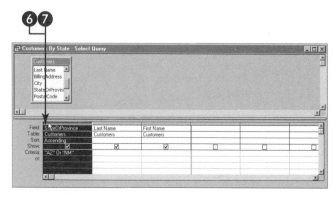

8 In the Sort cell in the Last Name field, select Ascending.

Your query window should look like the accompanying illustration.

9 Switch to Datasheet view.

The query is sorted by state/province and then by last name within each state/province.

But when you moved the StateOrProvince field in Design view, it also switched places in Datasheet view. You don't want it to switch places in Datasheet view, so you'll move it back in the next step.

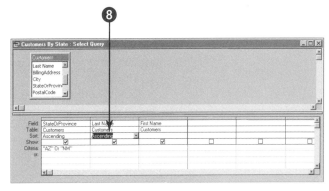

You can move any column in Datasheet view without moving it in Design view, so, in this case, even though Design view is set up to sort each field from left to right, Datasheet view will display the fields in any order you want.

10 In Datasheet view, point to the StateOrProvince column header.

11 Click when the pointer becomes a down arrow.

The StateOrProvince column is selected.

12 Drag the selected column header to the right.

13 Drop it on the right side of the First Name column.

Now Datasheet view displays fields the way you want, as shown in the accompanying figure, even though in Design view, the fields are in a different order to support the sort.

14 Close the query and save your changes.

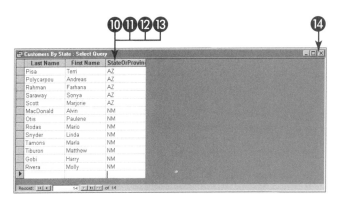

Setting parameters for a query

CUSTOMIZING QUERIES

It's great to be able to set criteria to get the specific records you want, but every time you change your criteria you have to open the query in Design view and set new criteria.

If you change criteria often (for example, if you want to see customers from a different state each time), you can create a *parameter query*, which asks you for your criteria each time it opens. All you have to do is type in your request, and the query pulls up the records you want. Parameter queries can find anything you can set a criteria for, such as orders placed in March, dried fruits, or customers in Nova Scotia. A parameter query is a more user-friendly query, which makes it easy for users who are unfamiliar with Access to pull up the records they need.

Setting parameters for a query

Instead of setting new criteria in Design view each time you want to query the Customers table for records from a different state, you can turn your query into a parameter query that asks you for the state you want each time it opens.

By making the Customers by State query a parameter query, Nora in Marketing will be able to use your query to get the records she wants herself.

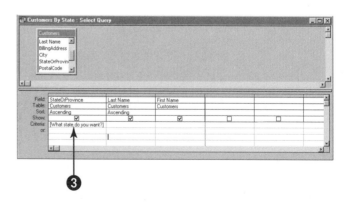

❶ Open the Customers by State query in Design view.

❷ Remove the criteria you set in the StateOrProvince field (select the criteria and press Delete).

❸ In the Criteria cell in the StateOrProvince column, type **[What state do you want?]**.

Be sure you type the square brackets. (Drag the column border to the right to make the column wider.)

Every time you run the query, a dialog box will ask you which state you want and will use your entry as a query criteria.

❹ On the toolbar, click View.

The Enter Parameter Value dialog box appears with the question you typed, as shown in the accompanying figure.

5 Type **ca** and click OK.

The query runs and returns all the records for customers in California.

6 Close the query and save your changes.

7 Open the query and type **Manitoba** in the Enter Parameter Value dialog box; press Enter.

The query opens and displays records for customers in Manitoba.

8 Close the Customers by State query.

USING CALCULATIONS IN QUERIES

Queries can do more than simply pull records: they can calculate the data in those records, to give you information such as how many orders and how much money came in from each state last month, or the total cost of each order plus tax and shipping.

To calculate data, you add extra fields that perform calculations on the other fields in the query.

In the next several exercises, you'll create a two-table query and then use that query to consolidate records and calculate giftpak prices raised by ten percent. Finally, you'll create a crosstab query that shows the number of each fruit in each giftpak, to see if there's a preponderance of certain fruits.

Creating a two-table query

Adrienne in Shipping has been assigned the task of cleaning out the catalog mailing list by removing inactive customer names. She needs a list of customer names and order dates to see who hasn't ordered anything recently. To pull out the information she wants, you'll create a query based on the Customers and Orders tables.

If you were to open the Relationships window, you'd see that the Customers table is not currently related to any other tables, but in a query it doesn't matter whether a permanent relationship exists. In the course of creating this query, you'll create a temporary relationship between the Customers table and the Orders table. This

Creating a two-table query

relationship is possible because both tables have a Customer ID field of matching data type and size (in the Customers table, the field is an AutoNumber data type; in the Orders table, it's a Number data type of Long Integer size).

1 On the Queries tab, click the New button.

The New Query dialog box appears.

2 In the New Query dialog box, double-click Design View.

A new query window and the Show Table dialog box appear.

3 In the Show Table dialog box, double-click Customers then double-click Orders.

4 Close the dialog box.

The Customers and Orders tables are added to the table pane, as shown in the accompanying figure.

Both tables have a Customer ID field; you'll relate the two tables using this field.

5 Drag the Customer ID field from the Customers table.

6 Drop it on the Customer ID field in the Orders table.

A relationship line, also known as a *join* line, appears between the two fields.

TIP *To remove a relationship, or join line, right-click the line; then click Delete.*

This query is going to find names and order dates.

7 In the Customers table, double-click First Name.

8 In the Customers table, double-click Last Name.

9 In the Orders table, double-click Order Date.

The three fields are added to the QBE grid, as shown in the accompanying illustration.

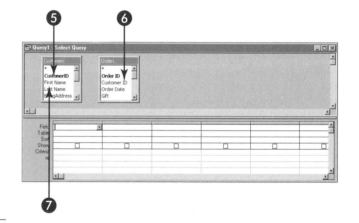

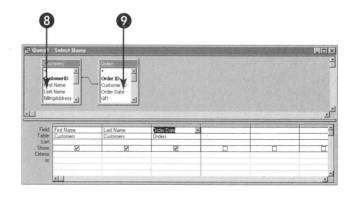

Concatenating names in one field

🔟 Switch to Datasheet view (on the toolbar, click View).

Your query shows a list of all customer names and order dates, as shown in the accompanying illustration.

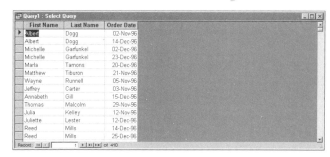

Concatenating (joining) names in one field

This is the information that Adrienne needs, but you can make it look a little nicer by combining the First Name and Last Name in a single column. This is called concatenation, and it's one of the calculations Access can perform for you.

❶ Switch to Design view.

❷ In the QBE grid, click the gray bar at the top of the First Name field to select it.

❸ Press Delete.

The First Name field is removed from the QBE grid.

❹ In the Last Name field, type **Customer:[First Name]&" "& [Last Name]**.

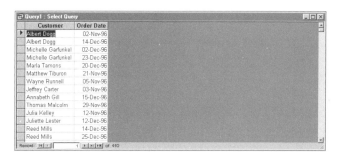

*The **Customer:** part of this expression gives the concatenated column the header "Customer". The names of the fields you are joining are enclosed in square brackets and must be spelled and spaced correctly, including spaces. The & (ampersand) is the mathematical operator that joins the two fields and the space between them. Be sure you type the space between the two quotation marks because it separates the two names.*

Make the column wider by dragging the right side of the column header, if you need to.

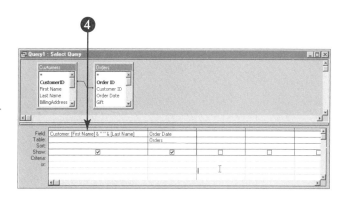

❺ Switch to Datasheet view.

Your query should look like the accompanying illustration.

❻ Save the query as Customers Order Dates

Setting an order date criteria

Setting an order date criteria

You can make this list more useful to Adrienne by querying the records for orders since November 15, 1996. These are recent orders, so Adrienne won't scratch these customers from the catalog list.

1 Switch the Customers Order Dates query to Design view.

2 In the criteria cell for the Order Date field, type **>11-14-96**.

3 Press Enter.

When you press Enter, Access converts your entry to the proper expression syntax.

4 In the sort cell for the Order Date field, select Ascending.

5 Switch to Datasheet view.

Your query dynaset should look like the accompanying illustration.

6 Save the Customers Order Dates query.

TIP

To print the query results, open the query in Datasheet view and click the Print button on the toolbar. If the query results are a long, narrow list, you may want to select File ➤ Page Setup and select the Portrait option button on the Page tab before you print the datasheet.

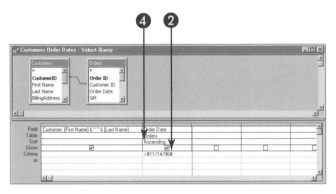

Creating a query that consolidates data

Jerome in Marketing wants to know the total number of giftpaks ordered in each state or province. You can get this information from the Customers and Orders tables (along with the Order Details table), but you don't have to create a new query; you can save the Customers Order Dates query with a new name and then tweak it to get the summary data that Jerome wants.

The Customers Order Dates query should still be open.

The Order Details table is identical to the Order Items table you created in Lesson 5, but has been filled in with data so you can practice calculations.

1 On the File menu, select Save As/Export.

2 In the Save As dialog box, be sure the Within The Current Database option button is selected.

3 In the New Name box, type **Orders by State**.

4 Click OK.

A copy of the Customers Order Dates query is saved with the name Orders by State.

5 Switch to Design view.

6 Delete both fields from the QBE grid (click the gray bar at the top of each field and press Delete).

7 Right-click in the table pane, then click Show Table.

8 Add the Order Details table, then close the Show Table dialog box.

The Order Details table already has a permanent relationship with the Orders table, and that relationship shows up automatically.

9 From the Customers table, add the StateOrProvince field to the QBE grid.

10 From the Order Details table, add the Quantity field to the QBE grid.

The relationships between the three tables enable Access to match individual giftpaks in the Order Items table with the customer states in the Customers table. Your query window should look like the accompanying illustration.

Jerome wants the orders totaled by state, so next you'll group the orders by state to consolidate them.

11 Right-click anywhere in the QBE grid, then click Totals.

A new row, Total, appears in the grid below the Table row.

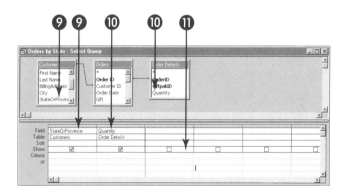

12 Click in the Total cell in the Quantity field.

13 Click the drop-down arrow and select Sum.

NOTE *Confused about whether to select Count or Sum? The Count function counts the number of Quantity fields from each state, while the Sum function sums these fields. The Quantity field in one customer order can consist of two — or three or ten — giftpaks, for a Quantity count of one, but a Quantity sum of two. When in doubt, look at a sample of the individual records, perhaps orders from Alaska, and count what you want on your fingers; then try both Count and Sum and see which gives you the answer you're looking for.*

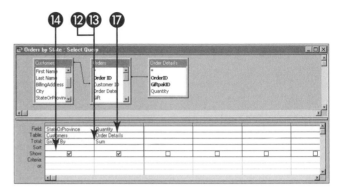

While you're at it, you'll sort the results by state/province, in ascending order.

14 In the Sort cell in the StateOrProvince field, select Ascending.

15 Switch to Datasheet view.

Your query dynaset should look like the accompanying illustration.

The field name Access has set, SumOfQuantity, is a less-than-wonderful caption for the column, so you'll change it (the caption, not the field name).

16 Switch to Design view.

17 In the QBE grid, right-click in the Quantity field, then click Properties.

The Field Properties dialog box appears.

18 In the Caption box, type **Total Giftpaks**.

19 Click the X close box to close the dialog box.

20 Switch to Datasheet view.

Your query dynaset should look like the accompanying illustration.

21 Save and close the query.

Creating a query that calculates data

Creating a query that calculates data

What would Fruitsweets giftpak prices be if they were raised by ten percent? Would the prices still seem reasonable?

You can find out by creating a query that calculates a ten percent increase in each giftpak price. To create this query, you need price data from the Giftpaks table.

1 On the Queries tab, click the New button.

2 In the New Query dialog box, double-click Design View.

3 In the new query window, add the Giftpaks table.

4 From the Giftpaks table, add the GiftpakName and Price fields.

Your query window should look like the accompanying illustration.

5 Save the query as **Increase Prices**.

6 In the QBE grid, in the empty field next to the Price field, type the expression **10% Increase: [Price]*1.1**.

7 Switch to Datasheet view.

Your query dynaset should look like the accompanying illustration.

The column of increased prices is not very intuitive, so you'll change the format of the number display.

8 Switch to Design view.

9 Right-click the new Increase field in the QBE grid, then click Properties.

10 In the Field Properties dialog box, click in the Format box.

11 Select Currency, then close the dialog box (click its X close box).

12 Switch to Datasheet view.

Your query dynaset should look like the accompanying illustration.

13 Save and close the query.

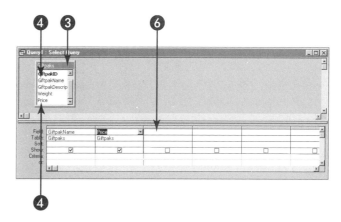

Drag here to resize rows

Creating a crosstab query

NOTE *The row heights are tall because the query has inherited display characteristics from the tables— you raised the row heights in the Giftpaks table (in Lesson 3) to display the Giftpak descriptions better.*

You can resize the rows in the query datasheet the same way you did in the table datasheet, by dragging a record selector border.

Creating a crosstab query

Some data is difficult to read in a list format because so much information is presented. Loan tables, for example, are traditionally displayed in a crosstab format, with loan amounts down the left side of the table and interest rates across the top; payment amounts for a given loan amount at a specific interest rate can be looked up in the center of the table. You can create crosstab queries in Access if you need to present a similar kind of data.

In this exercise, you'll create a crosstab query that shows the number of each fruit contained in each giftpak, with the giftpak names listed on the left side and the fruit names listed across the top. This type of query is easiest to create using a wizard.

You need the Giftpak names from the Giftpaks table, and the fruit names from the Fruits table; these two tables are related through the Giftpak Details table. To create a crosstab query that combines data from two or more tables, you first need to create a query that combines the data you want; then create the crosstab query from that query. The Fruits by Giftpak query has already been set up (if you want to, open it and take a look before you start this exercise).

1 On the Queries tab, click the New button.

2 In the New Query dialog box, double-click Crosstab Query Wizard.

The wizard starts and the first wizard step appears, as shown in the accompanying illustration.

3 Select the Queries option button.

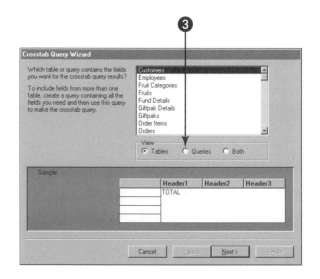

④ Select Fruits by Giftpak, then click Next.

The second wizard step appears, as shown in the accompanying illustration.

⑤ In the second wizard step, double-click GiftpakName, then click Next.

The third wizard step appears, and FruitName is already selected as the column heading.

⑥ Click Next.

The fourth wizard step appears.

⑦ In the Functions list, click Sum, then click Next.

The fifth wizard step appears, and the name that Access has selected will do fine.

⑧ Click Finish.

The crosstab query is created, as shown in the accompanying illustration.

⑨ Save and close the query.

SKILLS CHALLENGE: CREATING A NEW CROSSTAB QUERY

In this Skills Challenge, you'll create a crosstab query of employee investments in retirement funds.

First you need to add a bit more data to the Fund Details table; then you need to create a simple query that shows what portion of their retirement allotment each employee invests in each fund; finally, you create the crosstab query that displays that data in a crosstab format.

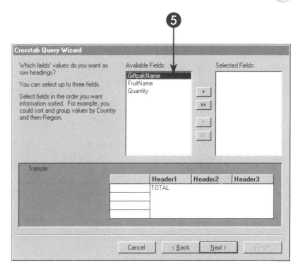

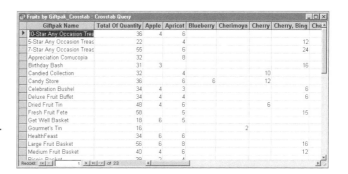

Skills challenge

1 Open the Fund Details table.

2 Add the following data:

Name	Funds and percentages		
McGinty	GetRichQuick Fund – 25%	Bahamas Portfolio – 75%	
Petrof	GetRichQuick Fund – 30%	Bahamas Portfolio – 35%	Stocks'r'Us – 35%
Willson	GetRichQuick Fund – 75%	Stocks'r'Us – 25%	
Andrews	GetRichQuick Fund – 40%	Bahamas Portfolio – 40%	Stocks'r'Us – 20%
Krauser	Bahamas Portfolio – 40%	Stocks'r'Us – 60%	

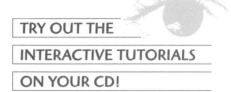
 Do you remember how to create a table relationship in the query design window?

 NOTE *If you don't see Nora McGinty's name in the Employees table, remember that in Lesson 3 you changed Nora Sparrow's name to Nora McGinty because she got married.*

3 Close the Fund Details table.

4 Create a new query in Design view.

 Do you remember how to sort a query by two or more fields?

5 Add the Employees table, the Fund Details table, and the Retirement Funds table.

6 From the Employees table, add a field that concatenates First Name and Last Name.

3 *Do you remember where to enter criteria?*

7 From the Fund Details table, add the Percent field.

8 From the Retirement Funds table, add the FundName field.

9 Save the query as **Retirement Allotments**.

10 Close the query.

 4 *Do you remember how to create a query parameter?*

11 Create a crosstab query based on the Retirement Allotments query.

12 Make employee names the row headings, and fund names the column headings.

13 Use the Sum function for the data in the body of the table.

Your completed crosstab table should look like the accompanying illustration.

TROUBLESHOOTING

You've learned how to generate a lot of useful information by using queries. The following solutions might answer some questions that came up during this lesson.

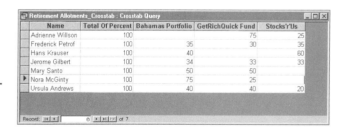

Problem	Solution
The two tables I want to query won't join.	If they have a many-to-many relationship, you'll need to create a junction table to join them (see Lesson 5 to learn about junction tables).
I typed my parameter in the Criteria box, but it doesn't work.	Be sure you type square brackets around the parameter phrase.

(continued)

Wrap up

Problem	Solution
How can I open my query without the parameter dialog box?	Open the query in Design view and remove the parameter.
My First Name and Last Name concatenation isn't working.	Check the spelling of the field names. They must be spelled and spaced exactly as they are in the table. (Remember, field names, not field captions.)
A field in my QBE grid isn't showing up in my query datasheet.	Make sure the field's Show box (in Design view) is checked. If you accidentally clicked it and cleared it, the field will be hidden in the datasheet.

WRAP UP

Before you finish, let's go over some of the things you learned in this lesson:

- You learned how to query single and related multiple tables.

- You learned how to set criteria and sort orders to generate more useful dynasets.

- You learned how to create user-friendly parameter queries.

- You learned how to calculate fields and how to summarize records.

- You learned how to create a crosstab query for a different data layout.

For more practice, try adding the Order Date field to the Orders by State Query and then set criteria for orders placed in November 1996 (between 10/31/96 and 12/1/96).

In the next lesson, you'll learn how to create forms that make data entry more efficient.

Beyond Basics

This part covers forms and reports and includes the following lessons:

- Lesson 7: Creating a Form — this lesson introduces you to forms and custom form design.

- Lesson 8: Finishing a Form — this lesson takes form design further and teaches you to customize and personalize your forms.

- Lesson 9: Creating Reports — this lesson teaches you to create and customize reports.

To begin working the book lessons in this part, instead of beginning with Lesson 3 or earlier, use the practice database file named `FSPart3.mdb` and begin with Lesson 7.

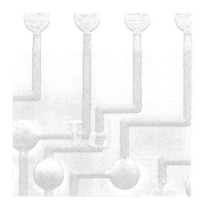

Creating a Form

GOALS

In this lesson, you'll master the following skills and concepts:

- Creating queries for forms
- Adding a calculated field to a form's query
- Creating forms using wizards
- Reconfiguring a form
- Combining a main form with a subform

Get ready

GET READY

To complete this lesson, you'll need to start Access 97 and open the Fruitsweets database (refer to Lesson 1 if you need help opening the Fruitsweets database).

When you finish these exercises, you'll have mastered the skills required to create useful forms that will speed up data entry and ensure a greater degree of accuracy.

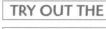

TRY OUT THE

INTERACTIVE TUTORIALS

ON YOUR CD!

BEGIN WITH DESIGN

You can whip up a simple data-entry form for a table or query by clicking the New Object: AutoForm button and letting the form wizard do the work for you, but the most useful forms can't be whipped up by a form wizard—they're complex and require planning and effort on your part (although you can have the form wizard whip up part of your form to save you time). The focus of this lesson is the planning and construction of a complex form, and along the way you'll learn myriad construction techniques you can use to build both simple and complex forms.

In this lesson, you'll create one of the most useful types of forms there is: an Orders form to take orders for Fruitsweets giftpaks. Many databases need a form similar to the one you'll create—a medical or legal office, to enter details of client visits; a horse show, to enter competitors in its events; or a school, to enroll students in its classes.

The Orders form needs to be able to:

- Look up customers by their CustomerID number

- Edit an existing customer's information

- Enter a new customer in the Customers table and then enter the new customer ID number in the Orders table

- Enter shipping information and payment information in the Orders table

- Enter the ordered items into the Order Details table

- Calculate the customer's order total

A good plan for your Orders form is to create a combination of forms:

- A main form that enters all of the information needed by the Orders table, including shipping and payment information and the customer ID

- A subform that displays the customer's name and address, so you can verify that you have the correct customer ID and edit that information if you need to

- Another subform that enters the giftpaks being ordered into the Order Details Table (this subform should also display the total number of giftpaks being ordered)

PLAN AHEAD

Before building a complex form, determine what information the form will need and in what order you'll build its parts. Planning will save you considerable time in the long run. In fact, a pencil and paper come in handy at this stage.

The Visual Bonus on the next page contains a sketch of some of the planning that goes into the Fruitsweets Orders form and the final form that you'll build from the plan.

SUBFORMS AND CONTROLS

A *subform* is simply a form within a form, as you can see in the Visual Workout. The *main*, or outer, form is the primary form, and the subform is *nested*, or embedded, in the main form. Using a subform in a main form allows you to display and edit related records from two different tables in the same form, which can save considerable time in the course of a busy workday.

Subforms and controls

Planning the Orders Form

The Orders form you'll build will look similar to the accompanying illustration when it's finished. You'll begin building the form in this lesson, and you'll complete it in Lesson 8.

The plan for the Orders form.

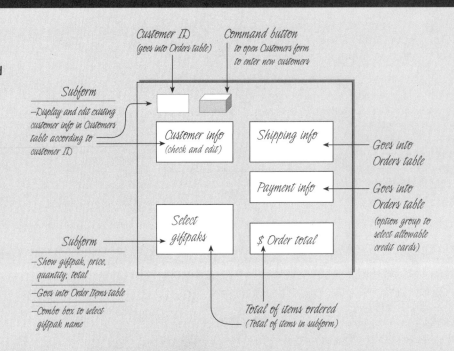

Customer ID
(goes into Orders table)

Command button
to open Customers form to enter new customers

Subform
—*Display and edit existing customer info in Customers table according to customer ID*

Customer info
(check and edit)

Shipping info

Payment info

Select giftpaks

$ Order total

Goes into Orders table

Goes into Orders table
(option group to select allowable credit cards)

Subform
—*Show giftpak, price, quantity, total*
—*Goes into Order Items table*
—*Combo box to select giftpak name*

Total of items ordered
(Total of items in subform)

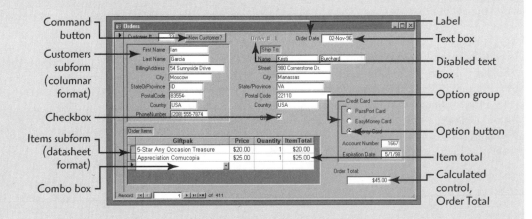

The finished Orders form.

Command button

Customers subform (columnar format)

Checkbox

Items subform (datasheet format)

Combo box

Label

Text box

Disabled text box

Option group

Option button

Item total

Calculated control, Order Total

Subforms and controls ◀

A subform and main form are connected by a linking field. In the Orders form you'll build, the main form and the Customers subform are linked by the Customer ID field, which both the Orders table and the Customers table share. The linkage between the two forms enables the Customers subform to show the customer information for the Customer ID number that's entered in the main form. The Items subform is connected to the main form by the Order ID number, which is shared by the Orders table and the Order Details Table. This link enables the Items subform to display the giftpak records associated with the Order ID number in the main form.

TIP *You can embed as many subforms in a main form as you want, and you can nest forms up to two deep—a subform can contain a subform.*

You can use a form wizard to create a main/subform combination for you, by selecting two related tables in the first wizard step—the wizard merges all the fields in both tables into a main/subform combination—but you have greater control over the finished form when you create the main/subform combination yourself. In this lesson, you'll use the form wizard to create the separate forms; then you'll embed and link the subforms in the main form yourself.

Forms and subforms can be based on either tables or queries; which you choose depends on what you want to do.

NOTE *Subforms perform faster when based on queries that include only the necessary fields, rather than on tables, because the extra fields in a table slow down subform performance. If your goal is simply to enter data directly into a single table, then you should base your form (not a subform) directly on the table without an intermediary query.*

In the Orders form you're going to build, the main form will be based on the Orders table, and the subforms will both be based on queries you'll create specifically for the forms.

Any form is really just a plateful of *controls*, which are the text boxes, option buttons, combo boxes, and so on that you click or type in to enter data in the underlying tables. In creating the form layout,

Creating queries for forms

you organize its controls so that you can enter data easily, accurately, and in a logical order.

NOTE *Even though a subform is a form in its own right, it's also a control, called a* subform control, *when it's nested in the main form.*

A control is either *bound*, which means it's connected to a specific field in a specific table and can display or enter data in that field, or *unbound*, which means it sits on the form to provide extra information. For example, all labels on forms are unbound controls. An unbound control is not attached to any underlying fields and cannot enter data in tables.

An unbound control can also calculate information displayed by other controls; for example, a *calculated control* can multiply the value in the Price control by the value in the Quantity control and display the resulting product.

You'll use several different kinds of controls, both bound and unbound, in your Orders form.

CREATING THE UNDERLYING QUERIES

Before you create your forms, you should create any queries on which you want to base them.

For the Orders form, the main form will be based directly on the Orders table, but the form's two subforms will both be based on queries, and you'll create the queries first.

Creating queries for forms

Your subforms will be based on queries created specifically for them.

The Customers subform and its underlying query will display most of the fields in the Customers table. The underlying query must also include the CustomerID field from the Orders table, so the subform can later be linked to the main form.

The Items subform and its underlying query will enter giftpak names and quantities the customer orders and will display the price of each giftpak. It will also include an item total that multiplies the price of a specific giftpak by the quantity ordered, and you'll add that field to the query in the exercise following this one.

In this exercise, you'll create the Customers subform query first and then you'll create the Items subform query.

1 On the Queries tab, click the New button and double-click Design View.

2 Add the Orders table and the Customers table to the query window; then close the Show Table dialog box.

TIP *You can create a permanent relationship between the Customers and Orders tables if you want to; they are unrelated in this book only for the purposes of teaching.*

3 Join the two tables by dragging the CustomerID field from the Customers table to the CustomerID field in the Orders table.

4 From the Orders table, add the CustomerID field to the QBE grid.

5 From the Customers table, add all fields *except* CustomerID and Catalog to the QBE grid.

Your query should look like the accompanying illustration.

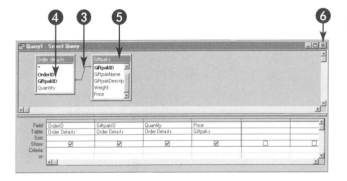

NOTE *It's important to use the CustomerID field from the Orders table, not the Customers table, so that the Customer ID number you enter in the Orders form will be entered in the Orders table.*

6 Save the query as **Customers subform qry** and close it.

Next, you'll build the Items subform query.

7 On the Queries tab, click the New button.

8 Double-click Design View.

9 Add the Order Details table and the Giftpaks table to the query window.

Adding a calculated field to a form

The two tables are already joined by a permanent relationship.

10 From the Order Details table, add the OrderID, GiftpakID, and Quantity fields to the QBE grid.

11 From the Giftpaks table, add the Price field to the QBE grid.

Your query should look like the accompanying illustration.

12 Save the query as **Items subform qry** (don't close it).

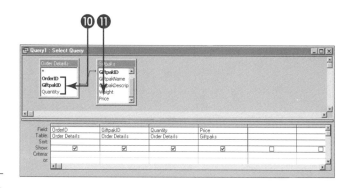

Adding a calculated field to a form's query

In your Items subform, you want to show an Item Total, so that in an order for three Fresh Fruit Fetes, for example, you can see the total cost immediately. The Item Total will be a calculated field that multiplies the value in the Price field by the value in the Quantity field.

You could create a text box in the subform that performs the calculation, instead of performing the calculation in the query and then showing the result in the subform, but here's a good place to plan ahead, because later you'll create a calculated control in the Orders main form that sums all of the Item Totals for the order. The control that sums the Item Totals can't use another calculated control in its calculation, but it can sum controls that display a value from a query. So, you'll create a field in the query that calculates the Item Total and shows that value in the subform; then you'll create a text box in the Orders main form that sums the Item Total values shown in the subform.

Creating forms using wizards

In this exercise, you'll create the calculated Item Total field in the Items subform query. The Items subform query should still be open.

1 Click in the first empty field column in the QBE grid.

2 In the field cell, type **Item Total: [Price]*[Quantity]**.

3 Press Enter.

Your query window should look like the accompanying illustration.

4 Switch to Datasheet view to check the calculated field.

The query shows all of the records in the Order Details Table and prices for each giftpak in the list; wherever the Quantity is two or more, the Item Total field shows a total for the number of giftpaks ordered.

5 Save and close the Items subform query.

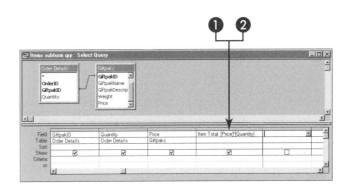

CREATING THE FORMS

Your subforms will be based on the queries you created in the previous exercises, and your main form will be based on the Orders table. You'll use the form wizard to create each one quickly.

Creating forms using wizards

The purpose of the Customers subform is simply to display customer information. Its purpose is twofold: to ensure that you have the correct Customer ID entered in the Orders table and to edit customers' information if their names or addresses have changed.

The purpose of the Items subform is to enter the customer's giftpak order in the Order Details Table. Giftpak prices and item totals are included in the Items subform, so you can see the breakdown of prices (and if a customer asks "How much is that?", you can tell them).

The purpose of the Orders main form is to enter data directly in the Orders table.

Creating forms using wizards

With this plan in mind, you'll create all three forms in this exercise, beginning with the Orders main form.

1 On the Tables tab, click the Orders table to select it.

2 On the toolbar, click New Object: AutoForm. 📇▾

The Form wizard creates a simple columnar form that contains all the fields in the Orders table, like the accompanying illustration.

3 Close the new form.

4 When prompted, save it with the name **Orders**.

Next you'll create the Customers subform.

5 On the Forms tab, click New.

6 Then double-click Form Wizard.

The first wizard step appears.

7 In the Tables/Queries box, click the drop-down arrow.

8 Select Query: Customers subform qry (you'll have to scroll down to find it).

The fields in the Customers subform query appear in the list of available fields; you want all the fields except the CustomerID field in your form.

9 Click the right double-arrow button.

All the fields are moved into the Selected Fields list.

10 Scroll up the list and select CustomerID.

11 Then click the left single-arrow button.

The CustomerID field is moved back to the Available Fields list, as shown in the accompanying illustration.

12 Click Next.

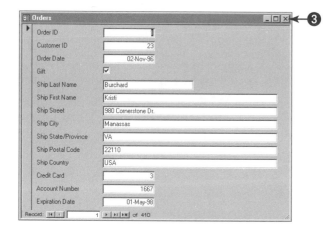

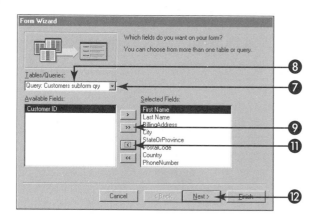

⑬ The default layout Columnar is suitable; click Next.

⑭ Select the Standard style, then click Next.

⑮ Title your form **Customers subform** and click Finish.

TIP *"Customers subform" is the form's caption, and appears in the form's title bar. If you want to change the caption (the title) of the form later, open the form in design view, and open the Properties dialog box for the form. On the Format tab, type a new title in the Caption box, then save and close the form.*

The new form is completed and saved; it should look similar to the accompanying illustration.

Later you'll reconfigure this form to make it fit on the Orders form.

⑯ Close the Customers subform.

Next you'll create the Items subform.

⑰ On the Forms tab, click the New button, then double-click Form Wizard.

⑱ Create a new form from the Items subform qry query.

⑲ Add the GiftpakID, Quantity, Price, and Item Total fields.

⑳ Select Datasheet layout and Standard style.

㉑ Name the form **Items subform**.

Your finished form should look similar to the accompanying illustration.

㉒ Close the Items subform.

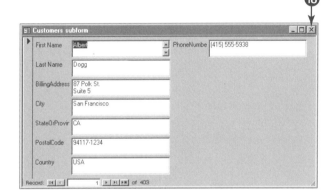

Reconfiguring a form

Reconfiguring a form

In this exercise, you'll reconfigure the Customers subform, so it's compact and readable.

1 Open the Customers subform.

The labels are truncated, and the text boxes are inappropriately sized and too far apart.

2 Switch to Design view.

3 Maximize the window, so you can see all of the controls.

TIP *You can maximize a window by clicking the Maximize button or by double-clicking the window's title bar.*

Each text box is too tall (they need to display only single lines of data), and they are all the same length. You need to make them shorter and change the widths to suit the data.

4 Click the Phone Number text box to select it.

5 Then drag the bottom handle up until the text box is approximately one line tall (the same height as the labels), as shown in the accompanying illustration.

You can speed up the process by resizing several controls at once.

6 Click one of the tall text boxes.

7 Then press and hold down the Shift key while you click the remaining tall text boxes.

All the text boxes you click are selected, and when you drag a sizing handle for one, all the selected controls will resize identically, as shown in the accompanying illustration.

8 Make all the labels the same height.

9 Select each text box in turn and drag the right-side handle to make the text box narrower, until your form looks similar to the accompanying illustration.

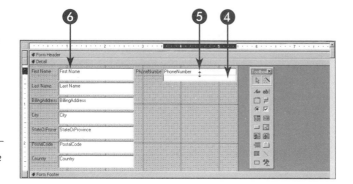

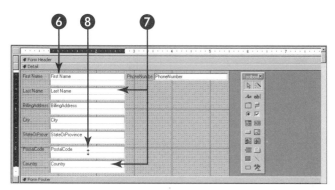

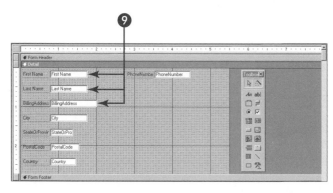

10 Click on a blank part of the form to deselect the controls.

11 Click on the Last Name text box and hold down the mouse button.

When you press the mouse button, the pointer becomes a small hand (as shown in the accompanying illustration), and you can move the control and its attached label to another position on the form.

12 Move each text box/label combination into new positions until your form resembles the accompanying illustration.

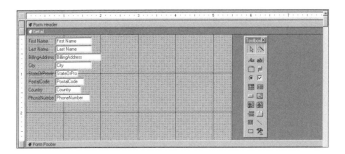

Now you need to align the controls and fit the labels to their text. These next steps can be a bit confusing at first, but once you've done it, you'll see how easy it is to reposition and align controls.

13 Starting at the lower right corner of the group of controls, drag to draw a rectangle that touches all of the controls; then release the mouse button.

All of the controls are selected.

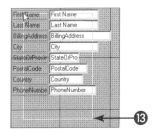

14 Move the entire group of controls about one inch to the right (click anywhere in the group and, with the hand icon, move the group).

15 Click away from the group to deselect the controls.

16 Click the First Name label to select it.

17 Move the pointer over the small box in the upper left corner of the label, until the pointer becomes a hand-with-a-pointing-finger icon.

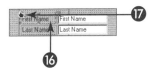

TIP

You can move a label separately from its attached text box (and vice versa) by dragging the box in the upper-left corner.

18 Drag the First Name label about ½" to the left.

Creating a Form — 7

Reconfiguring a form

19 Starting at the lower-right corner of the group of labels, drag to draw a rectangle that touches all of the labels (but not the text boxes).

20 On the Format menu, point to Align; then click Left.

The left edges of the selected controls are aligned with the left edge of the left-most control.

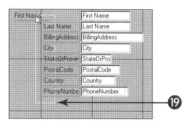

21 While the labels are selected, on the Format menu, point to Size, then click To Fit.

The labels are each sized to fit their text.

22 While the labels are selected, on the Format menu, point to Align and then click Right.

23 While the labels are selected, move the group of controls to the left, against the left side of the form (all of the controls move together).

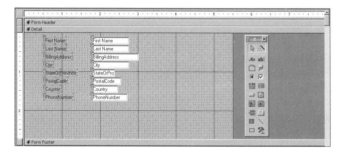

24 Click away from the controls to deselect them.

25 Then move the First Name text box to the left, until it is near but not touching the First Name label (as shown in the accompanying illustration).

You can move a control separately from its attached label by dragging the box in the upper-left corner of the control, just as you did with the label in Step 11.

26 Drag to select all of the text boxes (but not the labels) and on the Format menu, point to Align, then click Left.

The labels and text boxes are all neatly aligned.

27 Point to the top border of the Form Footer bar, and when the pointer becomes a two-headed arrow, drag upward until the border is just below the bottom-most controls.

28 Point to the right edge of the form grid, and when the pointer becomes a two-headed arrow, drag to the left until the edge of the grid is close to the right-most control.

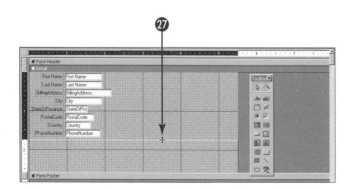

Your form should look like the accompanying illustration.

㉙ Switch to Form view.

㉚ Click the Restore Window button (in the upper-right corner), so the window is not maximized.

㉛ Click Window Size to Fit Form.

> **NOTE**
>
> *The Size To Fit Form command is unavailable when the window is maximized.*

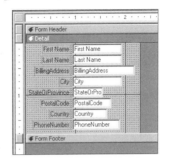

Your Customers subform should look like the accompanying illustration.

If any text boxes contain truncated data because they're too narrow, switch to Design view and lengthen the text boxes.

㉜ Save and close the Customers subform.

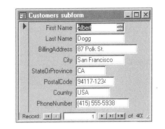

CREATING THE MAIN FORM/SUBFORM COMBINATION

Combining a main form with a subform

Now that you've created your main form and two subforms, you can drag the subforms onto the main form, drop them in place and connect them.

❶ Open the Orders form in Design view.

❷ Maximize the window.

❸ Drag the lower-right corner of the form grid down and to the right to make it larger (you need to make room for the subforms).

❹ Move, resize, and align the controls, so the form resembles the preliminary layout in the accompanying illustration.

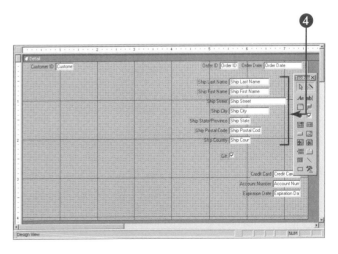

Main forms/subforms

Remember, to move a control separately from its label (or vice versa), drag the small box in the upper-left corner of the control. The pointer should look like a hand with the index finger pointing.

5 Click the Restore Window button to make the window smaller.

6 Click the database window to bring it on top of the Form window (you may need to move the Form window a bit to click the database window).

7 In the database window, on the Forms tab, drag the Customers subform.

8 Drop it in the Form window.

The blank rectangle that is the Customers subform is called a *subform control* when you are looking at the main form's Design view.

9 Move the Customers subform control into position below the Customer ID label and text box.

10 Click the database window.

11 Drag the Items subform from the database window.

12 Drop it below the Customers subform control in the Form window.

13 Maximize the Form window.

Your Form window should look similar to the accompanying illustration.

14 Right-click the Customers subform control.

15 Click Properties.

The Subform/Subreport dialog box appears, as shown in the illustration on the next page. You'll use this dialog box to link the subform to the main form by linking the Child Field (from the subform) to the Master Field (from the main form).

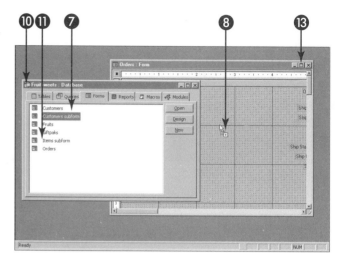

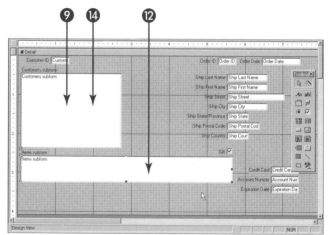

16 Click in the Link Child Fields box.

17 Then click the Build button (the small button with the three dots that appears to the right of the Link Child Fields box, not the toolbar button).

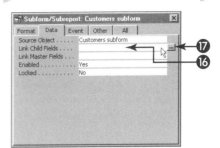

 If you get a message telling you to install the Advanced Wizards, save the form, close Access, and close any other programs you have running. Pop your Office 97 CD-ROM into the CD-ROM drive, click

Start ➢ Settings ➢ Control Panel, and double-click the Add/Remove Programs icon. Select Office 97; then click Add/Remove Programs; then click Add/Remove Programs again. Select Access; click Change Option; then click the Advanced Wizards checkbox and click OK. Click Continue and follow your computer's instructions. Finally, start Access again and continue with the lesson.

The Subform Field Linker dialog box appears, and Access has selected appropriate linking fields for the subform and main form — in this case, the Customer ID field in both forms.

18 Click OK.

The linking fields appear in the Properties dialog box, and the sub- and main forms are now linked.

 Instead of closing and reopening the Properties dialog box, you can simply click the Items subform control; the Properties dialog box will switch to the new control.

19 Follow Steps 14 through 18 to link the Items subform to the main form, using the OrderID field to link them.

20 Then close the Properties dialog box.

NOTE *You may notice that the Master Field name is Order ID (with a space) and the Child Field name is OrderID (no space). This is how the field names in the two tables are spelled; the Subform Field Linker dialog box has saved you untold frustration by spelling each field name precisely.*

㉑ Save the form.

㉒ Switch to Form view.

Your Orders form should look similar to the accompanying illustration.

The Orders form is usable now, even if it's not very elegant or error-proof. If you repeatedly click the Next Record navigation button at the bottom of the main form, you'll see the correct customer information and items ordered for each existing Fruitsweets order. The two subforms show only the records that correspond to the order shown in the main form.

㉓ Close the Orders form.

SKILLS CHALLENGE: ADDING PICTURES TO A FORM

In this Skills Challenge, you'll learn about another type of control, called an *image control*, that holds pictures.

Fruitsweets has decided to make the database more visual, by adding a company logo to forms and reports and by keeping photographs of employees in their database records. The employee photos can be scanned and saved as bitmap images and stored in the Employees table. You'll add a picture of the company logo to a new Employees form, and you'll add some employee photos to the Employees table and form.

Pictures are contained in *image controls* and *object frames*, which can be bound to a table field (suitable for the employee pictures) or unbound, which means the picture sits on the form and doesn't change (which is what you want for the company logo). For

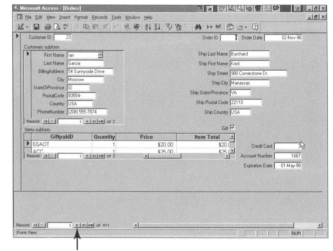

Next Record navigation button for main form

TRY OUT THE

INTERACTIVE TUTORIALS

ON YOUR CD!

unbound pictures like the company logo, you'll want to use an image control because image controls load much faster than unbound object frames. For a picture stored in a table, like an employee photo, you'll want to use an object frame because you can open and change the graphic image easily from within the form.

First, you'll add the new picture field to the Employees table; then you'll create an AutoForm for the table and enter an employee photo. Access will automatically create a bound object frame for the new field in the AutoForm. Finally, you'll add an image control to the new form and insert the company logo in the control.

1 Open the Employees table in Design view.

2 Add a new field named **Photo**.

3 Give it a data type of OLE Object.

4 Save the table.

5 Close the table.

6 On the Tables tab, click the Employees table to select it.

7 On the toolbar, click the New Object: AutoForm button.

The Form wizard creates a new form named Employees, as shown in the accompanying illustration.

The large box labeled "Photo" is an object frame that's bound to the Photo field in the Employees table. You can insert a scanned photograph of a Fruitsweets employee in this control to store his or her picture in his or her record, along with his or her name, address, and other personal information. The picture will be visible only in the form, but the embedded picture information will be stored in the table.

8 Save the new form with the name **Employees**.

 How can you tell what table or query a form is based on?

9 Locate the record for Jerome Gilbert (it should be record number 2).

10 Right-click the image control.

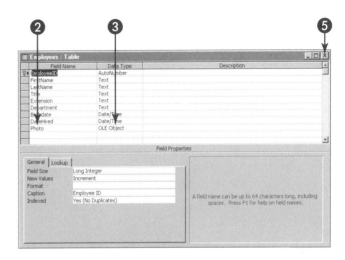

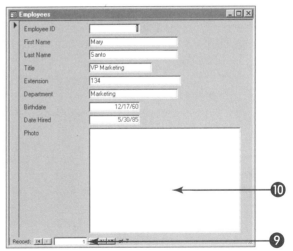

Skills challenge

⑪ Click Insert Object.

⑫ In the Insert Object dialog box, click the Create From File option button.

⑬ Click the Browse button.

⑭ Navigate to your Access One Step at a Time folder.

⑮ Double-click the file named `Gilbert.bmp`.

2 *How can you delete a partial record you've entered?*

⑯ In the Insert Object dialog box, click OK.

The picture is inserted in the control, and the embedded picture information is entered in Gilbert's record in the Employees table. But the picture doesn't fit the frame, so you need to resize the frame.

⑰ Switch to Design view.

⑱ Drag the lower-right corner of the control up and to the left to make it smaller, as shown in the accompanying figure.

⑲ Switch back to Form view. Your form should look similar to the accompanying illustration.

To make an inserted object fit the frame on your form, you can change the frame's Size Mode property (on the Format tab of the frame's Properties dialog box). The default size mode is Clip, which leaves the picture unchanged but only shows as much as will fit in your frame, so you must resize the frame to fit the picture. Stretch mode stretches and alters the dimensions of your picture to fit the frame's dimensions precisely. Zoom mode alters the picture's dimensions to fit your frame but without stretching the picture out of its original proportions.

Now you can add an unbound image control to the Employees form, and insert the Fruitsweets logo.

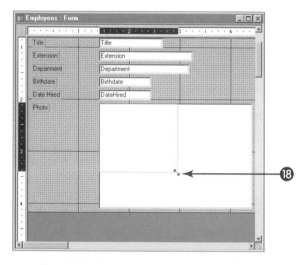

⑳ Switch to Design view.

㉑ Right-click on the Detail bar.

㉒ Then click Form Header/Footer.

A header and footer are added to the form.

 3 *How can you move or resize several controls at once?*

㉓ Drag the top of the Detail bar downward until the Header area is about one inch tall.

㉔ In the Control toolbox, click the Image button.

㉕ Then click in the form header.

The Control wizard places an image control in the form header and then opens the Insert Picture dialog box.

㉖ Double-click the `Logo.bmp` file.

The Logo picture is inserted in the image control.

㉗ Drag the image control into position, as shown in the accompanying illustration.

 4 *Do you remember how to align several controls with one another?*

㉘ Scroll to the bottom of the form grid.

㉙ Drag its bottom border up to the bottom of the form footer. This action hides the form footer. You don't need it because you have nothing in it.

 5 *How can you quickly resize a label to show all of its text?*

㉚ Switch to Form view.

㉛ Click Window Size to Fit Form.

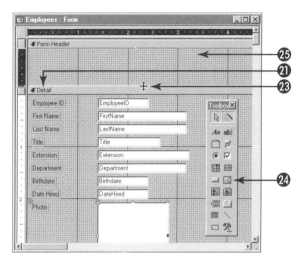

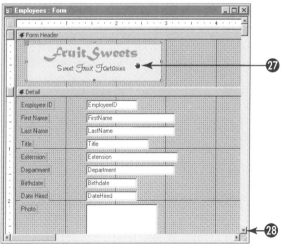

Troubleshooting

Your form, with Gilbert's record displayed, should look similar to the accompanying illustration.

TIP

If your form is too big, remember to switch to Design view and drag the edges of the grid to make it smaller.

 6 *Do you remember how to combine two related forms into a subform/main form?*

32 Save and close the Employees form.

TROUBLESHOOTING

You've learned the basics of form building, using the Form wizard, and then tweaking the result to get exactly what you want. The following solutions might answer some questions that came up during this lesson.

Problem	Solution
I've finished a new form and used a lot of numbers in testing it. How can I make AutoNumber start over and replace the used up numbers?	You must replace the AutoNumber field in the underlying table with a new AutoNumber field. First, delete any relationships the underlying table has in the Relationships window; then, in Design view, delete the AutoNumber field (if it's a primary key, delete the primary key first) and insert a new field row where the previous field row existed, setting it as an AutoNumber data type. Replace the primary key, if you need to, and replace any relationships you deleted in the Relationships window. The new field will begin at 1 and will renumber all of the records in the table.

Problem	Solution
I can't select "Size to Fit Form" because it's grayed out.	Make sure the Form window is not maximized (click the Restore Window button in the upper-right corner).
I can't make my subform/main form work.	If the field on one side of the subform/main form link is an AutoNumber data type, make sure the field on the other side is data type Number and size Long Integer.
All of my records show up in my subform, instead of just the records connected to my main form.	Be sure the Child Field and Master Field are linked. Open the main form in Design view and right-click the subform control. On the shortcut menu, click Properties; then, on the Data tab, click in the Link Child Fields or Link Master Fields box; then click the Build button. Select matching fields in the Child Fields and Master Fields boxes. (If you type in the field names yourself, be sure they're spelled precisely, so they match the names in the corresponding tables.)
I inserted a scanned photo into the bound object frame on my Employees form, but all I see in the frame is a small portion of the photo. How can I show the entire picture?	You need to change the Size Mode property of the bound object frame to Zoom (on the Format tab in the frame's Properties dialog box). The photo will then reduce or magnify to fit your frame's dimensions without warping.

Wrap up

WRAP UP

Before you finish, let's go over some of the things you learned in this lesson:

- You learned about the various controls you can use in your forms.

- You learned how to use the Form wizard to create forms and how to modify those forms to suit your purposes.

- You learned how to create queries specifically for your forms and how to add a calculated field to a query, so you can display its value in your form.

- You learned how to move and resize controls in a form to create a more useful layout.

- You learned how to combine separate forms into a subform/main form combination in which the combined forms are related and work together.

  For more practice, try this:

- Add Nora McGinty's picture to her employee record (the image is named Mcginty.bmp and is in your Access One Step at a Time folder).

- Add some image controls and object frames to various forms and insert other bitmap files you either have in your computer or create in Windows Paint.

- Make a Retirement Fund Details subform in the Employees form.

  In the next lesson, you'll make several changes in the Orders form to make it easier to use and more attractive.

Finishing a Form

GOALS

In this lesson, you'll master the following skills and concepts:

40 MINUTES

- Tweaking the Customers subform
- Changing a text box format
- Tweaking the Items subform
- Adding a combo box to a form
- Adding a calculated control to a form footer
- Adding a calculated control
- Adding an option group to a form
- Adding a command button that opens another form
- Setting the tab order
- Disabling controls
- Testing the new form
- Formatting the new form
- Setting up a form for printing

Get ready

GET READY

To complete this lesson, you'll need to start Access 97 and open the Fruitsweets database (refer to Lesson 1 if you need help). If you started Lesson 7 using the FSPart3 database, continue to use it for the remainder of the lessons in this book.

    When you finish these exercises, you'll have mastered the skills required to make a form more accurate and easier to use. You'll know how to replace text boxes in a form with more useful controls such as combo boxes and option groups, and you'll know how to create calculated controls that will calculate the answers you need.

TRY OUT THE
INTERACTIVE TUTORIALS
ON YOUR CD!

FINE-TUNING YOUR FORMS

The changes you'll make in the next several exercises include:

- Changing the text in labels to friendlier wording

- Removing the navigation buttons from the two subforms to prevent accidental selection, which might introduce errors into existing orders (your Orders form never requires navigation buttons in either of its subforms)

- Replacing the Credit Card text box with an option group (a group of option buttons) to make data entry easier and more accurate

- Adding a text box to the main form to calculate a total for the order

- Adding a command button that opens the Customers form, so you can add a new customer to the Customers table

- Disabling the Order ID text box so it can't be selected (because it's an AutoNumber field, you can't enter a value in it, and selecting it is distracting to the data entry process)

- Replacing the Giftpak text box in the Items subform with a combo box, so you can select a giftpak name from a list

Fine-tuning your forms

What Goes on in the Orders Form

The Orders form is a typical and very useful data entry form, but its "very usefulness" makes it somewhat complex. This Visual Workout will dissect the form, so you can see how the parts work together and why some parts are built the way they are.

The Orders form.

Enter customer # (if new customer, enter # and then press F9 to display new data in subform)

Remove navigation buttons and record selectors from subforms

Change a column width to fit entries

Click to enter new data in Customers table

Click to enter a new order

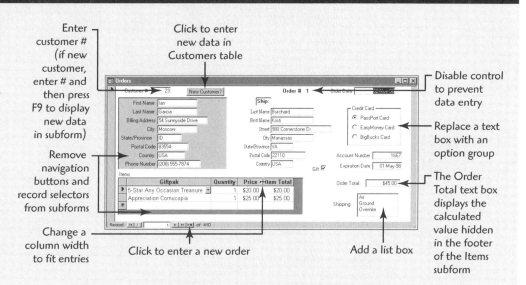

Disable control to prevent data entry

Replace a text box with an option group

The Order Total text box displays the calculated value hidden in the footer of the Items subform

Add a list box

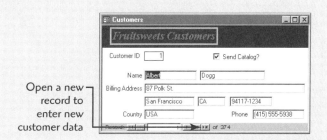

Open a new record to enter new customer data

The Customers form.

continued

8

Finishing a Form

Tweaking the Customers subform

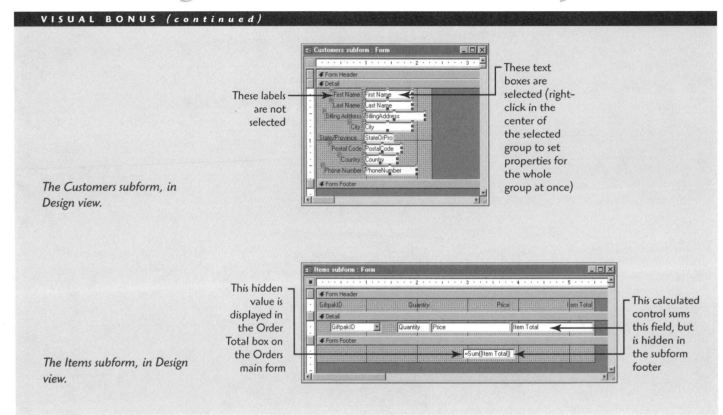

These labels are not selected

These text boxes are selected (right-click in the center of the selected group to set properties for the whole group at once)

The Customers subform, in Design view.

This hidden value is displayed in the Order Total box on the Orders main form

This calculated control sums this field, but is hidden in the subform footer

The Items subform, in Design view.

Tweaking the Customers subform

The purpose of this subform is to let you check the customer information, so you can be sure you have the correct customer ID entered and can edit a customer's information if, for example, their address has changed. In this form, the record selector, scroll bars, and navigation buttons are unnecessary clutter, so you'll remove them.

Tweaking the Customers subform

NOTE *The Orders form opens to display the first record in the underlying Orders table; if you change any data there, you'll be changing an existing record. To enter a new order, you must click the New Record scroll button that's in the Navigation area at the bottom of the Orders form.*

The Orders form should be open in Form view.

1 Open the Orders form in Design view.

2 Double-click the Customers subform control.

The Customers subform opens in Design view. Drag the lower-right corner of the window to make it larger if you need to.

3 In the subform, right-click in the gray area outside the form grid.

4 Click Properties.

The Properties dialog box appears, and it should say Form in the title bar.

5 In the Properties dialog box, click the Format tab.

6 In the Scroll Bars box, click the down arrow and select Neither.

7 In the Record Selectors box, click the down arrow and select No.

8 In the Navigation Buttons box, click the down arrow and select No.

9 In the Dividing Lines box, click the down arrow and select No.

10 Close the Properties dialog box by clicking its X close box.

11 Save the Customers subform.

12 Close the subform.

The Orders form is still open in Design view.

13 Drag the bottom of the Customers subform control upwards about ¼ inch to make it a bit shorter (you may need to switch back and forth between Design view and Form view, adjusting the size until it looks right to you).

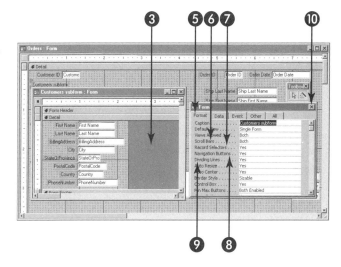

Changing a text box format

14 Select the Customers subform label, then press Delete.

The label is deleted.

15 Move the Customers subform control upward until it's just below the Customer ID controls.

16 In the Customer ID label, select the text "ID" and type # in its place.

17 Switch to Form view.

Your Orders form should look similar to the accompanying illustration.

18 Save the Orders form.

Changing a text box format

The Form wizard created the text boxes in the Customers subform with vertical scroll bars on their right sides. You don't need scrollbars in the text boxes, and they're visually distracting, so you'll remove them.

1 Switch the Orders form to Design view.

2 Double-click the Customers subform to open it in Design view.

3 Drag to select the group of text boxes in the subform.

The selected group of text boxes should look like the accompanying illustration (it may look as though the labels are also selected, but they're not; a selected control has handles all the way around its perimeter).

TIP

By selecting the text boxes as a group, you can reformat all of them in a single step.

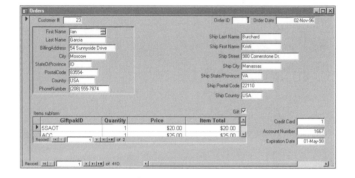

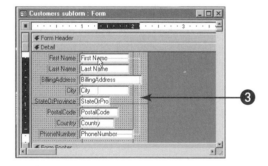

3

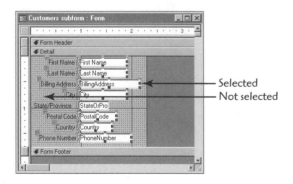

Selected
Not selected

4 Right-click inside the selected group of text boxes and click Properties.

The Multiple Selection properties dialog box appears.

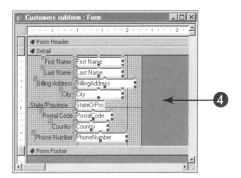

NOTE

If your properties dialog box does not say Multiple Selection in the title bar, repeat Step 4 and be sure you right-click in the center of the group of selected text boxes. Remember: The object you right-click is the object the properties dialog box applies to.

5 In the Multiple Selection properties dialog box, click the Format tab.

6 In the Scrollbars box, click the down arrow and select None.

7 Close the properties dialog box.

8 Save and close the subform.

9 Switch the Orders form to Form view.

Now text boxes in the Customers subform don't show scrollbars when they're selected.

Tweaking the Items subform

The Items subform suffers from some of the same problems as the Customers subform: It's impeded by the clutter of navigation buttons, and it needs some resizing. But it can retain its scrollbar, because the list of items ordered by a customer might be quite long, and the vertical scrollbar will help you see the different items in the list without having to make the subform much taller.

It also needs a more pleasing label.

1 Switch the Orders form to Design view.

2 Double-click the Items subform control to open it in Design view.

3 Right-click in the gray area outside the form grid.

Tweaking the Items subform

4 Click Properties.

The Properties dialog box appears, and should say Form in the title bar.

5 In the Properties dialog box, click the Format tab.

6 In the Record Selectors box, click the down arrow; then select No.

7 In the Navigation Buttons box, click the down arrow; then select No.

8 Close the Properties dialog box by clicking its X close box.

9 Switch to Datasheet view.

10 In the Items subform, double-click each column header to best-fit the column to its data, as shown in the accompanying illustration.

11 Close the Items subform.

12 In the Orders form, in Design view, drag the Items subform's control handles to make it a bit taller and narrower.

Switch back and forth between Form view and Design view if you need to, and adjust the subform control until it looks like the accompanying illustration.

NOTE *You want the Items subform to display all four columns and at least two or three records, but you don't want it to take up more space than necessary in the Orders form.*

13 In Design view, delete the word *subform* from the Items subform label.

14 Move the Items subform control up closer to the Customers subform control.

15 Switch to Form view.

16 Save (but don't close) the Orders form.

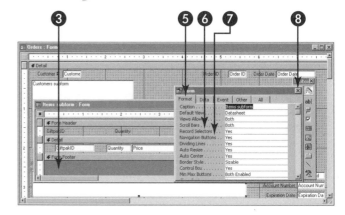

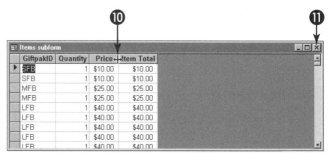

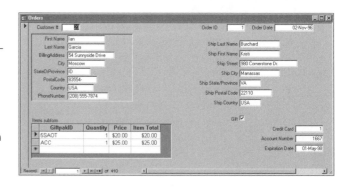

Adding a combo box to a form

Adding a combo box to a form

What's wrong with this picture? You have to look up giftpak ID codes
to enter a customer's order.

It will be a lot easier to select the giftpak name from a list, so
you'll replace the GiftpakID text box with a combo box, which looks
up giftpak names in the Giftpaks table and then enters your selection
in the Order Details table.

| NOTE | *The Order Details table is identical to the Order Items junction table you created in Lesson 5, but it has lots of data pre-entered, so you can use it to learn about forms and reports.* |

The Control Wizard will help you build the combo box.

1 Switch the Orders form to Design view.

2 Double-click the Items subform control to open it in Design view.

Drag the lower-right corner of the subform window to make it
larger if you need to.

3 Select the GiftpakID text box.

4 Press Delete.

The GiftpakID text box is removed from the form.

5 In the Control toolbox, be sure the Control Wizards button is
depressed.

The Control Wizards button should be highlighted, as shown in
the accompanying illustration.

6 In the toolbox, click the Combo Box button.

7 Then, in the Items subform, click in the center of the empty
space where the GiftpakID text box was.

A new combo box control and label are placed in the subform,
and the Combo Box wizard starts.

PART III: BEYOND BASICS   **155**

8

Finishing a Form

Adding a combo box to a form

8 In the first wizard step, you want the combo box to look up values in a table, so leave that option button selected and click Next.

The second wizard step appears, as shown in the accompanying figure.

9 Be sure the Tables option button is selected.

10 Select the Giftpaks table and click Next.

The third wizard step appears.

11 Double-click the GiftpakName field to add it to the Selected Fields list; then click Next.

The Fourth wizard step appears as shown in the accompanying figure.

12 Double-click the right border of the column header to widen it to fit all the entries in the list; then click Next.

The fifth wizard step appears.

13 Click the Store That Value In This Field option button.

14 Select GiftpakID from the list in the combo box and click Next.

The sixth wizard step appears and asks you for text for the label, but you're going to delete the label, so it doesn't matter what you enter here.

15 In the sixth wizard step, click Finish.

The wizard completes your new combo box, and your subform should look similar to the accompanying illustration.

16 Select the new label, and press Delete to remove it.

17 Move the new combo box into position in the row of controls.

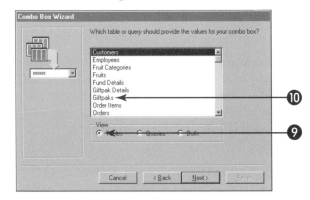

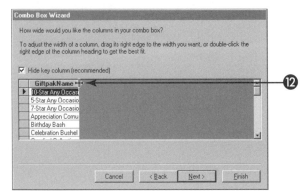

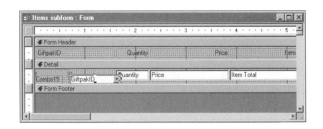

⓲ Switch to Datasheet view.

Your subform should look like the accompanying illustration, and you need to rearrange the columns and give the new combo box a better name.

⓳ ⓴

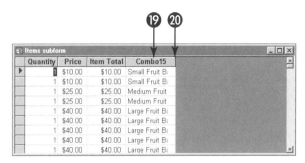

⓳ Click the new column header to select the column; drag the column header to the left until it's the leftmost column in the subform.

⓴ Double-click the right border of each column header to resize the columns.

㉑ Switch to Design view; then right-click the new combo box and click Properties.

㉒ In the Properties dialog box for the combo box, click the Other tab.

㉓ In the Name box, type **Giftpak**.

㉔ Close the Properties dialog box and save the subform; switch to Datasheet view.

Your Items subform should look similar to the accompanying illustration. You can select giftpak names from the new combo box, and the ID for the name you select will be entered in the Order Details table. The Price column in the subform will display the price for the selected giftpak, and the Item Total column will show the total for the quantity of each giftpak ordered.

When you open the Orders form, the Items subform will show only the records for the specific OrderID number in the main Orders form.

Next you'll create a calculated control—a text box that sums the Item Total fields for a single order.

ADDING CALCULATED CONTROLS

Your Orders form needs a text box that shows a price total for all the giftpaks included in an order. This is a two-part procedure: first you create a text box in the Items subform that sums the Item Totals for

8

Finishing a Form

Adding a calculated control to a form

all the giftpaks listed in the subform; then you create a text box in the Orders main form that displays the sum value you calculated in the subform.

This may seem like a convoluted approach, but here are the whys and wherefores behind it:

- A calculated control can't calculate other calculated controls — in other words, you can't sum controls that themselves calculate Price x Quantity.

- Therefore, you created a field in the underlying query that calculates the Price x Quantity for each giftpak ordered. You named it the Item Total field and displayed that field in the subform.

- Because the Item Total text boxes in the subform are *not* calculated controls, you *can* use a calculated control in the subform footer to sum them.

- The Datasheet format of the Items subform is very convenient because the list of items ordered may be any length, and you can see several items at once; but the Datasheet format hides the subform's header and footer, so the calculated control you create to sum the Item Totals will be hidden.

- You can get around the hidden attribute by placing an unbound text box in the main Orders form to display the value from the hidden control.

Adding a calculated control to a form footer

In this exercise, you'll create an unbound text box, a calculated control, in the Items subform footer to sum the values in the Item Total text boxes.

1 In the Items subform, switch to Design view.

Drag a corner to make the subform window larger if necessary.

2 Point to the bottom border of the Form Footer bar, and when the pointer becomes a two-headed arrow, drag it down about ½ inch.

A half-inch of form grid is displayed below the Form Footer bar.

3 In the Controls toolbox, click the Text Box button.

4 Click in the form footer area.

A new text box and label appear in the form footer.

5 Delete the new label (select the label and press Delete).

6 Click twice in the text box (not a double-click).

The text in the text box is replaced by a flashing insertion point, so you can type in the text box.

7 In the text box, type **=sum([Item Total])**.

8 Press Enter.

NOTE

If you type the function name, "sum", in lower-case letters and spell it correctly, it will be converted to upper-case letters when you press Enter; if you misspell the function name, it won't be converted to upper-case letters and that's your clue that you misspelled it. (This is also true of Excel.)

Be sure you type the parentheses and the square brackets and include the space in "Item Total".

9 Right-click in the text box and click Properties.

10 On the All tab, in the Name box, type **OrderTotal**.

The expression you typed in the text box is displayed in the Control Source box in the All tab. Your text box and Properties dialog box should look like those in the accompanying illustration.

11 Close the Properties dialog box.

12 Save and close the Items subform.

Because the subform footer is hidden, you won't see the results of your calculation expression until you display its value in a text box in the main Orders form, as you'll do in the next exercise.

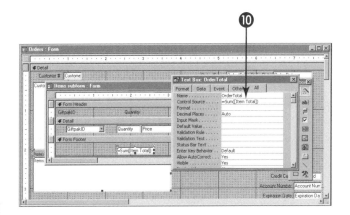

8

Finishing a Form

Adding a calculated control

▶ Adding a calculated control

The calculated control you just created is hidden in the subform's footer. In this exercise, you'll create an unbound text box in the main Orders form that displays the value from the text box in the Items subform footer (which is the total price of a customer's order).

Your Orders form should be open in Design view.

1 Maximize the form window so your work area is not cramped.

2 Place an unbound text box in the lower-right area of the Orders form; begin by clicking the Text Box button in the Controls toolbox.

3 Then click in the form window.

Your form should like the accompanying illustration.

4 Change the new label text to **Order Total**.

5 Right-click the text box; click Properties; then click the All tab.

6 In the Name box, type **MainTotal**.

7 In the Control Source box, type:
=[Items subform].[Form]![OrderTotal].

This expression identifies the specific control whose value you want to display in your text box. The expression uses an arcane programming language, but if you don't have the time or desire to learn Visual Basic language, you can use the Expression Builder to help you build expressions correctly.

8 In the Format box, click the down arrow; then select Currency.

Your Properties dialog box should look like the accompanying illustration.

9 Close the Properties dialog box and save the Orders form.

10 Switch to Form view.

Your Orders form should look similar to the accompanying illustration. The new Order Total text box shows the total price of the giftpaks shown in the Items subform.

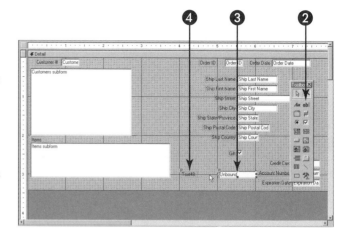

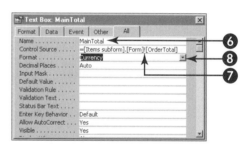

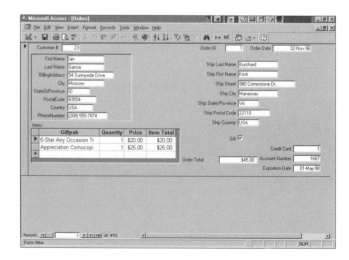

Adding a calculated control

The Expression Builder can help you write expressions in calculated controls (and in query fields) by spelling the names of fields and controls correctly and by placing them in the proper syntax. If you don't know Visual Basic (and let's face it, how many of us with real jobs have the time to learn programming languages?), the Expression Builder can be a great boon to productivity.

To open the Expression Builder for a control, right-click the control and click Properties. On the Data tab, click in the Control Source box and click the Build button — the small button with three dots that appears next to the Control Source box. In the Choose Builder dialog box, double-click Expression Builder.

The large box at the top of the Expression Builder dialog box is the Expression box, where your expression will be assembled. You can type in this box to amend an expression or select and delete parts of it. The buttons below the Expression box insert mathematical and logical operators. You can click buttons to insert an operator (such as + or Not) or you can type it.

The three boxes at the bottom of the Expression Builder contain expression elements, including the names of all the objects (forms, reports, tables, controls, fields, and so on) that have been saved in your database.

You can think of the three boxes as a succession of containers: the left box shows large containers, the center box shows the medium and small containers within the selected large container, and the right box shows objects contained in the selected medium or small container.

To use the Expression Builder to build the expression in your MainTotal control, follow these steps:

1. Open the Expression Builder for the MainTotal text box.

2. In the left box, double-click Forms.

3. Below Forms, double-click Loaded Forms.

4. Below Loaded Forms, double-click Orders.

5. Below Orders, double-click Items subform.

   The names of all the controls in the Items subform are displayed in the center box.

6. In the center box, double-click the OrderTotal control name.

   In the appropriate syntax, Access enters an expression in the Expression box that refers to the OrderTotal control in the Items subform.

7. Click OK.

   The full expression, including the = sign, is entered in the Control Source property box for the text box, and you're finished building the expression.

For more information about the Expression Builder, select Help ➤ Contents And Index; then click the Index tab and type **Expression**. In the list of help topics, double-click Expression Builder and poke around in the various help files.

Adding an option group to a form

ADDING OPTION AND COMMAND BUTTONS

Other types of controls are available to make data entry faster and more accurate, and the Control Wizard makes them easy to create. In the next two exercises, you'll create some additional controls for your Orders form: an option group for specifying credit cards for payment and a command button that opens a different form.

First you'll create an option group, which is a group of *option buttons* enclosed in a group box. The group box makes the option buttons within it work together as a group, separate from any other option buttons in the form.

Option buttons are designed to enter a number value from a list, beginning with 1. For example, if you create a group of four option buttons, they'll enter the numbers 1, 2, 3, and 4 in the underlying table field. You label the buttons so when a user clicks a particular one, its value is entered in the table. The advantage of option buttons is that the user is restricted to a single choice and doesn't have to remember which number value to enter; mistakes are difficult to make.

In your Orders form, you'll replace the credit card text box with an option group, so a user can simply click the customer's preferred credit card for payment.

Another control you'll add to your Orders form is a *command button.* Command buttons trigger macro commands that perform database actions for you, such as opening and closing forms, adding and deleting records, saving, printing, and more. *Macros,* automated procedures you'll learn more about in Lesson 10, don't do anything you can't do yourself with your mouse and keyboard, but they automate the procedures so, instead of going through the trouble of finding and opening the correct form, you simply click one button.

Command buttons can make data entry easier, and the Control wizard makes the creation of command buttons easier.

In your Orders form, you'll create a command button that opens the Customers form.

Adding an option group to a form

When a Fruitsweets employee takes a customer's order, it's important that the employee knows exactly which credit cards Fruitsweets accepts and that he or she enters the proper code for the card the customer wants to use. An option group makes this entry quick and accurate, by giving the employee specific card choices and then entering the proper value for the selected card into the underlying table.

In this exercise, you'll use the Control wizard (the easiest way) to create an option group for credit card selection. The option group will replace the Credit Card text box the Form wizard placed in the Orders form.

Your Orders form should be open.

1 Switch to Design view.

2 Remove the Credit Card text box and its label (select each control and press Delete).

3 On the toolbar, click Field List.

The list of fields in the table that the Orders form is based on appears, as shown in the accompanying illustration. (Drag the bottom border of the field list downward so you can see all the fields.)

4 In the Controls toolbox, click the Option Group button.

NOTE *When you click a control type in the Toolbox and then drag a field from the Field list, your actions tell Access that you want to create that specific type of control, bound to that specific field.*

5 Drag the Credit Card field from the Field list.

6 Drop it in a blank area on the form grid.

The Control wizard starts and the first wizard step appears, as shown in the accompanying illustration.

7 Type **PassPort Card**.

8 Press Tab.

9 Type **EasyMoney Card**.

10 Press Tab.

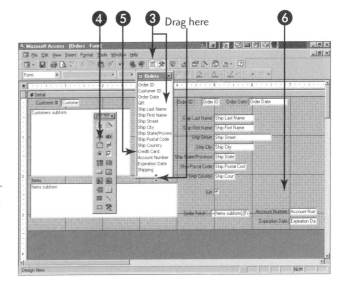

Drag here

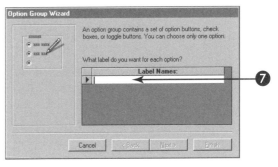

Adding a command button

⑪ Type **BigBucks Card**.

⑫ Press Tab.

⑬ Click Next.

The labels for your option buttons are entered in the wizard and the second wizard step appears, as shown in the accompanying illustration.

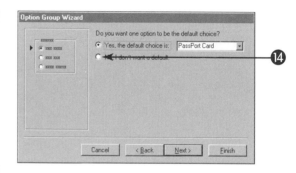

⑭ Click the No I Don't Want A Default option button; then click Next.

⑮ In the third wizard step, Access assigns values of 1, 2, and 3 to your labeled buttons. These values are suitable, so click Next.

⑯ In the fourth wizard step, Access wants to store the values in the Credit Card field in the Orders table, which is what you want, so click Next.

The fifth wizard step, in which Access wants your input on the format of the option group, appears, as shown in the accompanying illustration.

If you select different formats, the wizard shows you what each one would look like.

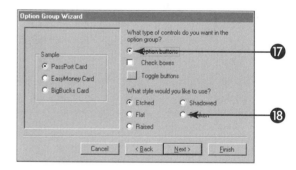

⑰ Select Option Buttons.

⑱ Select Sunken; then click Next.

⑲ For a caption, use the default **Credit Card**; then click Finish.

Your new option group should look like the accompanying illustration.

⑳ Close the Field list and save your form.

Adding a command button

When an existing customer calls to place an order and knows his or her customer ID number, you can enter it in the Orders form, and the customer's name and address will be displayed in the Customers subform, where you can check it. But what if the customer doesn't know his or her ID number, or is a new customer without a number?

NOTE *Don't confuse the Customers form with the Customers subform—they are two different forms.*

You need to open the Customers form, which is based on the Customers table, and either search for the name to get the ID number or enter the new customer information and then get the new number. Then you can enter the ID number in the Orders form, press the F9 key (see note below), check that the correct customer information is displayed, and continue taking the order.

NOTE *After you enter a new customer in the Customers table, you need to requery (rerun the underlying query) to update the Customers subform with the new record. To requery the subform, enter the new customer ID number in the Customer # text box; then press F9.*

To make it easy to open the Customers form, even for a user who isn't familiar with Access, you can add to the Orders form a command button that opens the Customers form.

1 In the Controls toolbox, click the Command Button button.

2 Click in the Orders form grid next to the Customer ID text box.

The Command Button wizard starts and the first wizard step appears, as shown in the accompanying illustration.

3 In the Categories list, click Form Operations.

The list of Actions changes to show a list of macro actions that are associated with form operations.

4 In the Actions list, click Open Form; then click Next.

5 In the second wizard step, click Customers; then click Next.

6 In the third wizard step, leave the Open The Form And Show All The Records option button selected; then click Next.

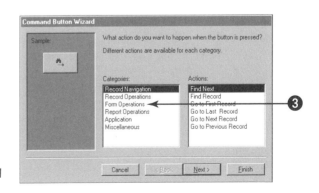

⑦ In the fourth wizard step, click the Text option button.

⑧ Then change the text in the box to read **New Customer?**.

Your fourth wizard step should look like the accompanying illustration.

⑨ Click Next.

⑩ In the fifth wizard step, name the new button **OpenCustomers** and click Finish.

⑪ Switch to Form view.

Your Orders form should look similar to the accompanying illustration.

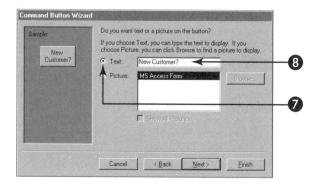

NOTE *Remember, to enter a new order, you must click the New Record scroll button at the bottom of the Orders form; to enter a new customer after clicking the New Customer? button, you must click the New Record scroll button at the bottom of the Customers form.*

New command button

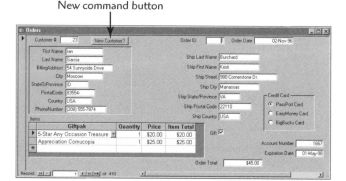

VALIDATING DATA ENTRY

It's important to the integrity of your data that your entries be valid: That is, the data you enter in each field should be appropriate, correct, and useful. For example, if someone takes an order and accidentally enters W Snackboxes instead of 2 Snackboxes, you don't have valid order data. Likewise, if someone enters an expired credit card for payment, you want to be aware that the credit card is invalid before you accept the order!

Access automatically checks the validity of data to a degree: for example, in the Quantity field in the Order Details table, you set the Data Type to Number; so, if you try to enter a letter instead of a number in the Quantity field (in either the Order Details table, or in the Items subform in the Orders form), you'll see an error message telling you that the value you entered isn't valid for that field.

But what if you want to be sure that a customer's credit card hasn't expired yet? You can set your own validation rule, for either a table field or for a control on a form.

If you set a validation rule for a table field, any control based on that field will automatically have the validation rule you set; but you can also set a validation rule for a control that applies only to the control and not to the table field or to other controls based on the table field.

Setting a validation rule and validation text

In this exercise, you'll set a validation rule for the Expiration Date text box on the Orders form, and you'll create your own error message for expired dates.

1 Switch the Orders form to Design view.

2 Right-click the Expiration Date text box and click Properties.

3 In the Properties dialog box, click the Data tab.

4 In the Validation Rule box, type **>Date()**.

The expression >Date() is a combination of the operator "greater than" (>) and the function Date(), which gives the current date; therefore, the rule says that a valid entry is greater than the current date.

You can use the expression builder to build validation rule expressions—click the Build box (the small box with three dots) to open the Expression Builder.

5 In the Validation Text box, type **Card is expired.**

If you enter a date that is expired—that is, current or past—an error message that says "Card is expired." will appear, and the expired date will not be accepted as an entry.

6 Close the Properties box and save the form.

8

Finishing a Form

Setting the tab order

POLISHING THE ORDERS FORM

You have only two remaining tasks: you need to set the tab order, so that pressing the Tab key moves the focus to different controls in a logical order, and you need to test the new Orders form. You won't change formatting options such as font and color until you've tested the form and made sure that everything works properly.

Setting the tab order

When you press the Tab key, the *focus* (the area of the form that is ready to accept data) moves to another control. The order in which the focus moves from control to control is called the *tab order*. The tab order can become quite illogical after you add and delete controls, but it's easy to reset it to make data entry logical and quick.

In this exercise, you'll set the tab order to move through the Orders form in a logical manner.

1 Switch to Design view.

2 Click View ➤ Tab Order.

The Tab Order dialog box appears, as shown in the accompanying figure.

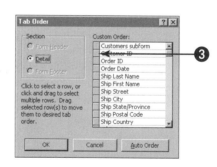

 NOTE *Tab order within a subform is set separately, by opening the subform in Design view and then setting its tab order.*

3 Click the gray box to the left of Customer ID to select it.

4 Drag the gray box for the selected control upward.

5 Drop it at the top of the list.

6 Drag the control names up and down until they're in this order:

Order Date

Customer ID

Customers subform

OpenCustomers

Order ID

Ship Last Name

Ship First Name

Ship Street

Ship City

Ship State/Province

Ship Postal Code

Ship Country

Gift

Items subform

CreditCard

Account Number

Expiration Date

MainTotal

7 Click OK.

8 Switch to Form view.

The Orders form opens to display Order #1, and the focus is in the first control in the tab order list, the Order Date text box.

9 Click Tab repeatedly to cycle through the controls in the form.

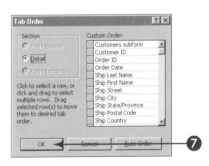

Tab Order [? X]

Section
○ Form Header
⦿ Detail
○ Form Footer

Click to select a row, or click and drag to select multiple rows. Drag selected row(s) to move them to desired tab order.

Custom Order:
Customers subform
Customer ID
Order ID
Order Date
Ship Last Name
Ship First Name
Ship City
Ship State/Province
Ship Postal Code
Ship Country

[OK] ◀ **7** [Cancel] [Auto Order]

NOTE

When you enter data in a subform, pressing Tab moves the focus within the subform. When you reach the last control in the subform, pressing Tab moves the focus to the next record in the subform instead of back to the main form. To move the focus back to the main form, press Ctrl+Tab.

Disabling controls

When you get to the PhoneNumber text box in the Customers subform, press Ctrl+Tab to get to the next control in the main form, the New Customer button. Do the same thing when you get to the end of the list of giftpaks in the Items subform.

Disabling controls

Here's another potential problem in data entry speed and accuracy: Some of the controls (such as Order ID and Order Total) should not have data entered in them. To make these controls off-limits to data entry, you can disable them by changing their properties.

In this exercise, you'll disable the controls that are off-limits to data entry.

1 Switch the Orders form to Design view.

2 Right-click the Order ID text box.

3 Click Properties.

4 In the Order ID properties dialog box, click the Data tab.

5 In the Enabled box, click the down arrow, then select No.

Disabling the control prevents it from receiving the focus when you click it or press Tab.

6 In the Locked box, click the down arrow, then select Yes.

Locking the control prevents a user from entering or editing its data.

> **TIP** While the Properties dialog box is open, click the Order Total text box to show its properties.

7 Follow steps 5 and 6 above to disable and lock the MainTotal text box.

8 Follow the same procedure to lock and disable the Price and Item Total text boxes in the Items subform.

9 Save and close both the subform and the Orders main form.

Now when you enter items in the Items subform, you cannot accidentally select the Price or Item Total controls.

Okay! You're finished building the functional form. Now you get to test it (the fun part) and then you can make it look great with formatting.

Testing the new form

It's a good idea to test a new form before you spend time making it pretty; testing first can save you a lot of time, because if some part of the form doesn't work, you may have to delete and replace it and the time you spent making it look aesthetically pleasing is wasted.

To test the new Orders form, pretend that an existing customer has called to place an order:

1 Open the Orders form.

NOTE *The Orders form opens to the first record in the Orders table—do not enter new data until you open a new record.*

2 In the navigation buttons at the bottom of the Orders form, click the New Record button.

A new record opens. The Date box has the focus because you set the tab order that way in the exercise "Setting a validation rule and validation text."

3 Enter today's date.

4 Enter an existing customer number (**#33**).

When you press Tab, the ID number is entered in the Orders table, and the related data from the Customers table is displayed in the Customers subform.

Testing the new form

⑤ Ask the customer if the address has changed. If they moved, you can change their address in the Customers subform.

TIP *After you make a change, you can satisfy yourself that it worked by looking the customer up in the Customers table.*

⑥ Now pretend this is a new customer. Click the New Customer? Button.

⑦ Enter new customer information (remember, this is only a test, so you can enter your own name and address if you like).

⑧ Take note of the new Customer ID number Access assigns.

⑨ Close the Customers form.

⑩ Enter the new Customer ID in the Orders form.

⑪ Press the F9 key to make the new customer address appear in the Customers subform.

The new customer information is displayed in the Customers subform.

TIP *Pressing the F9 key tells Access to requery the Customers table for current data. Once the query has been completed, the new record will appear in the Customers subform. To remember the keystroke, you can create a helpful label that says Press F9 to see new customer data. Place the label on the Orders form or in the Customers subform, wherever it will work best for you.*

⑫ Enter shipping name and address information (just make something up—this is only a test).

⑬ Enter an order in the Items subform—perhaps 3 SnackBoxes.

Check that the Items subform shows you the correct price and item total information.

⑭ Enter payment information.

15 Check the Order Total; then Tab to a new record.

Check the Orders table and the Order Details table to see if your entries were added to the tables correctly.

You can delete the test records directly from the tables or from the form.

- To delete the test order from Orders form, on the Edit menu, click Delete Record.

- To delete the test order from the tables, note the order number and then open each table in turn and delete the records for that Order ID number.

When you delete an order record, that Order ID number will not be used again. The AutoNumber data type prevents any number from being used again to avoid confusion about duplicate information.

16 When you finish testing your form, save it and leave it open in Form view.

Formatting the new form

Now that you know the form works the way you want it to, you can change the look of it to match the Fruitsweets company standard. In this exercise, you'll reformat several controls and the background color of the main form itself.

1 Switch to Design view.

2 Click in the form grid.

3 Click the down arrow next to the Fill/Back Color button on the toolbar.

The Fill/Back Color palette appears.

Formatting the new form

TIP

You can keep the palette displayed ("floating") on your screen if you drag its title bar away from the toolbar.

4 Click a pale blue color.

The Orders form background is colored pale blue (but the subforms remain gray).

5 Select all the shipping information labels as a group.

6 Then, on the toolbar, in the Font box, select the MS Serif font (or another you like better).

The label font is changed. Feel free to change any other label font on the form.

7 Select the Order ID text box.

8 On the toolbar, apply the following formats:

- From the Fill/Back Color palette, select Transparent.
- From the Special Effect palette, select Sunken.

9 Select the Credit Card label.

10 From the Fill/Back Color palette, select pale blue (the same color you chose for the form grid).

11 From the Control toolbox, add a label above the Shipping information area that reads **Ship:**.

12 Format the new label bold, transparent, and sunken.

So far, your form should look like the accompanying illustration.

13 Make more changes in your formatting, move controls around, and change label text, until your form looks similar to the accompanying illustration.

That's it! Your Orders form is ready to use!

14 Save the Orders form.

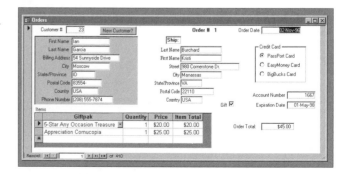

PRINTING A FORM

Your form contains all the information you want to send out with an order, and you can use it as a shipping invoice if you print it, but there are a few properties of the Orders form that need tweaking to make it print properly. You'll notice three particular printing problems: there are several duplicate entries in the Customers subform (for example, Ian Garcia's customer information is repeated several times instead of the once that's required); the individual order forms are run together instead of breaking onto separate pages; and some of the labels have truncated text.

You'll notice these problems when you look at the form in print preview, and then you'll make the necessary changes to fix the form's printing properties.

You can also save the form as a report, and then make changes to the report that include printing each order on a separate page automatically; then you can select several pages to print at one time, and they will print on separate pages.

Setting up a form for printing

In this exercise, you'll look at problems and create solutions for printing your Orders form.

1 Click File ➤ Print Preview.

A preview of the printed form page appears. The Customers subform shows duplicate entries, and the order forms are not separated onto individual pages.

To solve the duplicate customer information problem, you need to change a property in the underlying query. (The query shows duplicate information because it gathers customer data for each order the customer places—but the data is not duplicated in any tables, so don't worry about excess baggage in your database.)

2 Close the Orders form.

3 Open the Customers Subform qry query in Design view, and right-click in an empty space in the table pane; then click Properties.

The Properties dialog box for the query appears—the title bar reads Query Properties.

4 Click in the Unique Values box; click the down arrow; then select Yes.

5 Close the Query Properties dialog box; then save and close the query.

6 Open the Orders form; then select File ➢ Print Preview.

Now each Order form prints a single record of customer data, but the Order forms run together. You can print each order separately, one record at a time.

7 On the toolbar, click Close.

Print Preview closes, and the Orders form is open.

8 Select File ➢ Print.

The Print dialog box appears.

9 Under Print Range, click the Selected Records option button.

10 Click OK.

The single record displayed in the form will be printed. For each order record you want to print, you must navigate to the specific form record you want and repeat steps 8 through 10.

NOTE

To solve the problem of the truncated labels, open the form in Design view and lengthen each truncated label until it prints fully.

11 Close the Orders form.

Next you'll save the form as a report and break the individual orders onto separate pages.

⑫ On the Forms tab, right-click the Orders form name; then click Save As Report.

The Save Form As Report dialog box appears — the default name Orders is suitable.

⑬ Click OK.

The Report Wizard creates a report from your form.

⑭ Click the Reports tab, and double-click the new Orders report to open it.

The Orders report looks just like your Orders form, but the order records are not separated onto individual pages.

⑮ Switch the report to Design view; right-click the Detail bar (the horizontal gray bar that reads Detail, at the top of the window); then click Properties; then click the Format tab.

The Properties dialog box should read Section: Detail in its title bar.

⑯ Click in the Force New Page box.

⑰ Click the down arrow, and select After Section.

⑱ Close the Properties dialog box and save the report.

⑲ Click the View button to switch to Print Preview.

Now the report prints each order on a new page. You can print several specific orders by setting a page range in the Print dialog box. You'll learn more about reports in Lesson 9.

SKILLS CHALLENGE: MAKING THE FORM EVEN BETTER

In this Skills Challenge, you'll add a control to the Orders form that enters the customer's preferred shipping type. First you'll need to add a field to the Orders table that accepts the value. The control you'll add is a fixed-list list box, in which you select from a list you've entered in the control rather than from a list that's looked up in a table.

TRY OUT THE

INTERACTIVE TUTORIALS

ON YOUR CD!

8

Finishing a Form

Skills challenge

You'll also set the Data Entry property of the Orders form, so that when you open the form, instead of opening to the first record in the Orders table, it opens to a new record, ready for data entry. This prevents anyone from tampering with an existing order, because they won't be able to open it.

1 Open the Orders table in Design view.

2 Add a field named Shipping.

3 Give it a data type of Text.

4 Save the Orders table.

5 Close the Orders table.

 Do you remember where to change the settings for record selectors, scrollbars, and navigation buttons in a form?

6 Open the Orders form in Design view.

7 Display the Field list (click Field List on the Toolbar).

8 On the Controls toolbox, click the List Box button.

9 Drag the Shipping field from the Field list onto the Orders form grid.

 How can you change an attribute for several controls simultaneously?

10 In the first step of the List Box Wizard, select I Will Type In The Values That I Want.

11 In the second wizard step, type three labels into Column1: **Air**, **Ground**, and **Overnite**. These entries match the entries in the linked Shippers table.

 What's a good way to ensure accuracy in data entry?

12 In the third wizard step, store the value in the Shipping field.

13 In the fourth wizard step, name the field **Shipping**, then click Finish.

14 Close the Field list.

15 Switch to Form view.

Now you can add a shipping entry for any record in the Orders table by selecting a Shipping type in the list box. Your Orders form might resemble the accompanying illustration.

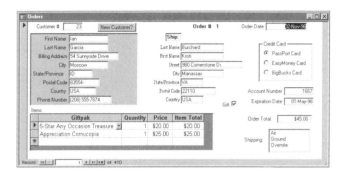

To make sure an employee taking an order starts in a new record, you'll set the Orders form to open to a new record instead of the first record in the Orders table.

 4 *How do you refer to a field name in a calculated control?*

16 Switch to Design view.

 5 *How can you change the tab order in a form?*

17 Set the tab order to give the Shipping list box the focus after the shipping address information has been entered.

18 Scroll down below the form grid.

19 Double-click the blank area below the form grid.

The Form Properties dialog box appears.

20 On the Data tab, in the Data Entry box, click the down arrow and select Yes.

The Orders form will no longer show existing orders; it will open only to a new record. This protects existing orders from being accidentally edited.

 6 *Do you remember how to copy the formatting (font, color, and so on) from one control to other controls?*

21 Save and close the Orders form.

8

Finishing a Form

Troubleshooting

TROUBLESHOOTING

You've learned how to make forms more useful, speedier, and more accurate by modifying the attributes and properties of different controls. The following solutions might answer some questions that came up during this lesson.

Problem	Solution
Why does my Orders form open to #23?	It opens to the first order in the Orders table, order #1, which was placed by customer #23 (the "23" you see is the customer ID).
I tried to create an option group in a form, but the Control wizard wouldn't start.	Be sure the Control Wizards button in the Control toolbox is turned on or depressed.
How can I see if my Items subform total is calculating correctly when it's hidden?	You can open the subform in Form view and see the text box in the footer. To open the subform in Form view, open it first in Design view; then right-click its Title bar and click Form view.
My Total Order calculated control in the Orders main form was working fine a minute ago, but now it's showing a #Name? error.	This is a bug in Access 97 that existed when this book went to press. If it still exists in your copy of Access 97, you can work around it like this: save and close your form, close the database and exit Access; then start Access and open the database and form. The error should disappear.
My Total Order calculated control has never worked. It shows a #Name? error.	Check that you've typed the form and control names correctly, including spaces; check that all the names are enclosed in square brackets; check that you have the proper syntax for your expression (see the sidebar Break for Expression Building in this lesson).

Problem	Solution
My Total Order calculated control shows an #Error? error.	The problem is most likely an error in the control being referenced (the calculated control in the subform footer). Check that the Sum expression in the Items subform footer is correct (see the previous problem *How can I see if my Items subform total is calculating correctly when it's hidden?*, and make sure you've typed *both* parentheses and *both* square brackets).
I can't see all four columns in my Items subform.	Make the columns narrower (in the Orders form, in Form view, drag the column heading borders) or make the Items subform control wider (in the Orders form, in Design view, drag the subform handles).
I entered the new customer number in the Customer # text box, but the new customer data doesn't appear in the Customers subform.	Press F9 to requery the Customers subform. Remember from Lesson 6 that a query is a dynamic set of records that exists when the query is run. The query underlying the Customers subform is run when you open the Orders form and, therefore, won't include customer records you add after the Orders form is opened. To show newly entered customer records, you run the query again, or *requery*, by pressing F9.

8

Finishing a Form

Wrap up

WRAP UP

Before you finish, let's go over some of the things you learned in this lesson:

- How to reconfigure and modify forms and subforms.
- How to create calculated controls.
- How to create option groups, combo boxes, and list boxes.
- How to format text and color in forms and controls.
- How to set a form's Data Entry property, so only new records can be shown/entered in a form.

  For more practice, try:

- Placing a Command button on the Customers form to close it after you enter a new customer
- Setting the Customers form open to a new record (to prevent accidentally editing existing customer data)
- Creating a Credit Cards table that contains the names and ID numbers of the credit cards in your option group and then relating the Credit Cards table to the Orders table and creating a query that shows the names of the credit cards used for each order
- Adding a fourth option button to the Credit Card group, for a fourth Credit Card type, and then adding the fourth card and its ID number to the Credit Cards table you created above

  In the next lesson, you'll learn how to create reports that display any data you choose—including calculated totals—in a professional-looking, easy-to-read format.

Creating Reports

GOALS

In this lesson, you'll master the following skills and concepts:

30 MINUTES

- Creating an AutoReport
- Printing a report quickly
- Printing a report with more options
- Creating a detail report with the Report Wizard
- Creating a grouped report
- Adding a new group level
- Changing the look of a report
- Creating customer mailing labels
- Creating a chart report

183

Get ready

GET READY

To complete this lesson, you'll need to start Access 97 and open the Fruitsweets database (refer to Lesson 1 if you need help).

When you finish these exercises, you'll have mastered the skills required to create printed reports that show your data to its best advantage, including grouping and sorting the details and calculating subtotals and totals.

Of course, you can simply print datasheet views of tables and queries, but datasheet views tend to be a sea of data with no trends apparent or summary data shown and, as such, are difficult to comprehend. When you create a report, you can show only the fields you need, can organize them into logical groups, can sort those groups into the order you want, and can create subtotals for each group and a grand total for the entire report. In addition, you can format the report to be an easy-to-read and professional-looking presentation by changing fonts, detail placement, colors, and lines.

In the interest of simplicity, all reports you create in this lesson will be based on queries that have already been created. It's a good idea to open these queries and take a look at how they were constructed if you want to create similar reports in your other databases.

TRY OUT THE

INTERACTIVE TUTORIALS

ON YOUR CD!

Report Structure and Elements

There are two kinds of reports: the *detail* report, which is nothing more than a list of record details, and the *grouped* report, which organizes records into groups and then subtotals the groups.

A report and its underlying query. A detail report takes raw data from a table or query and presents it in an attractive layout.

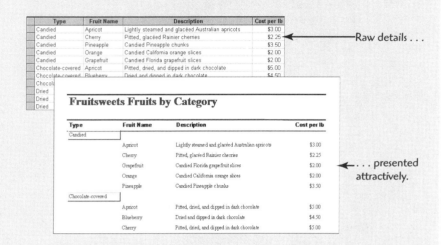

Raw details . . .

. . . presented attractively.

A grouped report. A grouped report organizes records into groups and includes summary information for each group.

Records are grouped . . .

. . . and groups are summarized.

continued

9

Creating Reports

Get ready

A report looks quite different in Design view than it looks in Print Preview, as this Visual Workout illustrates. Understanding what and where different report elements are will help you modify your reports after the wizard creates them.

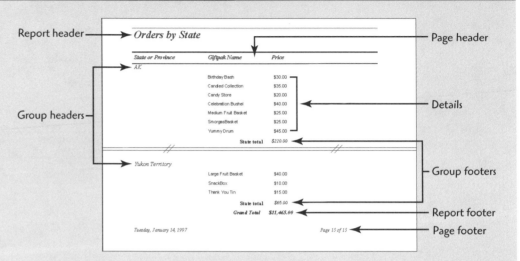

A report in Print Preview.

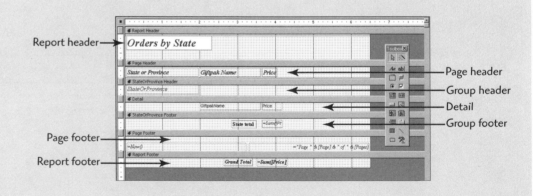

A report in Design view.

CREATING AND PRINTING A QUICK REPORT

The fastest way to create a report is by using AutoReport, although the results are often unsatisfactory. Nevertheless, on occasion an AutoReport comes in handy.

Printing a report is similar to printing a spreadsheet in Microsoft Excel or a document in Microsoft Word, so if you're proficient in either of those programs, printing will be a familiar procedure.

Creating an AutoReport

AutoReports offer you no choices, but are very fast—great for when you're running out the door to a meeting. You can base a report on either a table or a query, but you ought to base reports on queries for the same reason you base forms on queries: the report will load faster and will be easier to build because only the query fields will be used in the report.

In this exercise, you'll see how rapidly you can create a report with AutoReport.

1 On the Queries tab, select the Fruits By Giftpak query (but don't open it).

2 On the toolbar, click the down arrow on the New Object button.

3 Click AutoReport.

The New Object button and menu are shown in the accompanying illustration.

The AutoReport Wizard creates a report like that in the accompanying illustration.

The report is created rapidly, but it takes no input from you, and it isn't attractive. So, unless you're in a rush, you'll probably want to use the Report Wizard instead of the AutoReport Wizard.

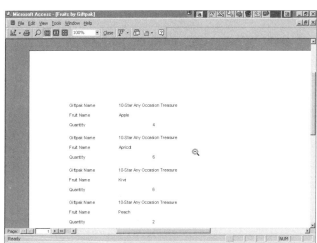

Printing a report quickly

NOTE To change the default style of the AutoReport, open any report in Design view. Select Format ➤ AutoFormat, and in the AutoFormat dialog box, select the style you want the AutoFormat Wizard to use (you can click the Options and Customize buttons for more alternatives). Then click OK to close the dialog boxes.

Printing a report quickly

Even though the Fruits by Giftpak AutoReport is rather unattractive, if you need to run off to a meeting with the report in hand, you can print it in even less time than it took you to create it.

1 Open the report in Print Preview.

TIP If the report is not open, you can simply select the name of the report on the Reports tab and print without opening.

2 On the toolbar, click Print. 🖨

The full report is sent to the printer without further input from you.

Printing a report with more options

You might want a bit more control over how your report is printed; for example, you might want to print your report in a portrait (tall) layout instead of a landscape (wide) layout, or you might want to print a single page from a long report.

1 With the report open in Print Preview, click File ➤ Print; or on the Reports tab, select the name of the report you want to print; then click File ➤ Print.

The Print dialog box appears.

② Select any printing options you want:

- To print specific pages—for example, the first two pages— click the Pages option button; then type the page numbers you want in the From boxes—for example, From **1** To **2**.

- To print more than one copy, in the Copies area, type the number you want in the Number Of Copies box.

- To change margins or column widths, click the Setup button and make those changes in the Page Setup dialog box.

③ In the Print dialog box, click OK.

The report is sent to the printer with your specified printing options.

④ Close the report without saving it.

USING THE REPORT WIZARD

The easiest way to create a report is to have the Report Wizard create the basic report for you and then modify it further until it's exactly what you want. A big advantage of using the Report Wizard is that it asks you for input when it creates your report, which means you have more choices than you do with an AutoReport and the finished report will require less tweaking.

Creating a detail report with the Report Wizard

In this exercise, you'll create a detail report, which is simply a list of records with no grouping or subtotals. A detail report is appropriate for a list of details such as the giftpaks and prices report that you're about to create.

In Lesson 6, Querying Your Tables, you created a query that showed what giftpak prices would be if they were increased by ten percent (the Increase Prices query). Now you'll create a report that presents the query results in a professional, easy-to-read layout that can be handed out at the next Fruitsweets executive meeting.

Creating a detail report

NOTE *Reports are best based on queries. The query contains only the details you want to show in the report, and the resulting report loads faster.*

① On the Reports tab, click the New button.

The New Report dialog box appears.

② Double-click Report Wizard.

The Report wizard starts, and the first step appears, as shown in the accompanying figure.

③ In the Tables/Queries combo box, click the down arrow.

④ Select Query: Increase Prices.

The field names in the Increase Prices query appear in the Available Fields list.

⑤ Click the right double arrow to move all three fields into the Selected Fields list.

⑥ Click Next.

The second wizard step appears, as shown in the accompanying figure.

In this report, there is no need to group records; you'll learn about this topic in the next exercise.

⑦ Click Next.

The third wizard step appears, as shown in the accompanying illustration. In this step, you'll set the sorting protocol for the list—you'll sort the list alphabetically by giftpak name.

⑧ In the 1 box, click the down arrow.

⑨ Click GiftpakName.

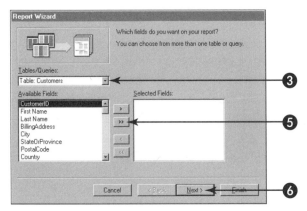

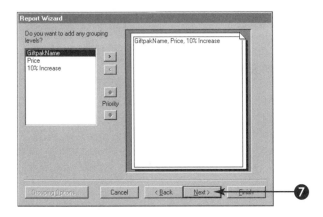

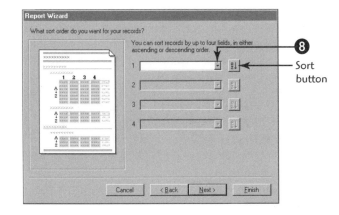

Sort button

NOTE *The sort button next to GiftpakName shows an ascending icon (A–Z) because that's the default sort order. If you click the sort button, the sort order is set to descending, and the sort button changes to show a descending icon (Z–A).*

⑩ Click Next.

The fourth wizard step appears and shows the report layout. The default layout (tabular and portrait) is good for this report.

⑪ Click Next.

The fifth wizard step appears and gives you six styles to choose from. Styles set the font formatting for the report elements.

TIP *You can get an idea of what each style looks like by clicking the style names and looking at the sample on the left side.*

⑫ Select Corporate.

⑬ Click Next.

The sixth wizard step asks you for a name for the report. The default name Increase Prices is good.

TIP *The name "Increase Prices" appears as both the title on the printed report and the caption in the title bar of the report on your screen. To change the caption later, open the report in Design view, then open the Properties dialog box for the report, and on the Format tab, change the text in the Caption box. To change the title on the printed report, open the report in Design view, then change the text in the label in the Header section.*

9

Creating Reports

Creating a grouped report

⓮ Click Finish.

The wizard creates your report, similar to the accompanying illustration.

This report looks good for a detail report. You can print it and take it to the Fruitsweets executive meeting with no further alterations.

⓯ Click anywhere on the report to get a zoomed-out view of the entire page. Close the report by clicking its X close box.

Creating a grouped report

Detail lists are useful, but sometimes you need to show more than a simple list: you need to show subtotals and totals. For example, you need to bring a report to the Fruitsweets executive meeting that shows monthly sales of each giftpak, subtotaled by month. The resulting report should look something like the accompanying illustration.

TIP

You'll achieve the results you want more directly if you plan and draw how you want the report to look before you create it.

Your report will be based on the query named Monthly Sales qry. You might want to take a look at the design of this query in order to understand the report; the query uses the following expression to sum the order amounts for each giftpak, each day:

Amount: Sum((([Order Details].[Quantity]*[Giftpaks].[Price]))

The query then groups the records by that expression. The expression tells Access to multiply the Quantity (from the Order Details table) by the Price (from the Giftpaks table) for each record in the query and then sum the products for all the records displayed in the query. In the report, this expression will show the sum for each giftpak in the month group, which you will understand more clearly after you create the report.

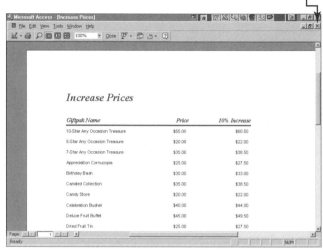

⓯

Increase Prices

Giftpak Name	Price	10% Increase
10-Star Any Occasion Treasure	$55.00	$60.50
5-Star Any Occasion Treasure	$20.00	$22.00
7-Star Any Occasion Treasure	$35.00	$38.50
Appreciation Cornucopia	$25.00	$27.50
Birthday Bash	$30.00	$33.00
Candied Collection	$35.00	$38.50
Candy Store	$20.00	$22.00
Celebration Bushel	$40.00	$44.00
Deluxe Fruit Buffet	$45.00	$49.50
Dried Fruit Tin	$25.00	$27.50

Total for Month ↓

Month A	Gift pak 1	$ XXX
	Gift pak 2	$ XXX
	Gift pak 3	$ XXX
	etc.	

Total for Month $ XXX

Month B	Gift pak 1	$ XXX
	Gift pak 2	$ XXX

Total for Month $ XXX

Grand total for Report $ XX,XXX

1 On the Reports tab, click the New button.

2 Double-click Report Wizard.

The Report wizard starts, and the first step appears.

3 In the first wizard step, in the Tables/Queries combo box, click the down arrow; select Query: Monthly Sales qry.

4 Click the right double arrow to move all three query fields into the Selected Fields list; click Next.

The second wizard step appears, as shown in the accompanying figure.

This step can be a bit confusing. You want to group your records by order date, so you can break the records into monthly groups.

5 In the left box, double-click Order Date.

In the right box, the layout changes to show Order Date by Month, as in the accompanying illustration.

TIP
If you want to group the records by a different time interval, such as Week or Quarter or Year, you can click the Grouping Options button and select a different Grouping Interval.

6 Click Next.

The third wizard step appears, asking for your preferences for sorting and summary information.

7 In the 1 box, select Order Date and an ascending sort order.

Your third wizard step should look like the one in the accompanying illustration.

8 Click the Summary Options button.

9 In the Summary Options dialog box, click the Sum checkbox.

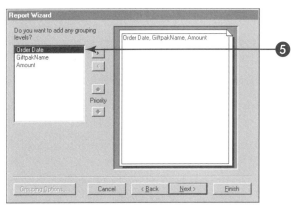

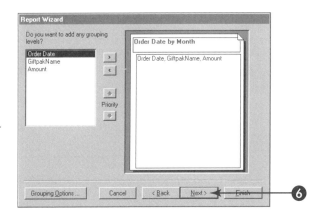

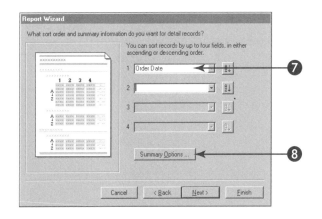

9

Creating Reports

Customizing a report's design

⑩ Click OK, then click Next.

⑪ In the fourth wizard step, leave the default option buttons (Stepped and Portrait) selected and click Next.

⑫ In the fifth wizard step, select the Bold style; click Next.

⑬ In the sixth wizard step, change the report title to **Monthly Sales**; click Finish.

Your report should look similar to the accompanying illustration.

TIP *You can see the report's details both close-up and overall by clicking the report page to zoom in and out.*

This report is not quite what you need, but you can fix it with just a bit of tweaking. Instead of showing the total for each giftpak each day, you want to show the total for each giftpak each month, and the total figures should be formatted as currency.

CUSTOMIZING A REPORT'S DESIGN

Many of your reports will be perfect just the way the wizard creates them, but on those occasions when the wizard can't create exactly what you need, you can alter, modify, and tweak the report design to suit you.

In this section, you'll make a number of changes to the Monthly Sales report, so it shows monthly subtotals for each giftpak, instead of details by date. You'll need to add a new grouping level for giftpak names and rearrange labels and text boxes.

If you switch the report to Design view, it should look like the accompanying illustration.

Click the page to zoom in or out

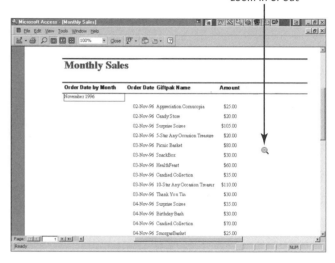

Report title label — Month group label — Column labels — Text boxes for detailed data

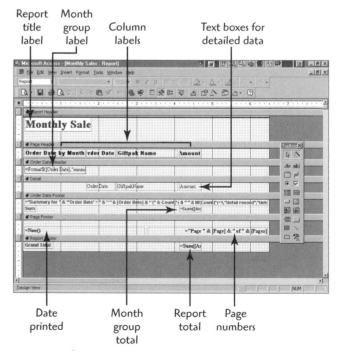

Date printed — Month group total — Report total — Page numbers

You need to remove the individual order dates and summarize the giftpak data within each month group. The trick here is to create a GiftpakName group and then move the Giftpak Name and Amount text boxes from the Detail section up into the new group header section, because a text box in the Detail section will always show all the record details (in this case, all the individual orders for each date), but the same text box in a group header section will group the record details and show a subtotal for the group.

A few other details will make the report look more professional: the sums for the groups and the report are numbers that need to be formatted as currency (yes, the Report Wizard ought to do this for you, but it doesn't . . .); the report would look more polished if each month's data was on its own page; and the month names will be more attractive if you remove the surrounding boxes and format the month names as bold and italic.

9

Creating Reports

ADDING A CALCULATION TO A REPORT

To create the group subtotals in the Monthly Sales report, you used a calculation that was performed in the underlying query. You can also perform calculations directly in the report, by creating an unbound text box in the report and then writing an expression in the text box. A summary calculation sums the details for the section in which you create it (for example, a summary calculation placed in a group section sums the records in each group, and a summary calculation placed in the report footer sums all the records in the report).

As an example, you could add a calculation to the Monthly Sales report that sums the quantity of Giftpaks sold each month, and the quantity sold over the entire report period. To create these calculations, start by opening the underlying query (Monthly Sales) and adding the Quantity field from the Order Details table. This makes the Quantity field available to the report for calculation.

Next, open the report in Design view. Click the Field List button — the Quantity field now appears in the Field List,

which means the report can perform calculations using the Quantity field.

Next, make the Order Date footer section taller, and place an unbound text box below the Sum label. Change the text box label to read **Quantity sold**, and in the text box, type the expression **=sum([Quantity])** (be sure to type the square brackets and the parentheses). You can check your calculation at this point by switching to Print Preview — the total number of giftpaks sold each month appears below the Amount sum for each month.

To sum Quantity for the entire report, place the same calculated control in the Report footer. Make the Report footer section taller, then copy the new text box and label. Click in the Report footer section and paste the text box and label. Switch back to Print Preview — the calculated control in the Report footer sums the quantity for the entire report.

Adding a new group level

Adding a new group level

In this exercise, you'll add a group for giftpak names and remove the individual order dates.

Be sure your report is in Design view when you begin this exercise.

1 Right-click an empty spot in the report grid.

2 Click Sorting and Grouping.

The Sorting and Grouping dialog box appears, as shown in the accompanying illustration.

3 Delete the second and third Order Date rows (they'll interfere with your Giftpak grouping).

> **TIP** *To delete a row, click in the gray record-selector box on the left of the row; then press Delete. When a message asks if you're sure about this, click Yes.*

4 Click in the first empty box in the Field/Expression column.

5 Click the box's down arrow and select GiftpakName.

Your dialog box should look like the accompanying illustration.

6 Be sure the GiftpakName row is selected (look for the right-pointing triangle in the record selector).

7 Then Click in the Group Header box.

8 Click its down arrow and select Yes.

9 Click the dialog box's X close box to close it.

A GiftpakName Header section appears in your report, between the Order Date Header section and the Detail section.

10 In the Page Header section, click the Order Date label and press Delete.

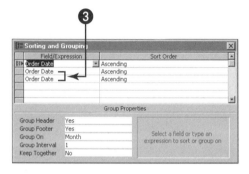

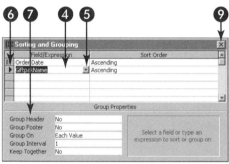

Changing the look of a report

⑪ In the Detail section, click the Order Date text box and press Delete.

⑫ Move the GiftpakName and Amount text boxes from the Detail section into the GiftpakName Header section.

> **NOTE** *Select and move text boxes the same way you did in forms, in Lesson 8. The GiftpakName Header section is simply a group header section; Access names each group according to its underlying field name.*

⑬ Drag the top border of the Order Date Footer bar up against the Detail bar. This removes extra line spacing in the report.

Your report should resemble the accompanying illustration. For each month, there is a list of all the giftpaks and the monthly order total for each.

⑭ Switch to Print Preview (click the View button 🔍 in the toolbar).

Your report should look like the accompanying illustration.

Now the data is grouped and summarized the way you want it: for each month, there's a list of the total amount of sales for each giftpak. In addition, the sales for each month are totaled at the end of each monthly group, and the total sales for the report are totaled at the end of the report (on page 4).

Changing the look of a report

A few more changes in the look of the report are in order:

- The subtotals and grand total need to be formatted as currency
- Each month's group should be kept together on the same page, instead of broken across pages
- The month names should be formatted as bold and italic, and the box should be removed

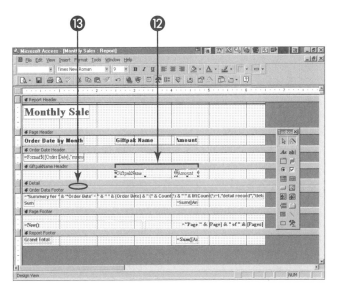

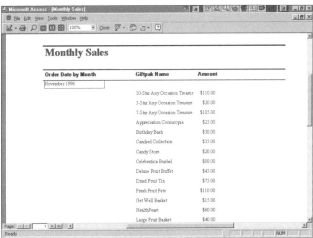

9

Creating Reports

Changing the look of a report

1 Switch to Design view.

2 On the right side of the Order Date Footer section, right-click the text box that contains the sum expression and click Properties.

3 In the Properties dialog box, on the Format tab, click the down arrow in the Format box and select Currency.

4 While the Properties box is open, click the sum text box on the right side of the Report Footer section.

The Properties dialog box changes to show properties for the sum text box in the Report Footer section.

5 Set the Format to Currency.

6 Close the Properties dialog box (click its X close box).

7 Widen the grand total text box (in the Report Footer section) by dragging the handle on either side. A width of 1½" is more than enough.

NOTE *By changing the format to Currency, you've made the displayed value wider. If you don't widen the text box, you may truncate the value.*

8 In the Report Design toolbar, click the Sorting And Grouping button. ▣

9 Click in the Order Date box.

10 Click in the Keep Together box at the bottom of the dialog box and select Whole Group.

11 Close the Sorting And Grouping dialog box.

12 Click the text box in the Order Date Header section (the text box that shows the month name) and format it as follows:

- Click the down arrow on the Line/Border Color button and click Transparent. ▣
- On the Formatting toolbar, click Bold. **B**

- On the Formatting toolbar, click Italic. *I*

- On the Formatting toolbar, in the Font Size box, type **12** and press Enter. 9 ▾

13 Switch to Print Preview.

Your report should look like the accompanying illustration.

NOTE

You can create a report that asks you for start and end dates by creating a parameter query (see Lesson 6). When you open the report, you'll be asked for the date parameters of data you want to see, and the report will show only that data.

14 Save and close the report.

OTHER QUICK AND USEFUL REPORTS

Access has a couple of wizards that create different kinds of reports: a Chart Wizard that charts your data and a Label Wizard that makes mailing labels to fit standard Avery labels.

In this exercise, you'll use the Label Wizard to create mailing labels from the Customers table.

Creating customer mailing labels

Adrienne in Shipping needs mailing labels for the next catalog mailing. You can create the labels she needs and print them out on standard Avery 5160 address labels in your laser printer. (If you use different labels or a different type of printer, you can make those selections in the wizard steps.)

You can easily create mailing labels for all the customers in the Customers table, but not all of them want a catalog, so you'll create mailing labels only for those customers who do want catalogs. You'll sort them out by basing the mailing labels report on a query that selects those records with a Yes in the Catalog field.

Monthly Sales

Order Date by Month	Giftpak Name	Amount
November 1996		
	10-Star Any Occasion Treasure	$110.00
	5-Star Any Occasion Treasure	$20.00
	7-Star Any Occasion Treasure	$105.00
	Appreciation Cornucopia	$25.00
	Birthday Bash	$30.00
	Candied Collection	$35.00
	SmorgasBasket	$25.00
	SnackBox	$30.00
	Surprise Soiree	$105.00
	Thank You Tin	$30.00
	Yummy Drum	$45.00
Summary for 'Order Date' = 11/2/96 (115 detail records)		
Sum		$5,075.00

Monday, January 13, 1997   Page 1 of 5

9

Creating Reports

Creating customer mailing labels

To understand how the query gives you the records you want, take a minute to open it in Design view and study its construction.

1 On the Reports tab, click the New button.

The New Report dialog box appears, as shown in the accompanying figure.

2 In the New Report dialog box, in the combo box near the bottom, click the down arrow and select Labels qry.

This is where naming your queries with the suffix "qry" is helpful. The tag enables you to distinguish queries from tables.

3 In the wizards list, double-click Label Wizard.

The Label Wizard starts, and the first wizard step appears, as shown in the accompanying figure.

4 In the labels list, select 5160 and click Next.

The second wizard step appears. The default font is fine for these labels, although you may change the font if you wish.

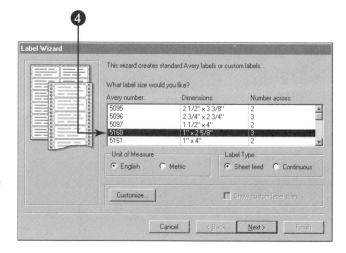

5 Click Next.

The third wizard step appears, as shown in the accompanying figure. This step is where you build your label.

6 In the Available Fields list, double-click First Name.

7 Type a space.

8 Double-click Last Name and press Enter.

The first line of your label layout is visible in the Prototype Label box.

9 Double-click Billing Address and press Enter.

10 Double-click City.

11 Type a comma and enter a space.

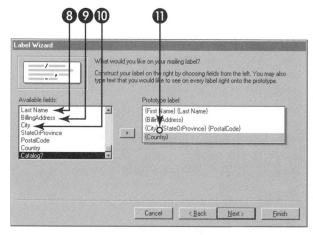

12 Double-click StateOrProvince; type a space; double-click PostalCode; press Enter; double-click Country.

TIP

If you make a typing mistake, click in the label and use the Backspace key and spacebar to correct it.

13 Click Next.

14 In the fourth wizard step, in the Available Fields list, double-click PostalCode, so the labels will be sorted by postal codes for easier mailing. Click Next.

15 In the fifth wizard step, name the report **Catalog Labels** and click Finish.

The wizard creates your labels. They should look similar to the labels shown in the accompanying illustration.

16 Print the Catalog Labels report and close the report.

Creating a chart report

In this exercise, you'll use the Chart Wizard to create a chart report that shows giftpak sales to date. The chart will be based on an existing query, the Monthly Sales qry, and will summarize all sales to date in a single bar chart.

NOTE

To use the Access Chart Wizard, you must have Microsoft Graph 97 installed. The Access 97 Typical installation does not include Microsoft Graph, so if you find you can't start the Chart Wizard, reinstall Access 97 and include all of the Access 97 accessory features.

1 On the Reports tab, click the New button.

2 In the New Report dialog box, in the combo box near the bottom, select Monthly Sales qry.

3 In the Wizards list, double-click Chart Wizard.

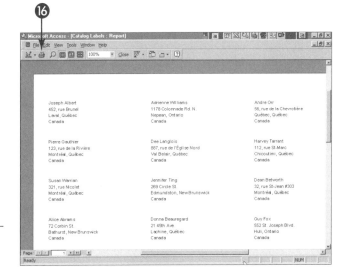

16

Creating Reports

9

Creating a chart report

The Chart Wizard starts, and the first step asks which query fields you want to include. Because this chart will summarize sales to date, you don't need to include the Order Date field.

4 Double-click GiftpakName and Amount and click Next.

The second wizard step asks which chart type you'd like.

5 Click the bar chart (the leftmost button in the second row) and click Next.

The third wizard step shows a layout for the chart data, with your categories (GiftpakName) on the vertical axis and the Amount on the horizontal axis. The Amount field button reads SumOfAmount because Access sums the data by default, which is appropriate for this sales chart.

TIP *To use a different summary function (for example, Min or Average), double-click the field button in the chart layout and select a different function from the list that's presented.*

6 Click Next.

The fourth (and last) wizard step asks you for a chart title and whether you want a legend. Leave the default title—you'll remove it and add a label to the report header later.

7 Click the No, Don't Display A Legend option button; then click Finish.

Access creates a report with your chart on it, but the chart is ridiculously small. Next you'll resize and modify the report so it's readable.

8 Click the View button to switch to Design view.

Your report is a chart object displayed in the report's Detail section. You'll make the chart object big enough to fill the page, add a report header that's a more pleasing chart title, and add a print date to the report footer. You'll also format the Amount axis to display dollars instead of simple numbers.

9 Double-click anywhere in the chart object.

A Microsoft Graph window opens with a sample datasheet displayed, and a chart window opens on top of the graph window. You'll modify the chart by making changes in the chart window.

To resize the chart to fit the report page, you must resize the chart window; you'll need to make the chart much bigger than the initial magnification will allow, so you'll reduce the magnification and then resize the chart. It's an unwieldy method, but you'll understand better after you follow these steps.

10 Click View ➢ Zoom.

11 Click the 50% option button and click OK.

12 Double-click the title bar of the Microsoft Graph window to maximize it.

13 Drag the lower-right corner of the chart window to make it taller.

14 Click the chart title, Monthly Sales qry, to select it and press Delete.

The chart title is deleted.

15 Double-click the horizontal axis at the bottom of the chart.

The Format Axis dialog box appears.

16 In the Format Axis dialog box, click the Number tab.

17 Select the Currency category.

18 Set Decimal Places to 0 and click OK.

19 Click File ➢ Update.

20 Click File ➢ Exit & Return to Report1:Report.

The report appears in Design view; your chart has been resized, so you need to resize the chart object that contains it so that the entire chart will be visible on the report page. You also need to change the report layout to Portrait because your bar chart will be tall and narrow rather than short and wide.

Creating a chart report

21 Select File ➤ Page Setup.

22 On the Page tab, click the Portrait option button; then click OK.

23 Drag the right edge of the page grid out to the 6" mark on the top ruler.

24 Then drag the top of the Page Footer bar downwards to the 8" mark on the side ruler.

25 Drag the chart object handles to resize it until it fills the page grid, both sideways and top-to-bottom.

26 Click the View button to switch to Print Preview.

27 Check the chart size.

If the chart is too big (if you can't see all of the chart, including the Amount axis at the bottom), return to Design view, double-click the chart object, and drag the chart window to make it smaller. Check the report's Print Preview and make changes to the chart window until the chart size looks right.

 NOTE *Be sure you select File ➤ Update and File ➤ Exit & Return To Report each time you modify the chart window.*

28 When the chart is sized the way you want it, return to Design view to create the report header and footer.

29 In the Controls Toolbox, click the Label button.

30 Click the Page Header section.

31 Type **Sales to Date** and press Enter.

The report title is created and selected.

32 In the Formatting toolbar, select a Font Size of 16.

33 Click Format ➤ Size ➤ To Fit.

34 Move the label to center it over the chart object.

35 Click Insert ➤ Date And Time.

36 In the Date And Time dialog box, click the Include Time checkbox to clear it, then click OK.

A text box, containing an expression that displays the current date, is created in the Detail section, at the upper-left corner of your chart object.

37 Move the date text box downwards into the center of the Page Footer section (drag the text box with the hand pointer to move it).

38 Click in the expression, on the right side of the equal sign.

39 Type **"Sales as of "&**.

The expression in the text box should read:
="Sales as of "&Format(Date(),"Short Date").

40 Switch to Print Preview.

Your Current Sales chart is complete.

41 Save the chart report as **Current Sales Chart** and close it.

To add a chart to an existing report or form, open the report or form in Design view and click Insert ➤ Chart. Click in the report or form where you want to insert the chart, and then follow the steps in the wizard to create the chart.

SKILLS CHALLENGE: CREATING TWO MORE REPORTS

In this Skills Challenge, you'll create a Report based on the Fruits by Giftpak query; then you'll create a report that shows employee investment allocation in the various retirement funds.

TRY OUT THE

INTERACTIVE TUTORIALS

ON YOUR CD!

9

Creating Reports

Skills challenge

■ Creating a Giftpaks report

First you'll use the Report Wizard to create a Giftpaks report, based on the Fruits by Giftpak query, and you'll modify the report to keep the groups printing together on the same page.

1 On the Reports tab, click the New button.

 Do you remember how to create an AutoReport?

2 In the New Report dialog box, double-click Report Wizard.

3 In the wizard steps, base the report on the Fruits By Giftpak query and include all the query fields in the report.

 Do you remember how to add a new group level to a finished report?

4 Group the data by GiftpakName.

5 Sort the data in ascending order by FruitName.

6 Choose a Stepped layout and Portrait orientation.

7 Choose a style you like and name the report **Giftpaks**.

 What's the difference between a text box in the Detail section and the same text box in a group header section?

Your finished report should look similar to the accompanying illustration.

TIP *To see the first two pages, as shown in the illustration, click the Two Pages button on the toolbar.*

 Do you remember how to format the value in a text box (as Currency, for example)?

8 Switch to Design view.

Two pages

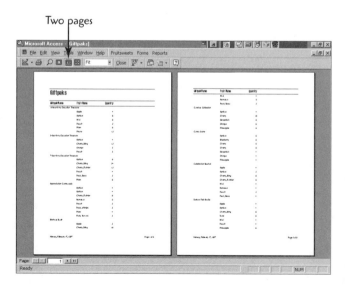

9 Click the Sorting And Grouping button on the toolbar.

10 In the GiftpakName field, set the Keep Together property to Whole Group.

11 Close the Sorting And Grouping dialog box.

12 Save and close the report.

■ Creating an Employee Funds report

Next you'll use the Report Wizard to create a report that shows employee investment in the various retirement funds, with subtotals, to make sure that each employee has 100 percent of their retirement money allocated.

This exercise uses the Fund Details table you created in the Lesson 5 Skills Challenge. If you haven't already created this table, you might want to go back to Lesson 5 and create it. It won't take long.

1 On the Reports tab, click the New button.

2 In the New Report dialog box, select the Fund Details table.

3 Double-click Report Wizard.

4 Place all three of the Fund Details fields into the report.

5 Group the report by Employee ID.

6 Set a Summary Option of sum for the Percent field.

7 Use a Stepped layout, a Portrait orientation, and the Corporate style.

8 Name the report Fund Details Report.

The finished report should look like the accompanying illustration.

9 Close your report.

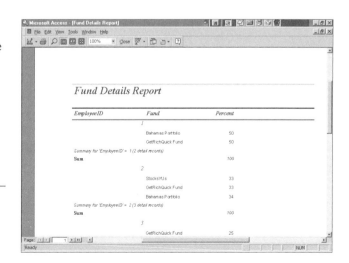

NOTE

If your table doesn't match the illustration, switch to Design view and change the labels, the sorting and grouping, and anything else that seems different.

Troubleshooting

This report looks great except that it's based on a table that doesn't contain employee names. The solution is to base the report on a query that combines the data in the Fund Details table with the names in the Employees table as shown.

 Do you remember how to create mailing labels in Access?

If you create a query like the one shown in the accompanying illustration, then you can re-create this report, and it will look like the one in the accompanying illustration.

 NOTE *You can refresh your memory of how to create a query by skimming through Lesson 6.*

TROUBLESHOOTING

You've learned how to create reports that list and combine details into subtotaled groups and how to tweak your reports to show more precisely what you want. The following solutions might answer some questions that came up during this lesson.

Problem	Solution
The Grand Total in my report doesn't have a $ sign, even though I formatted it as Currency.	Switch to Design view and widen the text box. When you format a number as currency (or bold, or a larger font or size), it becomes wider and may be truncated if you don't make its text box wider.
My Grand Total is only 1,780, but it should be 21,780.	Switch to Design view and widen the text box (see answer above).

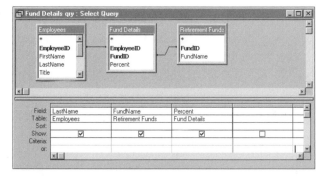

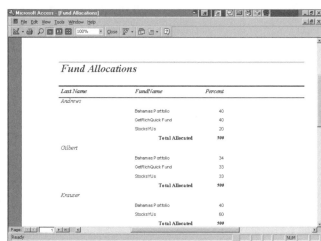

Problem	Solution
I switched my page setup from landscape to portrait orientation, and I'm getting extra, blank pages printed.	The page grid is still at landscape width and may have lines or other elements that stretch beyond the portrait page width. Resize or move any elements that extend too far to the right; then drag the right edge of the page grid to the left, to approximately the 6" mark on the Design view ruler.
In my Monthly Sales report, the GiftpakNames are cut off.	Widen the GiftpakName text box.
In my Fund Allocations report, I can't make the percents line up with the totals.	Format the detail percents and the total percents to right-align in their text boxes; then select both text boxes and click Format ➢ Align ➢ Right.
Where can I adjust margins?	Click File ➢ Page Setup, and set margins on the Margins tab.

WRAP UP

Before you finish, let's go over some of the things you learned in this lesson:

- You learned how to create a detail report that lists record details.

- You learned how to create a grouped report that consolidates details into groups and summarizes them.

- You learned how to create your own groups in a report.

- You learned how to format labels and text boxes.

- You learned how to create mailing labels.

    For more practice, try creating:

- Reports for all the tables and queries in the Fruitsweets database

Wrap up

- Reports for tables and queries in your personal databases

- The query and report shown at the end of the Skills Challenge

- The report shown in the Visual Workout at the beginning of this chapter

Finishing Touches

Part IV guides you through creating a simple application out of the Fruitsweets database, with custom features and automated performance so even a beginner can use the Fruitsweets database easily. It includes the following lessons:

- **Lesson 10: Automating Your Database with Macros**—this lesson introduces you to macros and explains what they are and how you can use them to automate database procedures.

- **Lesson 11: Creating a Switchboard**—this lesson covers creating a Switchboard form, which makes your database pushbutton easy to use.

- **Lesson 12: Creating Custom Toolbars and Menus**—this lesson teaches you techniques to further automate your database.

- **Lesson 13: Polishing and Publishing**—this last lesson shows you how to add elegant finishing touches and how to publish information in your database to the Internet or company intranet.

To begin working the book lessons in this part, use the practice database file named `FSPart4.mdb` and begin with Lesson 10.

Automating Your Database with Macros

30 MINUTES

GOALS

In this lesson, you'll master the following skills and concepts:

- Replacing a command button with one that runs a macro
- Creating a macro to show a form
- Testing a new macro
- Creating a macro to show a message
- Testing a new macro directly from the Macros tab
- Attaching a macro to a control

Get ready

GET READY

To complete this lesson, you'll need to start Access 97 and open the Fruitsweets database. For this exercise, you'll use the Fruitsweets database you've been working in throughout Part III.

When you finish these exercises, you'll know how to create Access macros to automate routine database tasks and procedures.

WHAT CAN MACROS DO FOR YOU?

Your Fruitsweets database is completely functional as it stands, and you'll have no trouble using it, because you're proficient in Access; however, a user who's less familiar with Access might get lost occasionally. A few macros can help such a user, by streamlining activities such as opening forms and printing reports, or by offering timely help in message boxes.

Macros are nonessential elements of a database that make it simpler and faster. If you're familiar with Microsoft Excel or Microsoft Word, you may have recorded macros previously, but Access macros are different. For one thing, Access has no macro recorder, so Access macros have to be built step-by-step (but that's not as difficult as it sounds). For another, while macros recorded in Excel and Word are designed to duplicate keystrokes and mouse actions, Access macros perform specific steps that you designate without recording every keystroke or mouse click.

In Lesson 8, you added a command button to the Orders form. This button runs a Visual Basic procedure that opens the Customers form. You didn't need to write or understand Visual Basic because the Command Button Wizard wrote the procedure for you; however, you can easily create a macro that does exactly the same thing without having to learn Visual Basic. While Visual Basic programming is much more powerful than macros and is useful (and sometimes necessary) in complex applications, it's also more time-consuming to learn. The advantage of using macros instead of Visual Basic is that macros enable you to automate your database more simply and quickly and perform a wider variety of procedures, including opening and closing any object in the database, printing reports or sending them to another program (such as Word or Excel), running queries, running strings of other macros, setting values in controls, applying filters, changing displays, and renaming objects.

To begin this lesson, you should have Access 97 started and the Fruitsweets database open.

▶ *Replacing a command button*

In this exercise, you'll open the Orders form and replace the current New Customer command button (which uses Visual Basic) with a command button that uses a macro to perform the same task.

Before you delete the existing command button, you'll take a look at the Visual Basic procedure the Command Button Wizard wrote.

① On the Forms tab, select the Orders form.

② Click the Design button.

The Orders form opens in Design view.

> **TIP**
>
> *Double-click the form's title bar, so you can see the entire form.*

③ Right-click the New Customer? command button.

④ Click Properties.

> **TIP**
>
> *You can also show a control's Properties dialog box by double-clicking the control.*

⑤ On the command button's Properties dialog box, click the Event tab.

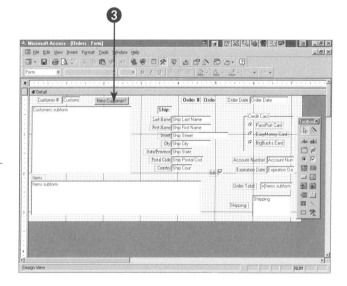

10

Automating Your Database with Macros

Replacing a command button

6 In the On Click box, click next to [Event Procedure].

A build button (with three dots in it) appears on the right side of the On Click box.

7 Click the build button.

A module window opens, as shown in the accompanying figure, showing the Visual Basic procedure the Command Button Wizard wrote.

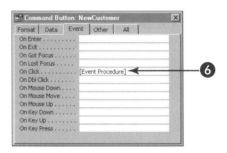

If you're unfamiliar with Visual Basic, this window may be a bit confusing. Don't worry—for this book, you won't need to understand any of what you see in the window.

8 Click the module window's X close box to close it.

9 Close the Properties dialog box.

The Orders form is still displayed in Design view, and the New Customer command button is still selected.

10 Press Delete to remove the New Customer command button.

11 On the Controls Toolbox, click the Control Wizards button to turn it off (it will not be highlighted when it's turned off).

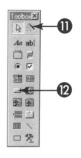

TIP *When the Control Wizards button is turned off, you can create controls without using a wizard.*

12 Click the Command Button button.

13 Click in the form where the previous command button was located.

A new command button appears. The button's label will read "Command" followed by a number (not necessarily the number you see in the illustration).

14 Double-click or drag through the label's text to select it, as shown in the accompanying illustration.

15 Type **New Customer?** and press Enter.

TIP *You can change the size and shape of the button by dragging the handles around the button's border.*

16 Right-click the new command button and click Properties.

17 In the Properties dialog box, click the Other tab.

18 In the Name box, type **NewCustomer**; then close the Properties dialog box.

Now you're ready to create a macro for the command button's On Click event.

The following Visual Bonus will give you a working reference for the macros you'll be building in this lesson.

10

Automating Your Database with Macros

Replacing a command button

An Access Macro

This Visual Bonus guides you through the bits and pieces of an Access macro.

Build a macro in the macro window.

Macros in a group named AutoKeys run when you press assigned keys.

Select View ➤ Macro Names to display the Macro Names column and create Macro groups

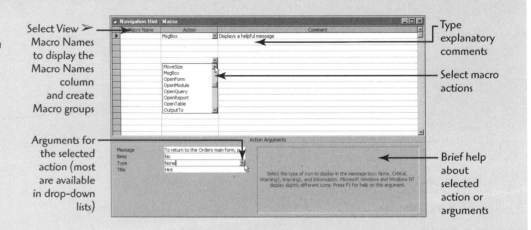

Type explanatory comments

Select macro actions

Arguments for the selected action (most are available in drop-down lists)

Brief help about selected action or arguments

Double-click an object, or right-click the object and click Properties to display the Properties dialog box

Each control has specific events associated with it

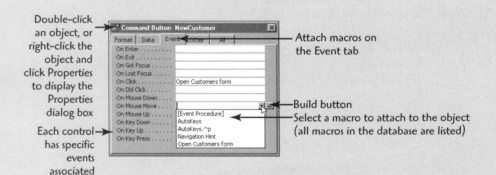

Attach macros on the Event tab

Build button

Select a macro to attach to the object (all macros in the database are listed)

Creating a macro to show a form

Now that you've replaced the wizard-built command button with a new command button, you'll create the macro the button will use to open the Customers form.

Your Orders form should still be open in Design view.

1 Right-click the command button, then click Build Event.

The Choose Builder dialog box appears.

2 In the Choose Builder dialog box, click Macro Builder.

3 Click OK.

An empty macro window and a Save As dialog box appear, as shown in the accompanying illustration. In the Save As dialog box, the name Macro1 is highlighted and ready for a new macro name.

4 Type **Open Customers Form**.

5 Click OK.

The macro window title bar shows the new macro name, and the insertion point is flashing in the first cell in the Action column, ready for you to select a macro action.

6 In the Action column, click the down arrow.

7 Scroll down the list and select OpenForm.

The OpenForm action is entered in the Action column, and the *arguments* for the OpenForm action appear in the argument pane, as shown in the accompanying illustration.

NOTE Arguments *tell Access how to carry out the action you set. In this case, arguments give Access information such as which form to open and what view to open the form in.*

8 In the argument pane, click in the Form Name box.

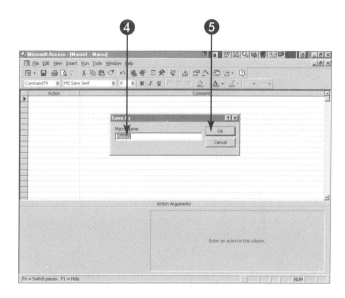

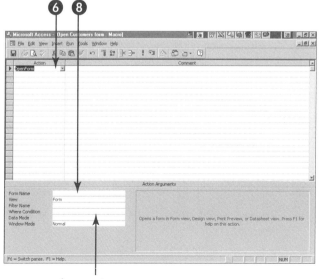

Argument pane

Creating a macro to show a form

TIP

It's a good idea to set arguments in the order in which they're listed (top to bottom) because what you set for one argument may affect your available choices in the arguments that follow.

9 Click the down arrow that appears in the Form Name box and click Customers.

10 Click in the Data Mode box then click the down arrow that appears.

11 Select Edit.

When the Data Mode box is selected, the helpful tip on the right side of the argument pane tells you that "Edit" allows you to edit existing records or add new ones, which is exactly what you want to be able to do, as shown in the accompanying figure.

TIP

If you want in-depth help with a specific action or argument, select it and press F1.

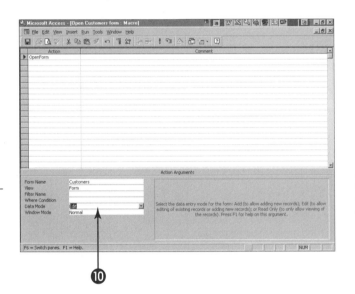

12 On the toolbar, click Save. 💾

13 Close the macro window by clicking its X close box.

There is one minor problem: the new command button is automatically placed at the end of the tab order for the form, but you want it positioned after the Customer # and before the Customers subform.

14 Click View ➤ Tab Order.

15 Select the NewCustomer control (at the bottom of the list).

16 Drag it up to the top, between Customer ID and Customers subform.

17 Click OK to close the Tab Order dialog box.

18 Switch the form to Form view.

TIP

To quickly create a macro that opens a specific form, report, or query, drag the name of the form, report, or query from the database window and drop it on the Action column in the macro window.

Testing a new macro

Now you can test the new macro and see if it works!

1 On the Orders form, click the New Customer? button.

The Customers form opens and shows the first record in the Customers table, as shown in the accompanying illustration.

NOTE

If your Customers form fills the screen, it's because you left it in maximized view last time you closed it. To resize it, click its Restore button (in the upper right corner of the form's window) and then click Window ➢ Size To Fit Form.

2 Close the Customers form.

3 Save and close the Orders form.

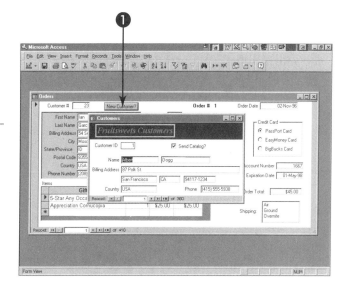

Creating a macro to show a message

When you created the subform controls in the Orders main form, you learned that the keystroke for moving the focus back to the main form from a subform is Ctrl+Tab. But other Fruitsweets employees who use the Orders form may not remember that keystroke.

You can help them by creating a macro that shows a helpful reminder message whenever a subform is entered; the message will say "To return to the Orders main form, press Ctrl+Tab", and it will have an OK button, so the user (who's typing madly while taking a customer's order) can simply press Enter to make the message disappear.

Creating a macro to show a message

1 In the database window, click the Macros tab.

One macro is listed in the macros tab: the macro you created in the second exercise. You created that macro in the Macro Builder for the command button, and it was automatically attached to the button; you'll create this new macro in the macro window and then you'll attach it to both subform controls.

2 On the Macros tab, click the New button.

A new macro window opens.

3 Click in the first cell in the Action column.

4 Click the down arrow; then scroll down to select Msgbox.

The Msgbox action's arguments appear in the arguments pane.

5 In the arguments pane, click in the Message box.

6 Type **To return to the Orders main form, press Ctrl+Tab.**

7 Click in the Beep box; then click its down arrow.

8 Select No; then click in the Title box.

9 Type **Hint**.

10 On the toolbar, click Save. 🖫

11 In the Save As dialog box, type **Navigation Hint**; then click OK.

12 Close the macro window by clicking its X close box.

The macro is complete. First, you'll test it from the Macros tab to be sure it works; then you'll attach it to the two subforms.

► Testing a new macro directly from the Macros tab

It's a good idea to test the macro right away, and you can do that directly from the Macros tab in the database window.

1 On the Macros tab, select the Navigation Hint macro.

2 Click the Run button.

Your message box appears.

3 Press Enter (or click OK) to close the message box.

► Attaching a macro to a control

Now that you know the macro works, you can attach it to the two subform controls in the Orders form.

1 In the database window, click the Forms tab.

2 Open the Orders form in Design view.

3 Right-click the Customers subform control and click Properties.

4 In the Properties dialog box, click the Event tab.

The Event tab shows the events available for a subform control, which are quite different from the events available for the command button you looked at in the first exercise.

5 Click in the On Enter box and click its down arrow.

A list of all the macros in the database appears.

6 Select the Navigation Hint macro.

The Navigation Hint macro is attached to the subform control.

7 While the Properties dialog box is open, click the Items subform control.

The Properties dialog box switches to show the properties for the Items subform control.

8 Repeat steps 5 and 6 to attach the Navigation Hint macro to the Items subform control.

10

Automating Your Database with Macros

9 Close the Properties dialog box.

10 Switch to Form view.

11 Save the Orders form.

12 Tab through the controls in the Orders form.

When you tab into the Customers subform, your message box appears, as shown in the accompanying illustration. Press Enter to close it; then press Ctrl+Tab to return to the Orders form and continue tabbing through the form.

 NOTE *"Tab through . . ." or "Tab into . . ." means "Press the Tab key to move the focus through or into . . .".*

13 Close the Orders form.

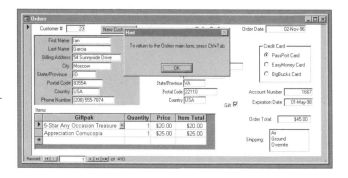

SKILLS CHALLENGE: CREATING ANOTHER MACRO

In this Skills Challenge, you'll create a macro to print the Catalog Labels report, and you'll attach it to a keystroke, so you can print the report simply by pressing the assigned keys.

Macros attached to keystrokes are special. They're named according to the keystrokes that run them (for example, Alt+C, or Ctrl+P) and are stored together in a *macro group* with a special name, "AutoKeys", that Access recognizes. A macro group is a collection of separate but related macros that are stored together under a single macro name.

In this Skills Challenge, you'll create an AutoKeys macro that runs when you press Ctrl+L.

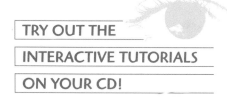

TRY OUT THE
INTERACTIVE TUTORIALS
ON YOUR CD!

 NOTE *Be careful about your choice of keystrokes: if you create a macro for a keystroke that is normally used in Access, such as Ctrl+C (to copy) or Ctrl+V (to paste), the macro action will replace the normal Access keystroke action.*

If you want to see a list of Access keystrokes, look up **shortcut keys** in the Access help files; but if you don't normally use a specific keystroke in Access, you won't miss it if you assign a macro to it.

1 On the Macros tab, click the New button.

A new macro window opens.

 Do you remember how to open a control's Properties dialog box?

2 Select Macro Names from the View menu.

A new column, Macro Names, is added to the macro window. You'll use the keystroke as the macro name and store it in a macro group named "AutoKeys".

 NOTE *Keystrokes are entered in Visual Basic syntax, in which the caret symbol (^) stands for Ctrl and the plus symbol (+) stands for Shift. For more information about keystroke syntax, ask the Office Assistant about AutoKeys or look up AutoKeys in Help ➢ Contents And Index on the Find tab.*

3 In the first cell in the Macro Name column, type **^l**.

 TIP *The ^ symbol is over the numeral 6 on your keyboard.*

 Do you remember where to attach a macro to a control event?

4 In the first Action cell, select OpenReport.

 How can you build a control without the wizard's help?

10

Automating Your Database with Macros

Skills challenge

5 In the argument pane, in the Report Name box, select Catalog Labels.

 4 *Do you remember where to give a control a logical (memorable) name?*

6 In the argument pane, be sure the View box reads Print. If it doesn't, select Print in the View box.

This action prints the report immediately without opening it.

 TIP *It's a good idea to type a short comment of your own in the Comment column to remind yourself later what the macro does.*

 5 *How can you find a list of macro actions?*

Your macro window should look like the accompanying illustration.

 6 *How can you get quick help about an action or argument?*

7 Save the macro with the name **AutoKeys** and close it.

 TIP *To create more keystroke macros for the Fruitsweets database, open the AutoKeys macro and add the new macros in that window, so they're all stored in the AutoKeys macro group.*

 7 *How can you test a new macro before you attach it to a control event?*

8 Test the new macro: From any database window, press Ctrl+L.

The Catalog Labels report prints out. Now you can simply tell your assistant to open the database and press Ctrl+L to print the

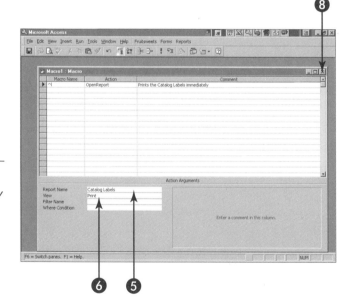

current mailing labels (remind them to put label stock in the printer!).

TIP

The Catalog Labels report is fairly long; if you don't want to print it, click Cancel in the Print message or turn off your printer.

TROUBLESHOOTING

You've learned a little bit about using macros to automate your Access database. By now you should know what Access macros are and what they can do for you, how to build a macro, what events are, how to attach a macro to a control event, how to group similar macros together, and how to create a keystroke macro. There's much more to explore if you decide you want to use macros frequently. The following solutions might answer some questions that came up during this lesson.

Problem	Solution
I can't create a command button without the darn wizard interfering!	In the Controls Toolbox, click the Control Wizards button to turn it off.
I want to create a command button with the wizard, but the wizard won't start.	In the Controls Toolbox, click the Control Wizards button to turn it on.
I created a keystroke macro named Shift+q, but when I press Shift+q, nothing happens.	Be sure the macro name is "+q", not "Shift+q".

continued

10

Automating Your Database with Macros

Troubleshooting

Problem	Solution
I can't find the On Click event for my subform.	A subform control doesn't have an On Click event, only On Enter and On Exit events. If you want to attach a macro to the On Click event of a control in a subform, you need to open the subform in Design view and then open the Properties dialog box for the control and attach the macro to its On Click event.
I don't want to see the Navigation Hint message anymore. How do I turn it off?	In the Properties dialog box for the subform control, on the Event tab, select the macro name and press Delete. This won't remove the macro from the database, just from the subform control.
I want to learn more about Access macros.	If you have Office Assistant installed, ask it about "macro"; if you don't have Office Assistant installed, select Help ➢ Contents And Index, and on the Find tab, type **macro**. You might also find the following book helpful: *Automating Microsoft Access with Macros* (Susann Novalis, 1996).
I want to learn more about Visual Basic.	If you have Office Assistant installed, ask it about "visual basic"; if you don't have Office Assistant installed, select Help ➢ Contents And Index and on the Find tab, type **visual basic**.

WRAP UP

Before you finish, let's go over some of the things you learned in this lesson:

- You learned how to create a command button without the wizard.

- You learned how to build a macro in the command button's Macro Builder.

- You learned how to build a macro in the macro window.

- You learned how to attach macros to control events.

- You learned how to build a macro that you run with a keystroke.

For more practice, create macros to open other forms and reports, open a query, close forms and reports, and display messages when text boxes are entered or exited.

In Part IV, you'll put what you've learned in previous lessons to work, creating an automated application with a switchboard and custom toolbars and menus. You'll also learn how to publish information from your database on the Web.

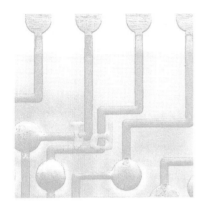

Creating a Switchboard

GOALS

In this lesson, you'll master the following skills and concepts:

- Creating and formatting a switchboard form
- Creating macros that open forms
- Creating command buttons in a switchboard
- Testing a switchboard

20 MINUTES

Get ready

GET READY

To complete this lesson's exercise, you need to start Access 97 and open the Fruitsweets database. For this exercise, you'll use the Fruitsweets database that you've been working in throughout Part III, or you can begin this lesson with the database FSPart4.mdb (on your practice CD-ROM).

    When you finish these exercises, you'll know how to create a switchboard form that makes your database push-button easy to use.

TRY OUT THE

INTERACTIVE TUTORIALS

ON YOUR CD!

WHY CREATE A SWITCHBOARD FORM?

Your Fruitsweets database is fully functional right now, but it's essentially a collection of interrelated database objects, usable by someone who knows Access but potentially mysterious to someone who doesn't.

    In this lesson, and in Lessons 12 and 13, you'll tie the database objects together into an *application*, a system of database organization that allows the user to focus on the data instead of on how to use Access. A primary component of any Access application is the switchboard, which is a form that serves as a central starting point for opening objects in your database.

    The switchboard is a form that contains command buttons; the command buttons run macros that perform tasks such as opening forms and reports. A user doesn't have to search through the database for forms and reports because the means of opening those objects is centrally located—on the switchboard.

    The switchboard shown in the accompanying illustration is the one you'll build in this lesson.

    As you can see, clicking a switchboard button to open a form is much more intuitive than clicking the Forms tab and then searching through the list of forms and subforms for the form a user needs.

    You've already learned everything you need to know to build your switchboard in earlier lessons; in this lesson, you'll put that information to use and also learn some quicker ways to work with command buttons and macros.

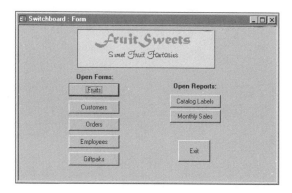

Creating a switchboard form ◀

To begin this lesson, you should have Access 97 started and the Fruitsweets database open.

Creating and formatting a switchboard form

In Lessons 7 and 8, you created forms by allowing the wizard to create the initial form and then modifying it to suit your needs. That was a good way to create a form with controls that were bound to fields in a table or query, but your switchboard won't be bound to any fields; it will simply run macros. To create your switchboard form, you'll begin with a blank form and add the buttons, macros, and graphic objects it needs.

In this exercise, you'll create and save a blank form and then format it and add the company logo.

1 On the Forms tab, click the New button.

2 In the New Form dialog box, double-click Design view.

A new, blank form appears, as shown in the accompanying illustration.

3 In the Controls Toolbox, be sure the Control Wizards button is turned off (it should not be highlighted).

4 In the Controls Toolbox, click the Image button.

5 Click in the center of the form grid.

The Insert Picture dialog box appears.

6 In the Insert Picture dialog box, navigate to your Access One Step at a Time folder.

7 Double-click the `Logo.bmp` filename.

The Fruitsweets logo appears in the form grid, as shown in the accompanying figure.

8 Drag the logo control to center it in the upper part of the form grid.

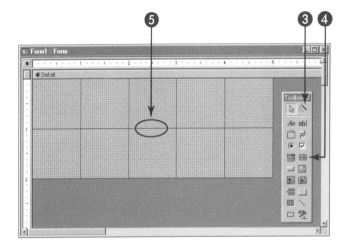

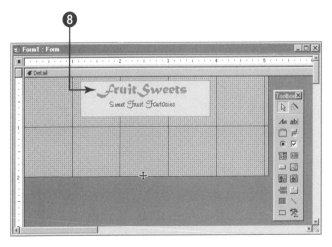

11

Creating a Switchboard

Creating a switchboard form

⑨ Drag the bottom of the form grid down until the form is about 3 inches long.

⑩ Right-click the form outside the form grid.

⑪ Click Properties.

⑫ In the Properties dialog box, on the Format tab, turn off the Scroll Bars, the Record Selectors, and the Navigation Buttons.

⑬ Close the Properties dialog box.

⑭ Save the form as **Switchboard**. 🖫

⑮ Switch to Form view. 🔲▾

⑯ Click Window, then click Size To Fit Form.

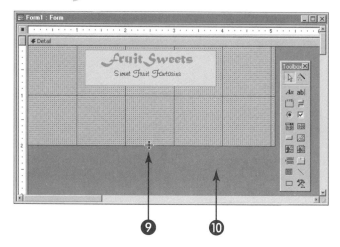

NOTE

Remember, if the form window is maximized, you cannot select the Size To Fit Form command; click the Restore button in the upper-right corner of the form window, then click Window ➢ Size To Fit Form.

Your form should look similar to the one shown in the accompanying illustration.

⑰ Close the Switchboard form.

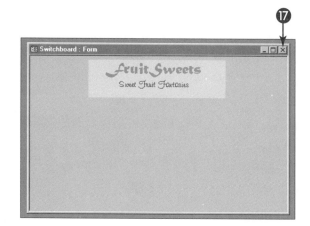

VISUAL BONUS

Building the Switchboard

This Visual Bonus shows how you'll build the switchboard.

The switchboard in Design view.

Add a picture in Image control

Drag macro name from the Macros tab onto form to create button

Make button text user-friendly

The ruler helps you size and place objects

Select the macro name in the button's Properties dialog box

Create identical buttons by copying and pasting

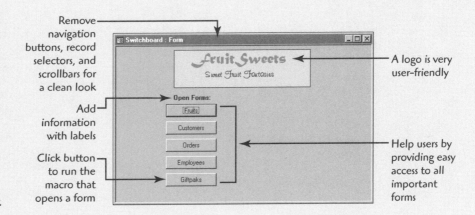

The switchboard in Form view.

Remove navigation buttons, record selectors, and scrollbars for a clean look

Add information with labels

Click button to run the macro that opens a form

A logo is very user-friendly

Help users by providing easy access to all important forms

continued

Creating macros that open forms

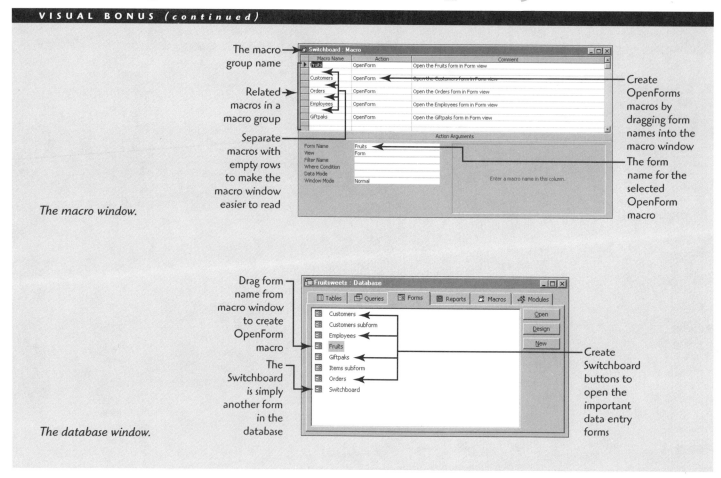

The macro group name

Related macros in a macro group

Separate macros with empty rows to make the macro window easier to read

The macro window.

Create OpenForms macros by dragging form names into the macro window

The form name for the selected OpenForm macro

Drag form name from macro window to create OpenForm macro

The Switchboard is simply another form in the database

The database window.

Create Switchboard buttons to open the important data entry forms

Creating macros that open forms

Next you'll create a group of similar macros that open all the important forms in the database. Because they're all similar, you'll store them in a macro group; the macros will be in one place, so they'll be easier to find and work with.

In this exercise, you'll learn some quick methods of creating the group of OpenForm macros.

Creating macros that open forms

NOTE

The "Open" macros are special—they're the only macros you can create by dragging a database object into the macro window.

1 On the Macros tab, click the New button.

A new macro window opens.

2 Save the new macro as **Switchboard**.

3 Click View.

4 Click Macro Names.

A Macro Name column is added to the macro window.

5 Click Window.

6 Click Tile Vertically.

The database window and the macro window are tiled vertically on your screen, as shown in the accompanying illustration.

TIP

Tiling windows is the quickest way to align them side-by-side, so you can drag objects from one window to the other; the Window ➢ Tile commands are available (and useful) in most Windows programs.

7 In the database window, click the Forms tab.

8 Drag the Fruits form name from the database window to the macro window.

9 Drop it on the first cell in the Action column.

NOTE

The cell the pointer tip is touching is the cell where the macro action will be dropped.

A new OpenForm action is created and the arguments are automatically filled in correctly.

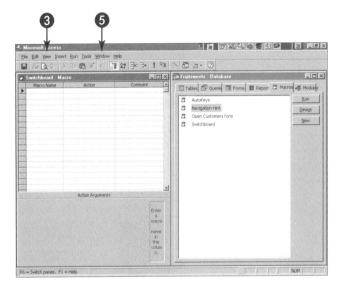

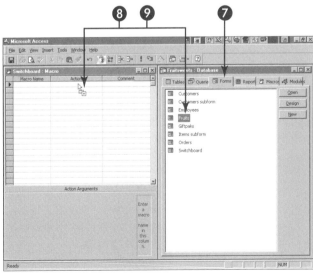

⑩ Repeat Steps 8 and 9 to create OpenForm actions for the Customers, Orders, Employees, and Giftpaks forms.

TIP

You can leave a blank row between each macro to make the macro window easier to read (as I have done), but skipping rows will not affect the macros — it's purely a matter of personal preference.

Your windows should look like the ones in the accompanying illustration.

All the macro actions have the same name, the group name Switchboard. Now you need to give them identifying names in the Macro Name column.

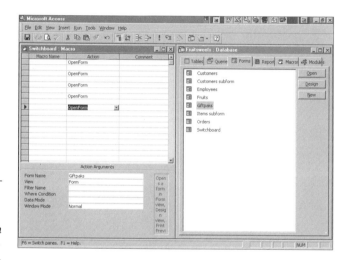

NOTE

A single macro in a macro window is referred to with a single name (for example, the Open Customers Form macro you created in Lesson 10), but macros in a macro group, such as these, will be referred to using the group name and the individual macro name. These macros will be referred to as Switchboard.Fruits, Switchboard.Orders, and so on.

⑪ In the Macro Name column, type the name of the form that each OpenForm action opens (hint: when you click in each macro row, the name of the form the macro opens appears in the argument pane).

TIP

To enter the form name in the Macro Name column more quickly, click in the row for the macro you are naming (the form name appears in the argument pane); select the form name in the argument pane and then press Ctrl+C (to copy the name); then click in the macro name cell for that macro; then press Ctrl+V (to paste the name).

Your macro window should look like the accompanying illustration (I've separated the macros for easier reading and typed comments to identify each macro).

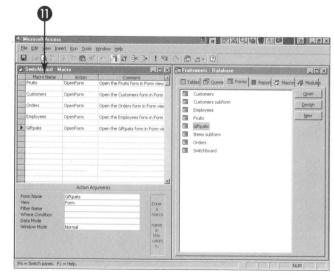

⑫ Save the Switchboard macro.

⑬ Close the Switchboard macro.

Now you're ready to create the command buttons that will run the macros in the Switchboard group.

Creating command buttons in a switchboard

You've previously created command buttons in two other ways: by using the wizard (which wrote a Visual Basic procedure) and without using the wizard (you created and attached macros to the button). Now you'll learn how to create buttons with attached macros the fast way, by dragging and dropping the macros onto the Switchboard form.

The database window should still be vertically tiled on your screen.

① On the database window, on the Forms tab, open the Switchboard form in Design view.

The Switchboard form appears in Design view, as shown in the accompanying illustration.

② In the database window, click the Macros tab.

The macro group name, Switchboard, appears in the list of macros.

③ Drag the macro name Switchboard to the form window.

④ Drop it below the logo.

A new command button with the macro group name appears on the Switchboard form.

⑤ Maximize the form window (click its Maximize button in the upper-right corner).

⑥ Move the new button to reposition it, as shown in the accompanying illustration.

Next you'll create copies of the button, and then you'll give them their individual names and macros.

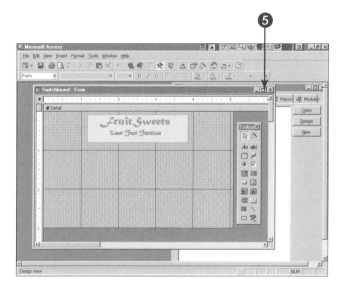

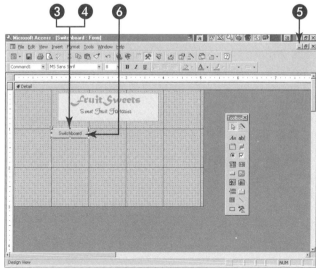

Creating command buttons

⑦ Click the new button to select it.

⑧ On the toolbar, click Copy. 📋

⑨ On the toolbar, click Paste four times. 📋

Four copies of the button are pasted below the original, for a total of five buttons.

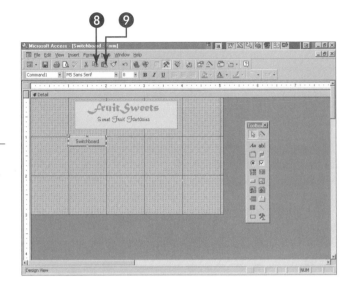

TIP

Copying and pasting controls is a fast way to create many identical controls on a form. You can also press Ctrl+C to copy and press Ctrl+V to paste.

⑩ Double-click the top button.

⑪ In its Properties dialog box, click the Event tab.

The button's On Click event shows the macro group name, Switchboard, but you need to change it to an individual macro name and then change the name on the button face.

⑫ Click in the On Click box.

⑬ Click the down arrow.

⑭ Select Switchboard.Fruits.

This is the complete name of the individual macro that opens the Fruits form.

⑮ In the Properties dialog box, click the Format tab.

⑯ Change the Caption to **Fruits**.

⑰ Repeat steps 12 through 16 to apply a different macro and caption to each button. Your form should look like the accompanying illustration when you finish.

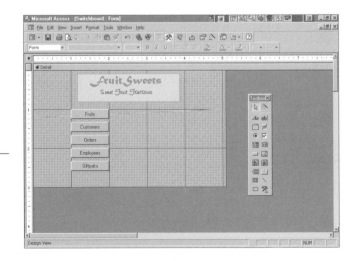

TIP

When you finish setting properties for one button, simply click the next button on the form to set its properties, instead of closing and reopening the Properties dialog box.

18 Close the Properties dialog box when you're finished.

19 Add a label above the column of buttons that reads **Open Forms:**.

> **TIP**
>
> *To add a label, click the Label button in the Controls Toolbox; then click above the buttons on the form, type the label text, and press Enter; then position the label where you want it.*

20 Switch the form to Form view.

21 Click the Resize button in its upper-right corner.

22 Click Window, then click Size To Fit Form.

Your Switchboard form should look like the accompanying illustration.

Testing a switchboard

Now is a good time to test your switchboard.

1 Click the Fruits button.

The Fruits form opens.

2 Close the Fruits form.

3 Test the remaining buttons to be sure they open the correct forms.

If any button opens the wrong form, check (and change) the macro name on the Event tab in its Properties dialog box.

4 Save the Switchboard form.

5 Close the Switchboard form.

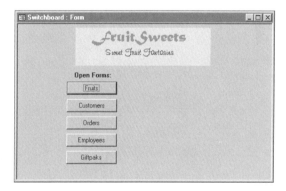

Skills challenge

SKILLS CHALLENGE: CREATING MACROS TO OPEN REPORTS AND EXIT THE DATABASE

In this Skills Challenge, you'll add a set of buttons that open important reports in Print Preview, and you'll add a button that closes the database.

TRY OUT THE

INTERACTIVE TUTORIALS

ON YOUR CD!

 Do you remember how to create a new form from scratch?

❶ On the Macros tab, open the Switchboard macro in Design view.

 Do you remember how to quickly create an OpenForm macro?

❷ Create macros in the Switchboard group to open the Catalog Labels and Monthly Sales reports (use the OpenReport macro action and set the View argument to Print Preview).

Remember to enter names for each new macro in the Macro Name column.

 How can you quickly create a command button to run a macro?

❸ Create command buttons on the Switchboard form to run those macros.

 Do you remember how to place a picture on a form?

❹ Add a label to the Switchboard that identifies those two buttons as opening reports.

 How can you remove scroll bars, record selectors, and navigation buttons from a form?

TIP *To define an access key for a button, type & (an ampersand) on the left side of the character in the button's caption (for example, to make the F in Fruits an access key, change the Fruits button's caption to &Fruits. Then, when you press Alt+F, the Fruits form opens just as if you had clicked the button).*

5 Test the new command buttons.

6 Create a macro in the Switchboard macro group that exits the database (use the Quit macro action, and in the argument pane, select Exit in the Options box).

NOTE *This action will not only close the database, it will also close Access.*

6 *How can you create a macro group?*

7 Add a command button captioned "Exit", which runs the Quit macro, to the Switchboard form.

Your Switchboard form should look similar to the accompanying illustration.

8 Test the new Exit button.

Access closes.

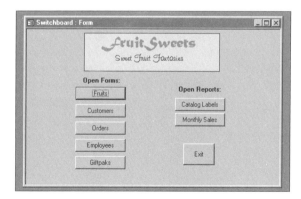

TROUBLESHOOTING

You've learned how to use a switchboard to add finishing touches to your database that begin to tie the separate objects together into a coherent application. The Switchboard makes the Fruitsweets database easier for a novice to use, reducing the time you must spend teaching others how to find their way around in your database. The following solutions should answer some questions that came up in this lesson.

Troubleshooting

Problem	Solution
I finished the first exercise, but when I switched my new Switchboard to Form view, there was a line running the full width of the screen and the Fruitsweets logo was not centered on the screen. How can I make my Switchboard look like the illustration at the end of the first exercise?	You need to perform the last step: click Window ➢ Size To Fit Form.
I dragged my macro onto my form window, but nothing happened.	Be sure you're dragging the macro name from the Macros tab in the database window, not from the macro window.
I double-clicked my command button to open the Properties dialog box, but all that happened was that the button name got selected.	If a control (like a button) is already selected, double-clicking won't accomplish what you want. Click away from the control to deselect it; then double-click on the control to open its Properties dialog box.
When I double-click the macro name on the Macros tab to open it, it runs the macro instead.	To open a macro window, you must click the macro name and then click the Design button.
I have a long list of OpenReport actions in my macro window. How can I remember which report each action opens?	Click in the row for a specific OpenReport action; the name of the report the selected action opens appears in the argument pane.

WRAP UP

Before you finish, let's go over some of the things you learned in this lesson:

- You learned how to create a new form from scratch.

- You learned how to create command buttons with attached macros by dragging and dropping the macro name onto the form.

- You learned how to create OpenForm macro actions by dragging and dropping database objects onto a macro window.

- You learned how to use macro groups to make working with macros more efficient.

  For more practice, try the following:

- Put command buttons on each of your forms and reports to close them (use the Close macro action)

- Put command buttons on each of your reports to print them (they should run only the PrintOut macro action)

- Create a second Switchboard form for reports and put a command button on the first Switchboard form to open the second Switchboard form (use the OpenForm macro action); then move all of your report command buttons onto the second Switchboard form (move the buttons by dragging and dropping or by cutting and pasting).

  In the next lesson, you'll learn how to create a custom toolbar and a custom menu bar for your application.

Creating Custom Toolbars and Menus

GOALS

In this lesson, you'll master the following skills and concepts:

20 MINUTES

- Creating a custom toolbar

- Adding buttons to a toolbar

- Creating a custom menu

Get ready

GET READY

To complete this lesson's exercise, you'll need to start Access 97 and open the Fruitsweets database. For this exercise, you'll use the Fruitsweets database that you've been working in throughout Part IV.

When you finish these exercises, you'll know how to create custom toolbars and menus that further automate your database.

TRY OUT THE
INTERACTIVE TUTORIALS
ON YOUR CD!

ADDING CUSTOM TOOLBARS AND MENUS

Custom toolbars and menus, like the Switchboard you created in Lesson 11, are nonessential database elements that turn your database into an application that even a novice can easily use. And in keeping with the Microsoft Windows tradition, the toolbar and menu you create in this lesson will be redundant, providing yet more means of opening forms and reports and exiting Access.

The toolbar and menu shown in the accompanying illustration are the ones you'll build in this lesson.

It might seem excessive to provide a switchboard, a toolbar, and a menu that perform identical actions, but some users are more comfortable with toolbars, and others with menus or forms, so if you create all three elements in your application, you've covered all the bases. Furthermore, once you know how to create each of these database elements, you'll be prepared to create toolbars and menus that each perform different actions. The possibilities are endless.

To begin this lesson, you should have the Fruitsweets database open.

New toolbar   New menu

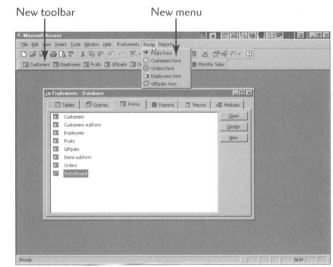

Creating a custom toolbar

Creating a custom toolbar that's open whenever the database is open is surprisingly simple. You can create a personal toolbar that contains only the normal Access toolbar buttons (but just the ones you use often, and nothing more) so that you have access to the buttons you use without the distraction of buttons you never use.

Adding buttons to a toolbar

You can also create a custom toolbar that contains buttons that run macros, and buttons that perform simple object-specific actions such as opening forms and reports.

In this exercise, you'll create a custom toolbar to hold application-specific buttons.

❶ On the View menu, point to Toolbars.

❷ Click Customize.

The Customize dialog box opens, as shown in the accompanying illustration.

❸ On the Toolbars tab, click the New button.

The New Toolbar dialog box appears, as shown in the accompanying illustration.

❹ Type the new toolbar name **Fruitsweets**.

❺ Click OK (or press Enter).

A tiny new toolbar with no buttons appears on your desktop, as shown in the accompanying illustration.

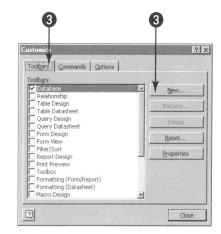

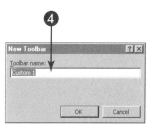

NOTE *When you click the Customize dialog box, the new toolbar will disappear behind the dialog box, so it's a good idea to drag the new toolbar off to the side, away from dialog boxes it might hide behind.*

Adding buttons to a toolbar

Now you'll put buttons on the new toolbar that open your application's forms and reports.

TIP *You can also add buttons to built-in toolbars using the following procedure.*

New toolbar
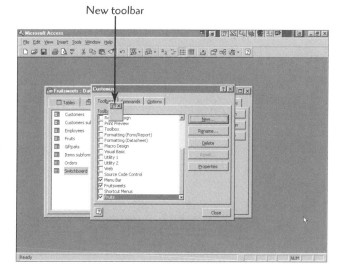

Adding buttons to a toolbar

1 In the Customize dialog box, click the Commands tab.

NOTE *Whenever you perform any toolbar-customizing procedures, the Customize dialog box must be open, even if you don't use it.*

The Commands tab contains all the built-in toolbar buttons, plus access to all your database objects and macros.

2 Scroll down the Categories list.

3 Select All Forms.

Buttons that will open your forms are displayed in the Commands window.

4 Drag the Customers form from the Commands window.

5 Drop it onto the new toolbar, as shown in the accompanying illustration.

A new button with a form icon on its face appears on the new toolbar.

6 Repeat Steps 4 and 5 to drag buttons for the Employees, Fruits, Giftpaks, and Orders forms onto the Fruitsweets toolbar.

The button faces are all identical, but you'll change that in the next few steps.

7 Right-click the first button on the Fruitsweets toolbar.

A shortcut menu, shown in the accompanying illustration, appears.

TIP *To change the ToolTip that appears when you point to the button, click Properties on the shortcut menu and then type a new ToolTip in the ToolTip box.*

8 On the shortcut menu, click Image And Text.

The name of the button appears in the button face, alongside the form icon.

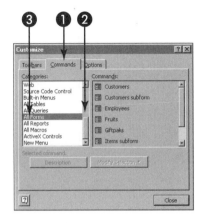

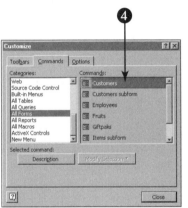

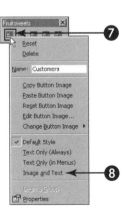

TIP

To change a button face, point to Change Button Image on the shortcut menu and select a different image from the collection displayed, or click Edit Button Image and create your own button face.

9 Repeat Steps 7 and 8 for each of the buttons on the toolbar.

The Fruitsweets toolbar should look similar to the accompanying illustration.

10 Repeat Steps 2 through 8 to add buttons for the Catalog Labels and Monthly Sales reports (you'll find them in the All Reports category).

11 Close the Customize dialog box.

12 Move the toolbar up to the top of the Access screen and dock it just below the existing toolbar (push it against the existing toolbar).

Your screen should look similar to the accompanying illustration.

The Fruitsweets toolbar, and any other object-specific toolbars, will be displayed whenever the Fruitsweets database is open.

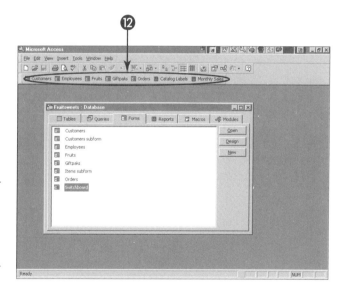

TIP

To hide or show the Fruitsweets toolbar, click View ➢ Toolbars, then click Fruitsweets on the submenu.

NOTE

To delete a custom toolbar, click View ➢ Toolbars ➢ Customize; then select the custom toolbar name and click the Delete button. You can delete custom toolbars or reset built-in toolbars, but you can't reset custom toolbars or delete built-in toolbars.

Creating a custom menu

Creating a custom menu

Creating a custom menu is also pretty simple—in fact, it's a lot like creating a toolbar. In this lesson, you'll create a custom menu the easiest way, and it will run the macros you created in Lesson 11 (the Switchboard macros that open forms, print reports, and quit Access). The menu will be added to your existing Access menu bar.

TIP *You can run any of your macros with custom menu commands.*

❶ Right-click the menu bar or any toolbar.

❷ On the shortcut menu, click Customize.

The Customize dialog box appears.

❸ On the Commands tab, scroll to the bottom and click New Menu.

A single command, New Menu, appears in the Commands box.

❹ Drag the New Menu command from the Commands box.

❺ Drop it on the Access menu bar.

A new menu is added to the menu bar.

❻ Right-click the new menu.

A shortcut menu appears, as shown in the accompanying illustration.

❼ In the Name box, type **Fruitsweets**.

❽ Press Enter.

The new menu is renamed Fruitsweets.

❾ In the Customize dialog box, on the Commands tab, select the category All Macros.

In the Commands box, all the macros in the database are listed.

❿ Drag the Switchboard.Fruits command to the Fruitsweets menu.

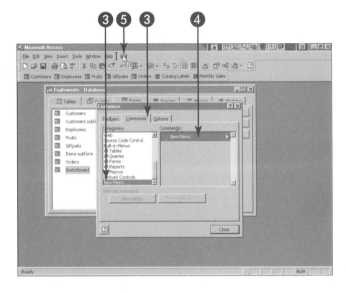

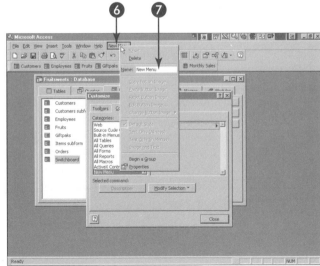

⑪ Drop it on the gray square that drops down from the Fruitsweets menu.

⑫ Drag all of the Switchboard macros onto the Fruitsweets menu list.

Your menu list should look like the accompanying illustration.

Next you'll give your menu commands more intuitive names.

⑬ On the Fruitsweets menu, right-click Switchboard.Fruits.

⑭ On the shortcut menu, in the Name box, change the name to **Fruits form**.

⑮ Repeat Steps 13 and 14 to change the names of the remaining menu commands to Customers form, Orders form, Employees form, Giftpaks form, Catalog Labels report, Monthly Sales report, and Quit Access.

Your menu should look like the accompanying illustration.

⑯ Close the Customize dialog box.

⑰ Test your new menu commands.

Fun, isn't it?

NOTE *Unlike a custom toolbar, which is part of the database and disappears when you close the database, a custom menu becomes part of Access and is displayed in every database you open. If you don't want your custom menu visible in each and every database, you must remove it permanently. To remove the custom menu, press and hold down the Alt key, then drag the menu away from the menu bar and drop it on the Access desktop.*

SKILLS CHALLENGE: CREATING MORE MENUS

In this Skills Challenge, you'll break the new Fruitsweets menu into three menus—a Forms menu, a Reports menu, and the Fruitsweets menu (which will have only the Quit Access command).

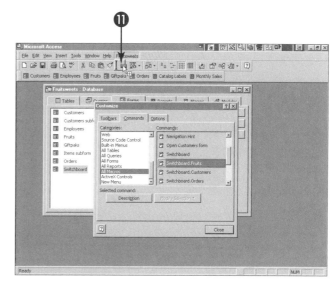

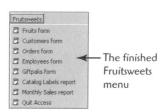

The finished Fruitsweets menu

TRY OUT THE

INTERACTIVE TUTORIALS

ON YOUR CD!

Skills challenge

1 Right-click the menu bar, then click Customize.

You can drag the Customize dialog box out of your way for the rest of the steps, but don't close it until the exercise is completed.

 Do you remember how to create a new toolbar?

2 Hold down Ctrl while you drag a copy of the Fruitsweets menu to the right of the original Fruitsweets menu, as shown in the accompanying illustration.

A copy of the Fruitsweets menu is created on the menu bar.

3 Repeat Step 2 to create a third Fruitsweets menu.

 What's a quick way to rearrange toolbar buttons?

4 Right-click the second Fruitsweets menu, and change its name to **Forms**.

5 Right-click the third Fruitsweets menu, and change its name to **Reports**.

 Do you remember how to change the ToolTip for a toolbar button?

6 Click the Fruitsweets menu to display its list of commands; then drag away from the menu all commands *except* the Quit Access command.

The Fruitsweets menu should contain only the Quit Access command.

 Do you remember how to add a new menu to the Access menu bar?

7 Click the Forms menu, then drag away from the menu list all commands except the forms commands.

The Forms menu should contain only commands to open forms.

 Do you remember how to add commands to a menu?

8 Click the Reports menu, then drag away from the menu list all commands except the reports commands.

The Reports menu should contain only commands to open reports.

Your menus should look similar to the ones shown in the accompanying illustrations (I changed the button faces on the Forms menu just for fun).

 You can change the button faces on the toolbar buttons to match the button faces on the Forms menu: click View ➤ Toolbars ➤ Customize; then right-click a button on the Fruitsweets toolbar; then point to Change Button Image and click the button face that matches the button face you selected for the corresponding menu command.

TROUBLESHOOTING

You've learned how to create more finishing touches for your database, including custom toolbars and custom menus that run both built-in procedures (such as those that open forms and reports) and macros. The following solutions might answer some questions that came up during this lesson.

Troubleshooting

Problem	Solution
How do I remove buttons from a toolbar?	Hold down the Alt key while you drag the button away from the toolbar.
How do I rearrange buttons on a toolbar?	Hold down the Alt key while you drag the buttons into new positions on the toolbar; you can also drag buttons from one toolbar to another and drag buttons a little apart to create space between them.
I accidentally deleted my custom toolbar; how can I get it back?	You can't; you must rebuild it.
I messed up one of my built-in toolbars while I was playing around with the Alt key; how can I return it to its original configuration?	Click View ➤ Toolbars ➤ Customize; on the Toolbars tab, click the name of the toolbar and then click the Reset button.
I dragged a menu command to my new menu, but when I dropped it on the menu, instead of adding the command to the new menu, a new menu was created.	This is a little tricky at first. You need to hold the dragged command over the menu until the menu list appears; then move the dragged command downward and drop it on the menu list, instead of on the menu name.
My custom menu won't go away when I close the Fruitsweets database.	Menus live in Access, not in individual databases. To remove the custom menu, you'll have to remove it permanently: press and hold down the Alt key while you drag the menu away from the menu bar. Drop the menu on the Access desktop, then release the Alt key. If you want to use the menu again, you must rebuild it from scratch.

WRAP UP

Before you finish, let's go over some of the things you learned in this lesson:

- You added a custom toolbar to your database.

- You added buttons to your custom toolbar.

- You added a custom menu to your Access menu bar.

- You added macro commands to your custom menu.

For more practice, create your own personal toolbar with only the buttons you commonly use; add more menus and menu commands to the Access menu bar; and change the icons for the commands in the new menus.

In the final lesson, you'll learn how to create an AutoExec macro to open the database with the Switchboard form displayed, and you'll learn how to publish data from the database on the Web.

Polishing and Publishing

GOALS

In this lesson, you'll master the following skills and concepts:

20 MINUTES

- Creating a startup macro
- Testing a startup macro
- Creating a query and report for a Web page
- Creating an HTML file for a Web page

Creating a startup macro

GET READY

To complete this lesson's exercise, you'll need to start Access 97 and open the Fruitsweets database. For this exercise, you'll use the Fruitsweets database that you've been working in throughout Part IV.

When you finish these exercises, you'll know how to create a startup macro that opens the Switchboard whenever you open the database and how to publish information from your database on the Web — either on your company intranet or on the worldwide Internet.

MAKING A GRAND ENTRANCE

In the last couple of lessons, you created several database objects that make the database easier for an Access novice to use: custom menus, a custom toolbar, and a switchboard form. But if a user must click the Forms tab, hunt through the long list of forms for the Switchboard, and then open the Switchboard to use it, just how much easier have you really made the database?

To make the database truly simple to use, you can have the Switchboard open automatically when the database opens. The easiest way to open a form when the database opens is to create a macro named "AutoExec". AutoExec is a macro name that Access recognizes, like the AutoKeys macro you created in Lesson 10. Access will run the AutoExec macro automatically when the database opens.

To begin this lesson, you should have the Fruitsweets database open.

Creating a startup macro

In this exercise, you'll create an AutoExec macro that automatically opens the Switchboard form when you open the Fruitsweets database.

1 On the Macros tab, click the New button.

A new macro window appears.

2 Click Window; then click Tile Vertically.

The database window and the macro window are tiled side-by-side.

3 In the Database window, click the Forms tab.

4 Drag the Switchboard form name from the Database window to the macro window.

5 Drop it in the Action column.

A new OpenForm macro action is created, with the action arguments filled in.

6 Save the macro as **AutoExec**; then close the Macro window.

7 Click Fruitsweets ➤ Quit Access.

The Fruitsweets database and Access close.

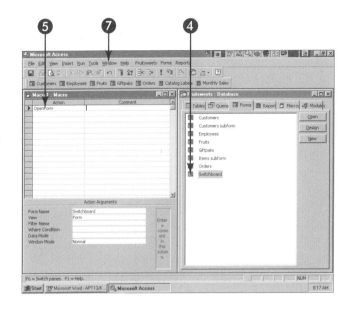

Testing a startup macro

Now you'll test the new macro.

1 Start Access.

Access starts normally.

2 Open the Fruitsweets database.

The database opens and then the Switchboard form opens. Your screen should look similar to the accompanying illustration.

TIP

To open the database without running the AutoExec macro, hold down the Shift key while you open the database.

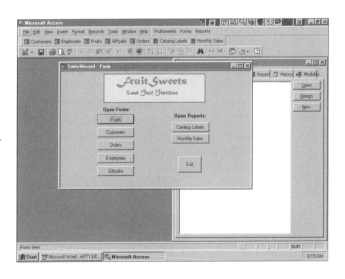

13

Polishing and Publishing

Creating a report for a Web page

PUBLISHING DATA ON THE WEB

This being the age of the Internet and the corporate intranet, Fruitsweets has decided to join the stampede and establish a presence on the Web. The basic element of a Web site is an HTML file, which formats your database information appropriately for publication on the World Wide Web.

HTML is an acronym for Hypertext Markup Language, which is a system for "marking up" a document so it's formatted for publishing on the World Wide Web.

Access makes it easy to create HTML files from a database object like a report. In these exercises, you'll create a report that shows a list of Fruitsweets giftpaks with descriptions and prices; then you'll create an HTML file from the report.

Setting up a Web site on a server is beyond the scope of this book; still, in this section, you'll learn the basics of creating functional HTML files, and you'll be ready with Web pages when you or your company's information systems troops decide to publish online.

Creating a query and report for a Web page

Access can create both static HTML files, in which the data doesn't change, and dynamic HTML files, in which the most current data in the database is shown in the Web page. This book covers only static files, which are simple to create and suitable for information such as a list of Fruitsweets giftpak names, descriptions, and prices.

In this exercise, you'll create a query and report that show just the information you want to publish on the Web page: a list of giftpak names, descriptions, and prices.

Creation of the query and report is covered quickly here; if you get lost, refer to Lesson 6 (Queries) and Lesson 9 (Reports) for help.

Creating a report for a Web page

TIP

To move the Switchboard form out of your way, you can either minimize it or close it. You won't need it for the remainder of this lesson.

1 Create a new query from the Giftpaks table.

2 Include the GiftpakName, GiftpakDescription, and Price fields.

In Design view, your query should look similar to the accompanying illustration.

3 Save the query as **Giftpak Descriptions qry**.

4 Close the query.

5 Use the Report Wizard to create a report from the Giftpak Descriptions qry query.

6 Supply the following information to the wizard:

- Include all three fields

- No grouping

- Sort by GiftpakName, in ascending order

- Use a Tabular layout and a Portrait orientation

- Use any Style you want

- Save the report with the name **Giftpak Descriptions**

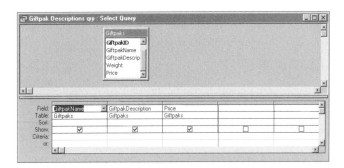

NOTE

Your chosen Style won't be translated into HTML formatting, so it doesn't matter which style you choose.

Your finished report should look similar to the accompanying illustration.

7 Close the report.

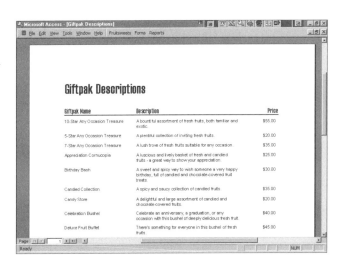

13

Polishing and Publishing

Creating an HTML file for a Web site

▶ ## Creating an HTML file for a Web site

In this exercise, you'll create an HTML file (a Web page) from your report.

1 On the Reports tab, select the Giftpak Descriptions report name, but don't open it.

2 Click File, then click Save As/Export.

3 In the Save As dialog box, verify that the To An External File Or Database option button is selected.

4 Click OK.

The Save Report 'Giftpak Descriptions' As dialog box appears, as shown in the accompanying figure.

5 Navigate to your Access One Step at a Time folder.

6 In the Save As Type box, select HTML Documents (*.html; *.htm).

7 Click the AutoStart checkbox.

TIP

AutoStart starts your Web browser, so you can see the new Web page as soon as you finish creating it. AutoStart won't dial your online service; it just starts the browser and displays your file as if you had surfed to it online.

Your dialog box should look like the one in the accompanying illustration.

8 Click Export.

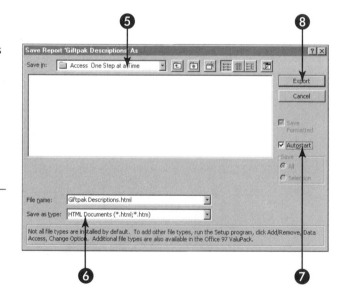

The HTML Output Options dialog box appears.

If you have an HTML template file that you use for a standard Web page layout—standard coloring, logos in the header and footer, and so forth—you can browse for the path to that file in this dialog box. If you don't have a template, Access will create the Web page in a standard, default (plain) style.

9 Leave the HTML Template box blank.

10 Click OK.

Your Web browser starts, and your new Web page is displayed, as shown in the accompanying illustration.

The report is two pages long; therefore, Access created two files (one file for each page). If you scroll to the bottom of the page, you'll see hyperlinks for navigation between the two pages. Click Next or Last to see the second page and then click First or Previous to return to the first page.

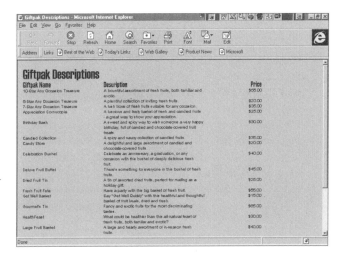

You can add the new file to your Favorites list and open it later by double-clicking it in your Favorites folder. In the Microsoft Internet Explorer, select Favorites ➢ Add To Favorites to add the page's path to your list of favorite Web sites; in other browsers, use whatever means are available for saving your favorite Web sites for a quick return.

11 When you finish playing with your new Web pages, close your browser.

Skills challenge

You are probably wondering how to create a product order form for your Web site, so that customers can order Fruitsweets giftpaks on-line. This is a more complex procedure than this book can demonstrate, because you'll need specific software that's not part of Access 97, but I'll tell you what you need to know to get started, and where to find more information.

If you attempt to publish any of your Fruitsweets forms as static HTML pages, you'll get the form datasheet (a table of the data underlying the form) rather than the fill-in form, in your HTML page.

The only way to publish a fill-in Access form as an HTML page is to save the form as an ActiveX Server page (also called an .asp file). To display or use an ActiveX Server page, both the page and your database must reside on a Microsoft Windows NT Server which is running both Microsoft Internet Information Server (version 3.0 or higher) and ActiveX Server. You must also have the Microsoft Access Desktop Driver loaded, and a valid DSN, or Data Source Name, designated in order to access the database. The DSN can be designated using the ODBC (Open Database Connectivity) Manager.

If you have all these requirements in place, you can use the Publish To The Web Wizard to publish your form as an ActiveX Server Web page. Users who open the page can add new records, and browse, update, and delete existing records — if you're putting an order form on the Internet, it's a good idea to use a separate form and table so you don't give random Internet surfers access to your Orders table. Better yet, create an HTML page that's an order form users can print out and mail in with a check or credit card number, or use an HTML program like Microsoft FrontPage to create a form users can fill in and send back as e-mail.

To create an ActiveX Server page, click File, then click Save As HTML, and follow the steps in the Publish To The Web Wizard. Fill in all the required information, such as Data Source Name and Server URL, and the wizard creates your page (but unless you have the required software mentioned above, you won't be able to open and view your page).

For more information, click Help ➢ Contents and Index, and on the Index tab, look up Publish To The Web Wizard. You can also find information on-line, at `http://www.microsoft.com/workshop/author/layout/layout.htm`.

SKILLS CHALLENGE: CREATING AN INTEGRATED WEB SITE

In this Skills Challenge, you'll create an integrated Web site consisting of two Fruitsweets tables and one report; then you'll create a home page with hyperlinks to these documents.

To accomplish this easily, you'll use the Publish To The Web Wizard and let it do all the work for you. You should still have the Fruitsweets database open.

TRY OUT THE

INTERACTIVE TUTORIALS

ON YOUR CD!

1 Click File; then click Save As HTML.

The Publish To The Web Wizard starts, and the first wizard step appears.

NOTE *You might want to read the text in each wizard step. It contains a lot of information—useful now while you perform this Skills Challenge, and later, when you're finished with this book.*

2 Click Next.

The second wizard step appears and looks like the one shown in the accompanying illustration.

 Do you remember how to tile windows, so you can drag and drop objects between them easily?

3 On the Tables tab, click the Employees checkbox.

4 Click the Fruits checkbox.

5 Click the Reports tab.

6 Click the Fruits by Category checkbox; then click Next.

The third wizard step appears. Here you can select a template that provides background graphics (you won't select one in this exercise).

 Do you remember how to set any macro to run automatically when the database opens?

7 Click Next.

8 In the fourth wizard step, leave the Static option button selected and click Next.

9 In the fifth wizard step, click the Browse button and browse to the Access One Step at a Time folder.

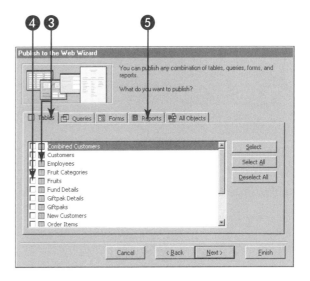

13

Polishing and Publishing

Skills challenge

10 Click Next.

 3 *Do you remember what file format static Web pages are saved in?*

11 In the sixth wizard step, click the Yes I Want To Create A Home Page checkbox.

12 Name the home page **Fruitsweets Data** and click Next.

13 In the seventh (and last) wizard step, click Finish.

The wizard creates Web pages for your three selected database objects and a home page with hyperlinks to each object.

 NOTE *The wizard does not start your browser automatically; so, to see the new files, you must open them yourself.*

14 From the My Computer window or the Windows Explorer window, navigate to your Access One Step at a Time folder.

15 Double-click the `Fruitsweets Data.html` filename.

Your browser opens and displays the home page the wizard created for you. It should look similar to the accompanying illustration.

16 Click the Fruits table. Look familiar?

The Web page is a snapshot of your Fruits table. The data on the Web page is static, so if data in the table changes, you'll need to create a new Web page to update the published data.

4 *Do you remember how to add the path to a Web page to your list of favorites in the Microsoft Internet Explorer browser?*

17 Close your browser.

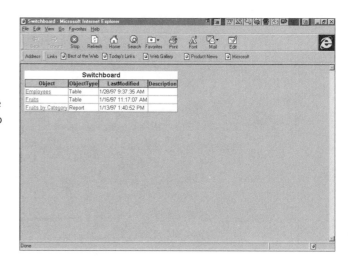

That's it! You've learned enough to be proficient in Access, and you have a good idea of what kinds of things you can do to make your database easy to use and to make the data available to other people, either by printing good-looking reports or by publishing on the Web.

If you want to study Access in depth, IDG Books Worldwide publishes several excellent books that will further your Access expertise. Check out *Access 97 Bible* (Cary Prague, 1997) and *Access 97 Secrets* (Prague & Foxall, 1997).

TROUBLESHOOTING

In this lesson, you learned how to open the Switchboard whenever the database starts and how to publish database information as a Web page. The following solutions might answer some questions that came up during this lesson.

Problem	Solution
My startup macro doesn't run when I open the database.	Be sure you spell the macro name correctly; it must be spelled **AutoExec**.
I added a new giftpak to the database, but it didn't show up on my Web page.	It won't. These are static HTML files, which means they don't change once you create them. To update the information on the Web page, create a new page.
I don't like the widths of the columns in my Web page table; how can I change them?	To change the column widths (or any other aspect) of your static Web page, change the layout in the original table, query, or report; then create a new Web page and delete the old Web page file.

Wrap up

WRAP UP

Before you finish, let's go over some of the things you learned in this lesson:

- You learned how to create a macro that runs automatically when you open the database.

- You learned how to create a static Web page (an HTML file) from a report.

- You learned how to use the Publish To The Web Wizard to create a set of integrated Web pages with a home page.

For more practice, create Web pages from other tables, queries, and reports.

Okay! Now you know Access!

For more ideas on ways you can use Access, check out Appendix B, Practice Projects, which contains a list of project ideas.

What's on the CD-ROM

One Step at a Time Software

The CD-ROM in the back of the book includes the exclusive *One Step at a Time On-Demand* software. This interactive software coaches you through the steps in the book's lessons while you work on a computer at your own pace.

USING THE ONE STEP AT A TIME ON-DEMAND INTERACTIVE SOFTWARE

One Step at a Time On-Demand interactive software includes the tutorials in the book so that you can search for information about how to perform a function or complete a task. You can run the software alone or in combination with the book. The software consists of three modes: Demo, Teacher, and Concurrent. In addition, the Concept option provides an overview of each topic.

- **Demo** mode provides a movie-style demonstration of the same steps that are presented in the book's steps, and works with the sample tutorial files that are included on the CD-ROM in the Exercise folder.

- **Teacher** mode simulates the software environment and permits you to interactively follow the steps in the book's lessons.

- **Concurrent** mode enables you to use the *One Step at a Time On-Demand* features while you work within the actual Access 97 environment. This unique interactive mode provides audio instructions, and directs you to take the correct actions as you work through the tutorials. (Concurrent mode may not be available to all tutorials.)

■ Installing the software

The *One Step at a Time On-Demand* software can be installed on Windows 95 and Windows NT 4.0. To install the interactive software on your computer, follow these steps:

❶ Launch Windows (if you haven't already).

❷ Place the *Access 97 One Step at a Time* CD-ROM in your CD-ROM drive.

3 Click the Start menu.

4 Select Run. The Run dialog box appears.

5 Type **D:\Setup.exe** (where D is your CD-ROM drive) in the Run dialog box.

6 Click OK to run the setup procedure. The On-Demand Installation dialog box appears.

7 Click Continue. The On-Demand Installation Options dialog box appears.

8 Click the Full/Network radio button (if this option is not already selected).

NOTE *Full/Network installation requires approximately 150MB of hard disk space. If you don't have enough hard disk space, click the Standard radio button to choose Standard installation. If you choose standard installation, you should always insert the CD-ROM when you start the software to hear sound.*

9 Click Next. The Determine Installation Drive and Directory dialog box appears.

10 Choose the default drive and directory that appears, or click Change to choose a different drive and directory.

11 Click Next. The Product Selection dialog box appears, which enables you to verify the software you want to install.

12 Click Finish to complete the installation. The On-Demand Installation dialog box displays the progress of the installation. After the installation, the Multiuser Pack Registration dialog box appears.

13 Enter information in the Multiuser Pack Registration dialog box.

14 Click OK. The Password Verification dialog box appears.

15 Click OK. The On-Demand Installation dialog box appears.

16 Click OK to confirm the installation has been successfully completed.

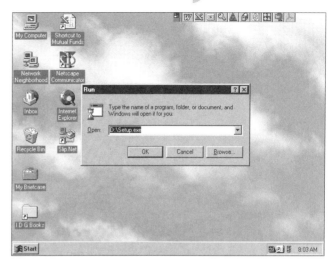

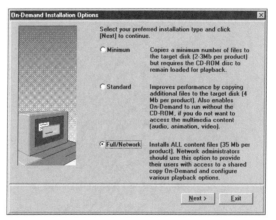

One Step at a Time Software

■ Running the software

Once you've installed the software, you can view the text of the book and follow interactively the steps in each exercise. If you run the *One Step at a Time On-Demand* software in Windows 98, we recommend that you don't work in Teacher or Concurrent modes unless you turn off the Active Desktop feature. However, Teacher mode or Concurrent mode may not work properly at all in Windows 98. At the time of the writing of this book, the final release of Windows 98 wasn't available, so we couldn't test all the topics in Teacher mode or Concurrent mode. To run Demo, Teacher, or Concurrent mode, follow these steps:

1 From the Windows desktop, click the Start menu.

2 Select Programs ➤ IDG Books Worldwide ➤ Access 97 One Step. A small On Demand toolbar appears in the upper-right corner of your screen.

3 Launch Access 97. See Appendix D, "Installing Access 97" for specific instructions.

4 Click the icon of the professor. The Interactive Training — Lesson Selection dialog box appears.

5 Select the Contents tab, if it isn't selected already. A list of the lessons appears, divided into parts.

6 Click the plus icon next to the Parts you want to explore. Lessons appear.

7 Click the plus icon next to the lesson you want to explore. Topics appear. If you wish to work in Concurrent mode, start with the first topic of any lesson because the software will direct you to open a specific file that you will use to complete the steps in that lesson.

8 Double-click a topic of your choice. A menu appears.

9 Select Concept, Demo, Teacher, or Concurrent (if available).

10 Follow the onscreen prompts to use the interactive software and work through the steps.

NOTE *In Demo mode, you only need to perform actions that appear in red. Otherwise, the software automatically demonstrates the actions for you. All you need to do is read the information that appears on screen.*
(Holding down the Shift key pauses the program; releasing the Shift key activates the program.) In Teacher mode, you need to follow the directions and perform the actions that appear on screen.

■ Stopping the program

To stop running the program at any time, press Esc to return to the Interactive Training—Lesson Selection dialog box. (To re-start the software, double-click a topic of your choice and select a mode.)

■ Exiting the program

Press Esc when the Interactive Training—Lesson Selection dialog box appears to exit the program. The On-Demand toolbar appears in the upper right corner of your screen. Click the icon that displays the lightning bolt image. A menu appears. Choose Exit. The On-Demand—Exit dialog box appears. Click Yes to exit On-Demand.

■ Installing additional On-Demand modules

You may install additional modules of On-Demand Interactive Learning and find out more about PTS Learning Systems, the company behind the software, by using a file on the CD-ROM included with this book. Follow these steps:

1 Start your browser.

2 Select File from the menu.

3 Select Open.

4 Type D:\info\welcome.htm, where D is your CD-ROM drive.

5 Click OK to view the contents.

A

What's on the CD-ROM

Using the practice database

USING THE PRACTICE DATABASE

The CD-ROM contains several practice files, including four databases.

The book and practice files are designed in such a way that you only need to use the Fruitsweets.mdb database file. You'll continue using the same database as you work through each lesson in the book. Because you'll build database objects in early lessons that you'll need in later lessons, you'll want to continue working in the same database.

If, however, you want to jump in at Part III, you can begin Lesson 7 with the FSPart3.mdb database file (copy it from the CD-ROM into your Access One Step at a Time folder). If you want to jump in at Part IV, you can begin Lesson 10 with the FSPart4.mdb database file (copy it from the CD-ROM into your Access One Step at a Time folder).

NOTE *If you find you're having problems building forms in Part III, the difficulties may be due to errors made in Part II, when you built some of the tables that are used by the forms. In that case, try using the database* FSPart3.mdb *to begin Lesson 7 and continue using it for the remainder of the book.*

Your CD-ROM contains the following files:

1. The Fruitsweets database, Fruitsweets.mdb—use this database to begin the book lessons at any point up to Lesson 3 and continue using it throughout the lessons if you start at the beginning and work your way through each lesson.

2. FSPart3.mdb, the Fruitsweets database as it exists at the end of Part II—you can use this database file if you want to begin the book lessons at Part III, Lesson 7 (continue to use this file throughout Part III).

3. FSPart4.mdb, the Fruitsweets database as it exists at the end of Part III—you can use this database file if you want to begin the book lessons at Part IV, Lesson 10 (continue to use this file throughout Part IV).

④ `FSFinal.mdb`, the Fruitsweets database as it exists at the end of the book lessons.

⑤ `New Mailing List.xls` and `Shippers.xls`, two Excel 97 files.

⑥ `Gilbert.bmp`, `Logo.bmp`, and `McGinty.bmp`, three bitmap files.

COPYING THE PRACTICE DATABASE

This procedure assumes your My Computer windows are set up so that only one window is open and the contents of that window change each time you double-click a folder in the list. If, instead, a new window opens each time you double-click a folder, many windows will be open on your screen.

TIP

To switch from many windows to a single window, double-click the My Computer icon and in the My Computer window, select View ➢ Options; on the Folder tab, click the Browse Folders By Using A Single Window option button; then click OK and close the My Computer window.

To copy the practice files, you'll create a new folder and copy the practice files into it:

❶ Put the practice CD-ROM into your CD-ROM drive (and ignore it for the moment).

❷ Double-click the My Computer icon on your desktop.

❸ In the My Computer window, double-click your hard drive icon (usually the C drive).

❹ In the list of folders, double-click Windows.

❺ In the list of folders in the Windows window, double-click Favorites.

❻ Select File ➢ New ➢ Folder.

A

What's on the CD-ROM

Copying the practice database

7 Type **Access One Step at a Time** and press Enter.

A new folder is created in your Favorites folder; when you want to quickly navigate the new folder in the future, you'll click the Look In Favorites button on the toolbar of any Open dialog box.

8 Double-click the new Access One Step at a Time folder.

The Access One Step at a Time folder will be empty; you'll copy your practice files into it in the next steps.

9 Double-click the My Computer icon on your desktop.

A second window opens; there should be a My Computer window and an Access One Step at a Time window open. You can drag their title bars to line them up side by side.

10 In the My Computer window, double-click your CD-ROM drive icon.

TIP

You can also select the CD-ROM drive from the drop-down list in the toolbar.

11 In the CD-ROM drive window, double-click the Exercise folder.

12 Choose Edit ➢ Select All or press Ctrl+A to select all the files in the CD-ROM window.

13 Drag any file in the selected group to move the whole group into the Access One Step at a Time window; then drop them (release the mouse button).

The files are copied into the Access One Step at a Time folder.

14 With all files still selected in the Access One Step at a Time folder, select Properties from the File menu and click the Read-only attribute check box so it's no longer checked.

15 Click OK to close the dialog box.

16 Close both windows.

17 Remove your CD-ROM and replace it in the envelope in the book.

Don't lose track of the CD-ROM—you may need to use the remaining database files later.

Now you are ready to begin your Access 97 training.

Practice Projects and Database Design

Practice projects

Now that you know how to customize an Access database to work for you, you'll want to keep your new skills honed. The best way to integrate and ingrain your new skills into your mental database of Access knowledge is to put those skills to work, creatively and often. As the saying goes, Practice Makes Perfect!

To help you practice and sharpen your skills, I've listed some ideas for other databases you can create in Access, along with a rough idea of the objects you'll want to include in each.

At the end of this appendix is a list of ideas, questions, and details to keep in mind when you plan a new database, to help keep the process going smoothly.

PRACTICE PROJECTS

The databases I've suggested are not simple, flat-file databases—you can create those more easily in Excel; rather, my suggestions are for more complex databases that require multiple, related tables for efficient data storage, and queries, forms, and reports to simplify data entry and extraction.

Pick a project you can use in real life; then get creative with it. Everything you need to know, you've already learned; refer to appropriate lessons in this book if you need to brush up on any aspect of your project.

■ Project 1: A competitive sporting event

For a project such as a gymnastics meet, horse show, or dog obedience trial, for example, you'll need tables for competitor information, family/owner/coach information, events, entry fees, event results; and junction tables between the competitors and events tables.

You'll want entry forms to enter all information that a competitor provides or that you might need to keep track of for official reasons.

You'll want reports for event rosters, winners in each event, point standings and championships, entry fees paid and owed, and a mailing list of all competitors for next year's competition.

Project 2: Sports league statistics

To keep track of Little League baseball, Pop Warner football, or youth soccer statistics, you'll need tables for player information, family and coach information, team information, league information, game locations, game times and schedules, game scores, and individual statistics.

You'll want entry forms to enter all information that a competitor provides, or that you might need to keep track of for official reasons, including game scores, individual statistics, and schedules.

You'll want reports for game scores, league standings, season statistics for each player, the season schedule, and, as always, a mailing list.

Project 3: A professional agency

To organize information for an entertainment, writers, or actors agency, you'll need tables for individual client information, venue (contractor) information, standard contract information, individual contract information, fees due and received, and other agencies (for referrals).

You'll want entry forms to enter all information that a client provides, including contract data, venue data, fees due and received, and referrals.

You'll want reports for client histories, specific contract information, venue/contractor schedules, fee schedules, and a mailing list for holiday greetings.

Project 4: School records

To maintain a database for a public school, college, parks and recreation department classes, or community extracurricular school, you'll need tables for class details, departments, student information, faculty information, class locations, and class schedules; and junction tables between classes and students and between classes and faculty.

You'll want entry forms to enter student information, faculty information, class details, and fees due and paid.

Practice projects

You'll want reports for a class/department catalog, class/student lists, faculty/class lists, grade reports, fees due and paid, and mailing lists.

■ Project 5: A retail business

A database for a bookstore or hardware or stationery store will need tables for products, suppliers, employees, and customers; and a junction table between customers and products (to track and target the sort of products specific customers are interested in).

You'll want entry forms to enter employee information, supplier information, customer names and addresses, products, and product availability.

You'll want reports for inventory and stock on hand, employee histories and birthdays, supplier contact phone lists, and customer mailing lists.

■ Project 6: A production business

A database for a business such as a bakery, woodworking shop, or furniture factory will need tables for equipment inventory, materials and supplies inventory, supplier information, employee information, product parts, finished product information and finished product inventory, orders/sales, invoices paid and due, customer information; and junction tables between materials/supplies and finished products (to track what materials are used to create each finished product) and between customers and finished products.

You'll want entry forms to enter new equipment and new supplies details, supplier information, product information, stock on hand, sales/orders information, and customer information.

You'll want reports for inventories of equipment, supplies, and finished products; sales/orders and parts/supplies lists for each finished product, a supplier phone list, and customer mailing lists.

■ Project 7: A professional services firm

A database for a law office or accounting or architectural firm will
need tables for client information, services offered and fee schedules,
billable time spent on individual projects/cases, and employee
information.

You'll want entry forms to enter client information and time
spent on individual projects/cases.

You'll want reports for client invoices detailing time spent and
lists of fees paid and due.

DESIGNING A DATABASE

A database is such an integrated project that a bit of planning before
you begin creating database objects will save you a lot of time in the
long run. If you don't plan ahead, you'll be forever recreating and
redesigning your database objects.

Start with a pencil and paper and begin sketching the results
you want and the objects you'll need to achieve those results; then
sketch the relationships between objects and the more detailed
requirements dictated by those relationships.

Some questions to keep in mind as you sketch are:

- What sets of data will I have? What logical tables should I create
  to store those sets of data efficiently?

- How will the various tables be related? Which tables will have
  many-to-many relationships and need junction tables to relate
  them to one another?

- What data will I be entering, and into which tables? How
  complex will my data entry forms need to be? Will they need
  subforms? How will the forms and subforms be related?

- What data type will each table field need, so that the matching
  fields in different tables can be related to one another?

- What output will I need in the form of reports? Does the data in
  some reports need to be grouped and subtotaled? How should
  the data be grouped? What expressions will I need?

Designing a database

- What queries will I need to create before I build each form and report? Do any queries need calculated fields in order to sum up the calculations in a report or form?

- Are there any ways macros can automate the process of entering and retrieving data?

You should end up with detailed sketches of each report, form, table, and query and notes about the relationships between them. The more time you spend in the planning stage, the less time you'll spend actually creating the database.

As you build the various database objects, take time to test each object with mock data as you go, so that you can catch problems before they are too deeply embedded in the database structure. Use easy mock data—short, easy-to-type names and round numbers—so that the results of calculations are easy to verify.

When you use mock data in a table that has a field with an AutoNumber data type, you'll notice that when you delete the mock data, you lose the numbers in the AutoNumber field— AutoNumber won't reuse numbers that were previously used, even if they've been deleted—but you can fix that. When you are finished designing and testing the database, you can create a new AutoNumber field for the table:

❶ Delete any relationships for the table.

❷ Delete the AutoNumber field.

❸ Create a new AutoNumber field in the table, identical to the one you deleted. (Be sure you designate the primary key again.)

❹ Recreate the table relationships.

The new AutoNumber field will begin at 1.

Now, the best way to get good at building databases is to build them! Building Access databases can be addictive—once you've created one, you'll want to create more, and each one will get easier. Enjoy!

Answers to Bonus Questions

Answers to Bonus Questions

This appendix contains the answers to the Bonus Questions from the Fitness Challenge in each lesson.

■ Bonus Question 1.1

Do you remember how to open a new record?

Click the New Record scroll button at the bottom of the table.

■ Bonus Question 1.2

How can you switch to Design view?

On the toolbar, click the View button.

■ Bonus Question 1.3

Do you remember how to size a form window to fit the form?

Select Window ➢ Size To Fit Form.

■ Bonus Question 1.4

How can you tell if this datasheet view is a table or a query?

Look at the title bar.

■ Bonus Question 1.5

How can you find out what table or tables a query is based on?

Switch to Design view.

■ Bonus Question 1.6

How can you see the entire page?

In Print Preview, click the report page with the zoom pointer.

Answers to Bonus Questions

■ Bonus Question 2.1

Do you remember how to start the New Database Wizard if Access is already open?

Select File ➢ New Database.

■ Bonus Question 2.2

How many tables are included in the Book Collection database?

Five tables are included in the Book Collection database.

■ Bonus Question 2.3

What is the purpose of the AutoNumber data type in the Author ID field?

AutoNumber is a consecutive number that is automatically assigned by Access, so that each record's ID number is unique.

■ Bonus Question 2.4

Do you remember how to delete a database from your computer's hard drive?

To completely delete a database, you need to delete it from the Recycle Bin (double-click the Recycle Bin icon on your desktop; then delete the database from the Recycle Bin list).

■ Bonus Question 3.1

Do you remember what keystroke copies data from the cell above?

Ctrl+' (apostrophe)

■ Bonus Question 3.2

Do you remember what a drop-down list is called?

A Combo box.

C

Answers to Bonus Questions

APPENDIXES **289**

Answers to Bonus Questions

■ Bonus Question 3.3

How can you tell which record is currently selected?

The right-pointing triangle in the record selector column points to the current record; a pencil icon in the record selector column means that changes in the current record are not saved yet.

■ Bonus Question 3.4

Do you remember how to save changes to a record?

Click in or select a different record.

■ Bonus Question 3.5

Do you remember how to delete a record?

Click the record's record selector; then press Delete.

■ Bonus Question 4.1

Which toolbar button can you click to search for a specific record?

The Find button.

■ Bonus Question 4.2

Which toolbar button sorts records from Z–A or 10–1?

The Sort Descending button.

■ Bonus Question 4.3

Do you remember how to raise row heights (from Lesson 3)?

Drag a border in the row selector column downward (with the mouse).

■ Bonus Question 4.4

How can you get a close-up view of the page preview?

Click the page with the zoom pointer.

Answers to Bonus Questions

■ **Bonus Question 4.5**

Do you remember how to reapply this filter the next time you open the Customers table?

On the toolbar, click Apply Filter.

■ **Bonus Question 5.1**

Do you remember how to set a primary key in a table?

In Design view, select the field row; then on the toolbar, click Primary Key.

■ **Bonus Question 5.2**

If a field has an AutoNumber data type, what data type and size does its related field have to be?

Number and Long Integer.

■ **Bonus Question 5.3**

Do you remember how to set up a many-to-many relationship?

Create a junction table, so that each of the tables in the many-to-many relationship has a one-to-many relationship with the junction table.

■ **Bonus Question 5.4**

Do you remember how to create a lookup field in a table?

In the field's Data Type, select Lookup Wizard and let the wizard create the lookup field for you.

■ **Bonus Question 5.5**

Do you remember how to change the width of a column in a table?

Answers to Bonus Questions

■ Bonus Question 5.6

When you save the Relationships window, what is saved?

The layout, or display, in the window (saving the layout does not affect the relationships).

■ Bonus Question 6.1

Do you remember how to create a table relationship in the query design window?

The same way as in the Relationships window—drag a field from one table and drop it on a matching field in the other table.

■ Bonus Question 6.2

Do you remember how to sort a query by two or more fields?

Select a sort order in each field's sort cell; then drag the fields into sort order, from left to right.

■ Bonus Question 6.3

Do you remember where to enter criteria?

In the QBE grid, in the field's Criteria cell.

■ Bonus Question 6.4

Do you remember how to create a query parameter?

Type the parameter message in square brackets in the field's Criteria cell in the QBE grid.

■ Bonus Question 7.1

How can you tell what table or query a form is based on?

Open the form in Design view; then double-click an area outside the form grid; in the Form Properties dialog box, on the Data tab, check the Record Source.

■ Bonus Question 7.2

How can you delete a partial record you've entered?

Select Edit ➤ Undo Current Field/Record.

■ Bonus Question 7.3

How can you move or resize several controls at once?

Drag through the controls, so that the rectangle touches them all; then move or resize the group.

■ Bonus Question 7.4

Do you remember how to align several controls with one another?

Drag to select the group you want to align; then select the Format ➤ Align command.

■ Bonus Question 7.5

How can you quickly resize a label to show all of its text?

Select the label; then select Format ➤ Size ➤ To Fit.

■ Bonus Question 7.6

Do you remember how to combine two related forms into a subform/main form?

Open the main form in Design view, then drag the subform name from the database window onto the main form grid; double-click the new subform control; then click Properties; click in the Link Child Fields box; then click the Build button and make sure Access has selected appropriate linking fields for the two forms (or select them yourself); click OK.

Answers to Bonus Questions

■ Bonus Question 8.1

Do you remember where to change the settings for record selectors, scrollbars, and navigation buttons in a form?

In the Properties dialog box for the form, on the Format tab.

■ Bonus Question 8.2

How can you change an attribute for several controls simultaneously?

Select the controls as a group, by holding down Shift while you click each control or by dragging to select them; then change the attribute.

■ Bonus Question 8.3

What's a good way to ensure accuracy in data entry?

Use controls such as option groups, combo boxes, and list boxes in your forms.

■ Bonus Question 8.4

How do you refer to a field name in a calculated control?

Enclose the field name in square brackets.

■ Bonus Question 8.5

How can you change the tab order in a form?

Open the form in Design view; then select View ➢ Tab Order; in the Tab Order dialog box, select and drag control names into the tab order you want.

■ Bonus Question 8.6

Do you remember how to copy the formatting (font, color, and so on) from one control to other controls?

Select the control you want to copy; then click the Format Painter button on the Standard toolbar; then click the control to which you want to copy the format.

■ Bonus Question 9.1

Do you remember how to create an AutoReport?

On the toolbar, click the down arrow on the New Object button; then click AutoReport.

■ Bonus Question 9.2

Do you remember how to add a new group level to a finished report?

In Design view, click the Sorting And Grouping button on the toolbar; in the Field/Expression column, add the field or expression name you want to group.

■ Bonus Question 9.3

What's the difference between a text box in the Detail section and the same text box in a group header section?

In the Detail section, the text box shows all the records in the underlying query or table; in a group header section, the same text box shows the records as consolidated groups.

■ Bonus Question 9.4

Do you remember how to format the value in a text box (as Currency, for example)?

Right-click the text box; then click Properties; on the Format tab, in the Format box, select a number format for the displayed value.

Answers to Bonus Questions

■ Bonus Question 9.5

Do you remember how to create mailing labels in Access?

On the Reports tab, click the New button; select the query or report you want to create labels from and then double-click Label Wizard.

■ Bonus Question 10.1

Do you remember how to open a control's Properties dialog box?

Double-click the control or right-click the control and click Properties.

■ Bonus Question 10.2

Do you remember where to attach a macro to a control event?

In the control's Properties dialog box, on the Event tab.

■ Bonus Question 10.3

How can you build a control without the wizard's help?

In the Controls Toolbox, click the Control Wizards button to turn it off.

■ Bonus Question 10.4

Do you remember where to give a control a logical (memorable) name?

In the control's Properties dialog box, on the Other tab, in the Name box.

■ Bonus Question 10.5

How can you find a list of macro actions?

Open a macro window and click the down arrow in any cell in the Actions column.

Answers to Bonus Questions

■ Bonus Question 10.6

How can you get quick help about an action or argument?

Click in the cell that contains the action or argument you want help with. A brief help tip is displayed on the right side of the arguments pane, and you can press F1 for more in-depth help.

■ Bonus Question 10.7

How can you test a new macro before you attach it to a control event?

In the Database window, on the Macros tab, select the macro name and click the Run button.

■ Bonus Question 11.1

Do you remember how to create a new form from scratch?

On the Forms tab, click the New button; then double-click Design View.

■ Bonus Question 11.2

Do you remember how to quickly create an OpenForm macro?

Drag the form name from the Forms tab in the database window to the Action column in the macro window.

■ Bonus Question 11.3

How can you quickly create a command button to run a macro?

Drag the macro name from the Macros tab in the database window to the Form grid.

■ Bonus Question 11.4

Do you remember how to place a picture on a form?

In the Controls Toolbox, click the Image control; then click in the Form grid; select a picture in the Insert Picture dialog box and click OK.

C

Answers to Bonus Questions

APPENDIXES **297**

Answers to Bonus Questions

■ **Bonus Question 11.5**

How can you remove scroll bars, record selectors, and navigation buttons from a form?

In the form's Properties dialog box, on the Format tab, select No or Neither for these settings.

■ **Bonus Question 11.6**

How can you create a macro group?

Create all the macros in one macro window; select View ➢ Macro Names to display the Macro Name column; save the macro window with the group name and enter individual names for each separate macro in the Macro Name column.

■ **Bonus Question 12.1**

Do you remember how to create a new toolbar?

In the Customize dialog box, on the Toolbars tab, click the New button.

■ **Bonus Question 12.2**

What's a quick way to rearrange toolbar buttons?

Hold down the Alt key and drag the buttons to new positions (this works even if the Customize dialog box is not displayed).

■ **Bonus Question 12.3**

Do you remember how to change the ToolTip for a toolbar button?

With the Customize dialog box displayed, right-click the button and click Properties; then type the new ToolTip text in the ToolTip box.

■ Bonus Question 12.4

Do you remember how to add a new menu to the Access menu bar?

In the Customize dialog box, on the Commands tab, select the New Menu category; then drag the New Menu command to the menu bar.

■ Bonus Question 12.5

Do you remember how to add commands to a menu?

In the Customize dialog box displayed, on the Commands tab, select the category that contains the command(s) you want to add to the menu; then drag commands to the menu and drop them on the dropped-down menu list.

■ Bonus Question 13.1

Do you remember how to tile windows, so you can drag and drop objects between them easily?

Select Window ➢ Tile Vertically.

■ Bonus Question 13.2

Do you remember how to set any macro to run automatically when the database opens?

Name the macro **AutoExec**.

■ Bonus Question 13.3

Do you remember what file format static Web pages are saved in?

HTML file format, or `* .html`.

■ Bonus Question 13.4

Do you remember how to add the path to a Web page to your list of favorites in the Microsoft Internet Explorer browser?

Open the page in the browser; then select Favorites ➢ Add To Favorites.

Installing Access 97

Get ready

This appendix contains instructions for installing Access 97.

GET READY

These instructions assume that you're loading Access 97 from a CD-ROM, that your CD-ROM drive is labeled (D:), and that you have sufficient space to support a typical installation (about 121MB).

INSTALLING ACCESS 97

Follow the instructions in your Microsoft Office 97 or Microsoft Access 97 documentation to install Access 97.

You may have done a "Typical" installation when you installed the software, but for the lessons in this book, you need to make one small change: you need to install the Access Advanced Wizards.

■ Installing the Advanced Wizards when installing Office 97

To install the Advanced Wizards when you first install the software, complete the following steps:

1 Run a "Custom" installation.

2 In the dialog box that allows you to choose options to install, click the Microsoft Access option; then click the Change Options button.

3 Click the Advanced Wizards check box; then click OK.

4 Click the Continue button and continue installing Office 97.

- **Installing the Advanced Wizards after Installing Office 97**

To install the Advanced Wizards after you've installed Microsoft Access 97, complete the following steps:

1 Close all open programs.

2 Click the Start button on your taskbar.

3 Point to Settings; then click Control Panel.

4 Double-click Add/Remove Programs.

5 Select Microsoft Office 97 and click the Add/Remove button.

6 In the Setup dialog box, click the Add/Remove button.

7 In the Maintenance dialog box, select Microsoft Access; then click the Change Options button.

8 Click the Advanced Wizards check box; then click OK.

9 Click the Continue button and continue to follow the steps without making any further changes.

This glossary contains simple definitions of the common computer terms you encounter in this book and in using Access 97. Although this section provides basic definitions of many terms, it's not exhaustive; don't forget that you can also use the Contents and Index command in the Access 97 Help menu to search for information on terms you may not understand.

A

access key A keystroke or key combination that performs the same activity as clicking a button or selecting a menu command (also called *hot key*). An example is pressing Ctrl+C to copy.

application A database in which related tasks have been organized and rendered simple and error-proof, so a user can focus on the job at hand rather than on how Access works.

AutoExec A macro name that Access recognizes; AutoExec macros run automatically when the database opens.

AutoForm A form that's created automatically by the Form Wizard with no user input.

AutoKeys A macro name that Access recognizes; AutoKeys macros attach macro actions to keystrokes.

AutoNumber A field data type that automatically stores a unique number for each record that's added to a table. Numbers generated by an AutoNumber field can't be changed or replaced. When relating tables, a field with the AutoNumber data type matches a field with a Number data type, size Long Integer.

AutoReport A report that is created automatically by the Report Wizard with no user input.

B

bound control A control that's tied to a specific field in a query or table to display the data in that field.

bound object frame An object frame that displays objects (usually graphic objects) that are stored in a table field; a bound object frame displays a specific object for each record in the table.

C

calculated control An unbound control (usually a text box) that contains an expression that calculates the values in other controls in a form or report.

calculated field A query field that contains an expression that performs calculations on the values in other fields in the query.

caption (field caption) The field column heading that's displayed in Datasheet view; it doesn't have to be identical to the field *name*.

cell In Datasheet view, the intersection of a row and a column.

check box

check box A control that displays Yes/No data graphically; a check mark in the check box means Yes and a blank check box means No.

combo box A control that allows you to select a value from a list or type a new value into the list; used by a Lookup Field to look up values in another table.

command button A button-shaped control that runs a macro or carries out an event procedure.

concatenate To join two values to display them as a single value; for example, if you concatenate a FirstName field to a LastName field, as in [FirstName]&[LastName], the two names are displayed as a full name in a single field.

control An object on a form or report that displays data, performs an action, or adds graphics to the form or report (examples are text boxes, image controls, option buttons, labels, command buttons, and subform controls).

criteria A limiting condition, such as "Arizona" or ">100"; used in queries and filters to show a limited set of records.

crosstab query A query that displays values in a spreadsheet-style table.

D

data The information stored in a table in a database.

data type A field property that determines what type of data the field can contain (for example: number, text, date/time, or Yes/No).

database A collection of data related to a particular topic; a single file that contains all the tables, queries, forms, and reports for that collection of information.

database objects Tables, queries, reports, forms, macros, and modules that are the functional parts of a database.

database tabs The tabs (like index card tabs) along the top of the database window that allow you to display a list of like objects in a database: tables, queries, forms, reports, macros, or modules.

database window The window that appears when you first open a database; it gives you access to all the objects in a database.

Datasheet view A view that displays records in a row-and-column format similar to a spreadsheet; this view allows you to see many records at the same time.

Design view A view that allows you to design and change tables, queries, forms, reports, and macros.

detail section The section of a report or form where individual records from an underlying table or query are displayed.

display format The format in which data are displayed in a form or report; doesn't alter the value of the data, only the format (for example, the number 1.234 can be displayed as 1.23 or 1 or $1.23 or 123%).

drag and drop The action of dragging an object from one place and releasing it in another place to move or copy the object to a new position. To drag an object, position the mouse pointer over the object and press and hold the mouse button while you move the mouse (and the object); to drop the object, release the mouse button.

dynaset The set of records that results from running a query or a filter.

E

expression A formula that calculates a value or defines a criteria; you can use an expression in any database object to calculate new values or to specify which records should be displayed.

Expression Builder An Access feature that helps you to build expressions by providing correctly spelled object names and correct expression syntax.

external table A table outside the open database (can be in another Access database or in a spreadsheet file or text file).

F

field A category of information, such as Last Name or Fruit Type; a column in a Datasheet view.

field list A list of all the fields in an underlying table or query; available by clicking the Field List button on a Design view toolbar for a form or report.

field selector The gray caption box at the top of a column in Datasheet view; it can be clicked to select the entire field.

filter A set of criteria you apply to records in a table, query, or form to show a specific subset of those records, and to hide any records not meeting the criteria.

focus The ability to receive user input through mouse or keyboard actions; only one object can have the focus at any given time: the object that's currently active and awaiting user input.

form A database object that holds controls for entering, editing, and displaying data from an underlying table or query.

Form view A view that usually displays data one record at a time, with added graphical elements for easier reading; this view is convenient for entering and editing data in tables.

G

group In a report, a collection of similar records that are grouped together.

group footer The section of a report where calculations or information that apply to a single group of records are displayed.

group header The section of a report where labels and information that apply to a single group of records are displayed.

H

hyperlink Colored and underlined text that you click to jump to an Internet or intranet Web page; usually begins with "http://". A hyperlink to a file on your computer consists of the path enclosed in # symbols, like this: `#c:\windows\personal\letter.doc#`

I

image control A control that displays a picture or other graphical image unrelated to any specific tables or records; similar to an unbound object frame, but faster to load.

import The process of copying data from another source (database, spreadsheet, and so on) into your open database.

input mask A control property that determines display format and limits the type of data that can be entered; it makes data entry faster and more precise.

insertion point A flashing vertical line that shows where typed characters will appear.

Internet A worldwide network of thousands of smaller computer networks.

intranet An internal organization network that uses Internet technologies, such as hyperlinks, to move between destinations on the network.

J

join A relationship between a field in one table and a field with the same data type in another table; a *join line* is the graphical representation of the relationship.

junction table A table that provides a link between two tables that have a many-to-many relationship; the junction table has a one-to-many relationship with each of the two tables it links.

L

label A control that displays informational text on a form or report (always unbound).

link The connection between a source file and a destination file.

linked table A table stored outside the open database, but from which the database can access records.

list box A control that displays a list of values from which you can select.

lookup field A field that looks up a list of values in another table; uses a combo box to present the list of values for selection.

M

macro A set of one or more actions that each perform a particular operation, such as opening a form or printing a report.

macro group A collection of related macros stored together under a single macro name.

many-to-many relationship A relationship between two tables in which each table can have many related records in the other table.

N

name (field name) The name by which Access recognizes a field; it does not have to be identical to the user-friendly field caption that

name (field name)

a field's column heading displays in Datasheet view.

navigation area The area at the bottom of a form, report, table, or query window where you can click scroll buttons to select specific records.

O

one-to-many relationship A relationship between two tables in which only one table (the *primary* table) can have many related records in the other table (the *related* table).

one-to-one relationship A relationship between two tables in which each table has only one related record in the other table.

option button A control in a form for entering a value in a specific field; it allows you to select only one of multiple choices.

option group A group of option buttons that works together to provide a limited selection of data entry choices.

P

page footer Text and/or graphics that appear at the bottom of each page in a

report (page footers often contain page numbers).

page header Text and/or graphics that appear at the top of each page in a report (page headers often contain column headings).

palette A small dialog box of choices that drops down when you click a toolbar button (such as the Fill/Back Color and Line/Border Color buttons); palettes can be dragged away from the toolbar to "float" in the Access window, so you can use them repeatedly without having to open them each time.

parameter query A query that asks for user-entered parameters—criteria—to determine which records to display.

primary key One or more fields in a table whose values uniquely identify each record.

primary table The table on the "one" side of a one-to-many relationship.

Print Preview A report view that shows how your report will look when it's printed.

property An attribute of an object that you can set to determine the object's behavior and characteristics.

Q

QBE (query by example) A technique for designing queries by dragging and dropping fields from tables into a grid in the query Design view window.

query A database object that shows specific data you want to work with; the data may be drawn from multiple related tables, may have several filters applied, and may include calculated expressions.

R

record A set of information that belongs together, such as a customer's name and address information, or details about a giftpak.

record selector The gray box at the left side of each record in a Datasheet view; you click the record selector to select the entire record.

related table The table on the "many" side of a one-to-many relationship.

relational database A database type in which information is stored in separate but related tables, which allows for nonredundant (and,

therefore, more efficient) data storage and retrieval.

relationship between tables The association between two tables that share a field with matching values; the matching fields allow the tables to be joined, so that a query can select data from both tables.

report A database object that presents data organized and formatted to your specifications.

report footer Text and/or graphics that appear at the very end of a report; report footers often contain summaries and grand totals.

report header Text and/or graphics that appear at the very beginning of a report; report headers often contain the report title and a company logo.

requery To run a query again; requerying updates a query dynaset with any new records that were added since the query last ran.

S

shortcut menu A menu of commands that appears when you right-click an object; the commands are those most commonly used for the object you right-clicked.

sort order The order in which records are displayed; records may be sorted in ascending order (A–Z or 1–9) or descending order (Z–A or 9–1).

status bar The bar at the bottom of the screen that displays information about the activity on your screen.

subform A form within another form.

subform control The rectangular control that represents the subform when the main form is in Design view; a subform control has properties that are different and separate from the properties of the subform itself.

T

tab order The order in which the focus moves from control to control on a form when you press the Tab key.

table A collection of data with the same subject or topic; data are stored in records (rows) and fields (columns).

text box A control that displays a value from a field or

from an expression's calculation; it's often used to enter or edit data in a field.

toolbar The horizontal bar that contains toolbar buttons that you can click to carry out menu or macro commands (in Access, the toolbar changes depending on which object and view are displayed).

toolbox Also called Controls Toolbox; the toolbar that contains the buttons for creating controls in Design view.

U

unbound control A control that's not tied to a specific field in a query or table; you can use an unbound control to display general information or to perform calculations on the values in other controls in a form or report.

unbound object frame An object frame that displays objects (usually graphic objects) that are not stored in a table; an unbound object frame always displays the same object regardless of which record is displayed.

underlying table or query The table or query that contains the data you want to display in a form or report.

URL Uniform Resource Locator; an address for a destination on the Internet or on an organization's intranet.

V

value The data contained in a single field in a single record; for example, a customer's first name or a record's ID number.

W

Web The World Wide Web, part of the Internet.

Web page A text document written with the HTML Web-authoring language, so that it can be published on the World Wide Web or an organizational intranet.

Web site One or more linked Web pages that are accessible through a home page on the World Wide Web or an organizational intranet.

wizards Access features that help you create database objects by asking you questions and then using your input to create the objects.

Z

zoom pointer The mouse pointer; takes the shape of a magnifying glass when you

move it over a report in Print Preview; clicking the zoom pointer magnifies and reduces the report view.

Glossary

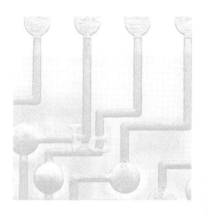

B–C

B

background patterns, 25
Between . . . And criteria operator, 105
bound controls, 128
browsers
    opening manually when publishing
        reports to Web, 268
    saving favorite sites in, 265
    starting with Autostart, 264
buttons
    adding to toolbars, 249–251
    changing images on, 251, 255
    defining access keys for, 243
    rearranging and removing from
        toolbar, 256
    on switchboards, 235

C

calculated controls
    adding to forms, 157–161
    creating with Expression Builder, 161
    defined, 128
    illustrated, 150
    troubleshooting errors with, 180–181
    See also controls
calculated fields, 130–131
calculations
    adding to reports, 195
    with queries, 115–116
    See also totals
captions
    changing form, 133
    changing text for onscreen reports,
        191
    defined, 75
    as field attribute, 72, 73, 74

illustrated, 11, 69, 70, 75
vs. field name, 68, 74
CD-ROM
    databases on, 10
    installing practice databases, 9
cells, dropping macros in, 237
changing
    the Office Assistant character, 19
    Properties dialog box, 153
    row height in Datasheet view, 41
Chart Wizard, 201–205
charts
    adding to existing reports, 205
    creating, 201–205
Child Field
    linking to Master Field, 138
    troubleshooting links with Master
        Field, 145
Clear Layout button, 81
Clip mode option (Properties dialog
    box), 142
Close command, 41
closing
    Access 97, 20
    databases with macros, 242–243
    Office Assistant, 19
    switchboards, 263
    tables, 41
    with X close box, 12
column labels, 194
columnar format, 126
columns
    changing width on Web page
        table, 269
    moving in Datasheet view, 107
    resizing width of, 149
    viewing in forms, 181
    See also fields

combining tables, 47–48
combo box
    adding to forms, 155–157
    illustrated, 12, 16
    in Orders form, 126
Combo Box Wizard, 155–157
Command Button Wizard, 164–166
command buttons
    adding to forms, 164–166
    changing size of, 217
    creating
        in switchboards, 235, 239–241
        without Control Wizards, 227
    defined, 162
    in Orders form, 126
    running macros with, 162, 215–218
comments, adding to macros, 226
concatenating names
    in one field, 101–102, 111
    troubleshooting First Name and Last
        Name, 120
concatenation expression, 102
consolidating data with queries,
    112–114
Control Source box (Text Box dialog
    box), 160
Control Wizards
    creating controls without, 217
    turning off and on, 227
controls
    about, 127–128
    attaching macros to, 223–224
    copying and pasting, 240
    disabling, 170–171
    moving, 136, 138
    See also calculated controls; command
        buttons
Controls toolbox, 15

continued

Index

D–E

continued

forms *(continued)*
  setting
    tab order for, 168–170
    validation rules and validation text, 167
  subforms and controls, 125–128
    designing, 126
    main forms and subforms, 127
  testing, 171–173
  troubleshooting, 144–145
    modifying forms, 180–181
  validating data entry, 166–167
  See also main forms; subforms; switchboards
Fruitsweets.mdb database, 10

G

grand totals, 208
greater than (>) criteria operator, 105
group footers, 186
group headers, 186
group levels, 196–197
grouped reports
  creating, 192–194
  illustrated, 185
grouping, reformatting and, 152
Grouping Options button (Report Wizard), 193

H

headers and footers
  adding calculated controls to footer, 158–159
  adding calculations to report footers, 195
  adding to forms, 143
  illustrated on report, 186

help, 18–19
  for AutoKeys, 225
  context-sensitive help in Design view, 69
  for criteria operators for queries, 106
  for Expression Builder, 161
  for macro arguments, 218, 220
  for macros, 228
  publishing fill-in forms on Web, 266
  for Visual Basic, 228
  See also Office Assistant
hiding and showing custom toolbars, 251
HTML (Hypertext Markup Language), 262
  creating HTML files, 264–266
  saving files in HTML format, 264
hyperlinks, 90

I

icons
  linked table, 49
  magnifying glass, 17
  Office Assistant, 19
  pencil, 43
  primary key, 73
  record selector, 14, 42
ID fields
  creating, 129
  illustrated, 13
  for junction tables, 85
ID numbers
  automatic, 27, 73
  reuse of, 173
  troubleshooting opening, 180
image controls, adding to forms, 140–144
images, button, 251, 255

Import dialog box, 45
Import Spreadsheet Wizard, 46
importing data, 45–46, 52–53
In A New Table option button (Import Spreadsheet Wizard), 46
In criteria operator, 105
indexed attribute, 75
Input Mask attribute
  adding punctuation with, 76
  defined, 75
insertion point, 42
installing Advanced Wizards, 139
Is Not Null criteria operator, 105
Is Null criteria operator, 105
Items subform
  in Design view, 150
  in Orders form, 126

J

join lines, 82, 110
junction tables
  creating, 85–88, 119
  creating relationships with, 88
  function of, 84
  illustrated, 69
  troubleshooting, 94

K

key combinations
  for backing up to previous field, 15
  replacing with macros, 224
key icon, 73
keystrokes
  avoiding Access keystrokes in macros, 224–225
  creating AutoKey macros, 226
  defining access keys for buttons, 243
  troubleshooting macro names for, 227

M-O

Q–R

queries (continued)
  selecting information for, 99
  setting
    order date criteria, 112
    parameters for, 108–109
  for a single table, 100–101
  sorting, 106–107
  troubleshooting, 119–120
  using .qry suffix, 130
  vs. filters, 98
Query Wizards, 99

R

reconfiguring forms, 134–137
record selector column, 70, 75
record selectors
  illustrated, 14, 41, 42
  removing from switchboards, 235
records
  defined, 2
  deleting, 44
    filtered, 62
  entering new, 166
  illustrated in table, 11
  reuse of deleted ID numbers, 173
  scrolling backward through, 40
  selecting grouping intervals for, 193
  typing first letters in lookup fields, 43
recovering databases, 32
Recycle Bin, recovering deleted
    databases from, 29, 32
refining forms, 148–150
  the Customers subform, 150–152
  the Items subform, 153–154
reformatting text boxes, 152
related table, 81
relational databases, 2, 3

relationship lines
  illustrated, 82
  removing, 110
relationships
  among tables, 81–82
  many-to-many, 81, 83–85, 89–93
  one-to-many, 69, 81
  one-to-one, 81
  setting up junction table, 88
  troubleshooting table, 94
  understanding, 80–81
Relationships window
  clearing, 81
  illustrated, 69
  many-to-many relationships, 83
  saving layout in, 89
Remove Filter button, 60
replacing text, 44
report header, 186
report title labels, 194
reports, 183–210
  about, 10, 11, 12
  adding
    calculations to, 195
    charts to existing, 205
    a new group level, 196–197
  changing look of, 197–199
  correcting errors, 32
  creating
    AutoReports, 187–188
    charts, 201–205
    detailed reports, 189–192
    grouped reports, 192–194
    macros to open, 242–243
    mailing labels, 199–201
    with parameter queries, 199
    queries and reports for Web pages,
      262–263
    for Web page, 262–263

  customizing design of, 194–195
  exercises creating mailing labels and,
      205–208
  opening with macros, 221
  parts of, 17–18
  previewing, 18, 186
  printing, 28, 188
  selecting printing options, 188–189
  troubleshooting, 208–209
  types of, 185
requerying
  subforms, 165
  table with F9 key, 172
  troubleshooting, 181
Required attribute, 73, 74
Reset button, restoring built-in toolbars
      with, 256
resizing
  charts, 203–204
  command buttons, 217
  forms, 144
  height of rows, 116
  rows, 41
  tables, 12
  width of columns, 149
Restore button, 221, 234
retrieving data, 55–66
  exercises for, 64–65
  filtering
    to find groups of records, 58–59
    related records, 59–60
  with OR filter, 60–62
  printing from datasheets, 63
  searching for specific records, 57–58
  sorting records
    by number fields, 57
    by text fields, 56–57
  troubleshooting sorting and filtering
      tables, 65–66

T

Now it's easy to remember what you just learned and more...

With *On-Demand*, you'll never rely on the help function again – or your money back.

...ducing *On-Demand Interactive Learning*™ — the remark-...software that actually makes corrections to your documents ...ou. Unlike the standard help function that merely provides ...ned" responses to your requests for help or makes ...write down a list of complicated instructions, *On-...and* lets you learn while you work.

...current Mode — makes the **changes for you** in your document.

...her Mode — *guides you* step-by-step to ...e changes safely outside your document.

...o Mode — *shows you* how the changes are ...e safely outside your document.

On-Demand take care of the software commands for you. ...follow the on-screen pointer and fill in the information, and ...l learn in the fastest and easiest way possible — without ...eaving your document.

In fact, *On-Demand* makes your work so easy, it's *guaranteed* to help you finish complicated documents neatly and on time. With over eleven years in software education and a development staff that's logged more than 5,000 hours of classroom teaching time, it's no wonder that Fortune 500 corporations around the world use *On-Demand* to make learning for their employees quicker and more effective.

"On-Demand Interactive Learning for Word 97. The best training title of this group..." —PC World

The Concurrent Mode Difference

Concurrent Mode guides you through learning new functions without having to stop for directions. Right before your eyes, a moving pointer clicks on the right buttons and icons for you and then lets you fill in the information.

"On-Demand lets me get my work done and learn without slowing me down." —**Rosemarie Hasson, Quad Micro**

...ES AVAILABLE FOR: Windows® 3.1, 95, NT, Microsoft® Word, Microsoft Excel, Microsoft PowerPoint, Microsoft Access, ...soft Internet Explorer, Lotus® SmartSuite, Lotus Notes, and more! Call for additional titles.

...AY GUARANTEE:
...*Demand* at the introductory price of **$32**⁹⁵ (U.S. dollars) for one title or pay **$29**⁹⁵ (U.S. dollars) each for two titles. That's a ...s of almost 10%. Use *On-Demand* for 30 days. If you don't learn more in a shorter period of time, simply return the software ...Learning Systems with your receipt for a full refund (this guarantee is good only for purchases made directly from PTS).

On Demand
Interactive Learning™

...all PTS at 800-387-8878 ext. 3053 or 610-337-8878 ext. 3053 outside the U.S.

PTS Learning Systems

IDG103197

IDG BOOKS WORLDWIDE, INC.
END-USER LICENSE AGREEMENT

READ THIS. You should carefully read these terms and conditions before opening the software packet(s) included with this book ("Book"). This is a license agreement ("Agreement") between you and IDG Books Worldwide, Inc. ("IDGB"). By opening the accompanying software packet(s), you acknowledge that you have read and accept the following terms and conditions. If you do not agree and do not want to be bound by such terms and conditions, promptly return the Book and the unopened software packet(s) to the place you obtained them for a full refund.

1. License Grant. IDGB grants to you (either an individual or entity) a nonexclusive license to use one copy of the enclosed software program(s) (collectively, the "Software") solely for your own personal or business purposes on a single computer (whether a standard computer or a workstation component of a multiuser network). The Software is in use on a computer when it is loaded into temporary memory (RAM) or installed into permanent memory (hard disk, CD-ROM, or other storage device). IDGB reserves all rights not expressly granted herein.

2. Ownership. IDGB is the owner of all right, title, and interest, including copyright, in and to the compilation of the Software recorded on the disk(s) or CD-ROM ("Software Media"). Copyright to the individual programs recorded on the Software Media is owned by the author or other authorized copyright owner of each program. Ownership of the Software and all proprietary rights relating thereto remain with IDGB and its licensers.

3. Restrictions On Use and Transfer.

(a) You may only (i) make one copy of the Software for backup or archival purposes, or (ii) transfer the Software to a single hard disk, provided that you keep the original for backup or archival purposes. You may not (i) rent or lease the Software, (ii) copy or reproduce the Software through a LAN or other network system or through any computer subscriber system or bulletin-board system, or (iii) modify, adapt, or create derivative works based on the Software.

(b) You may not reverse engineer, decompile, or disassemble the Software. You may transfer the Software and user documentation on a permanent basis, provided that the transferee agrees to accept the terms and conditions of this Agreement and you retain no copies. If the Software is an update or has been updated, any transfer must include the most recent update and all prior versions.

4. Restrictions On Use of Individual Programs. You must follow the individual requirements and restrictions detailed for each individual program in Appendix A, "What's on the CD-ROM," of this Book. These limitations are also contained in the individual license agreements recorded on the Software Media. These limitations may include a requirement that after using the program for a specified period of time, the user must pay a registration fee or discontinue use. By opening the Software packet(s), you will be agreeing to abide by the licenses and restrictions for these individual programs that are detailed in Appendix A, "What's on the CD-ROM," and on the Software Media. None of the material on this Software Media or listed in this Book may ever be redistributed, in original or modified form, for commercial purposes.

5. Limited Warranty.

(a) IDGB warrants that the Software and Software Media are free from defects in materials and workmanship under normal use for a period of sixty (60) days from the date of purchase of this Book. If IDGB receives notification within the warranty period of defects in materials or workmanship, IDGB will replace the defective Software Media.

(b) **IDGB AND THE AUTHOR OF THE BOOK DISCLAIM ALL OTHER WARRANTIES, EXPRESS OR IMPLIED, INCLUDING WITHOUT LIMITATION IMPLIED WARRANTIES OF MERCHANTABILITY AND FITNESS FOR A PARTICULAR PURPOSE, WITH RESPECT TO THE SOFTWARE, THE PROGRAMS, THE SOURCE CODE CONTAINED THEREIN, AND/OR THE TECHNIQUES DESCRIBED IN THIS BOOK. IDGB DOES NOT WARRANT THAT THE FUNCTIONS CONTAINED IN THE SOFTWARE WILL MEET YOUR REQUIREMENTS OR THAT THE OPERATION OF THE SOFTWARE WILL BE ERROR FREE.**

(c) This limited warranty gives you specific legal rights, and you may have other rights that vary from jurisdiction to jurisdiction.

6. Remedies.

(a) IDGB's entire liability and your exclusive remedy for defects in materials and workmanship shall be limited to replacement of the Software Media, which may be returned to IDGB with a copy of your receipt at the following address: Software Media Fulfillment Department, Attn.: *Access 97 One Step at a Time*, IDG Books Worldwide, Inc., 7260 Shadeland Station, Ste. 100, Indianapolis, IN 46256, or call 1-800-762-2974. Please allow three to four weeks for delivery. This Limited Warranty is void if failure of the Software Media has resulted from accident, abuse, or misapplication. Any replacement Software Media will be warranted for the remainder of the original warranty period or thirty (30) days, whichever is longer.

(b) In no event shall IDGB or the author be liable for any damages whatsoever (including without limitation damages for loss of business profits, business interruption, loss of business information, or any other pecuniary loss) arising from the use of or inability to use the Book or the Software, even if IDGB has been advised of the possibility of such damages.

(c) Because some jurisdictions do not allow the exclusion or limitation of liability for consequential or incidental damages, the above limitation or exclusion may not apply to you.

7. U.S. Government Restricted Rights.
Use, duplication, or disclosure of the Software by the U.S. Government is subject to restrictions stated in paragraph (c)(1)(ii) of the Rights in Technical Data and Computer Software clause of DFARS 252.227-7013, and in subparagraphs (a) through (d) of the Commercial Computer—Restricted Rights clause at FAR 52.227-19, and in similar clauses in the NASA FAR supplement, when applicable.

8. General.
This Agreement constitutes the entire understanding of the parties and revokes and supersedes all prior agreements, oral or written, between them and may not be modified or amended except in a writing signed by both parties hereto that specifically refers to this Agreement. This Agreement shall take precedence over any other documents that may be in conflict herewith. If any one or more provisions contained in this Agreement are held by any court or tribunal to be invalid, illegal, or otherwise unenforceable, each and every other provision shall remain in full force and effect.

my2cents.idgbooks.com

Register This Book — And Win!

Visit **http://my2cents.idgbooks.com** to register this book and we'll automatically enter you in our monthly prize giveaway. It's also your opportunity to give us feedback: let us know what you thought of this book and how you would like to see other topics covered.

Not on the Web yet? It's easy to get started with *Discover the Internet,* at local retailers everywhere (see our retailer list at IDG Books Online).

Discover IDG Books Online!

The IDG Books Online Web site is your online resource for tackling technology — at home and at the office.

Ten Productive and Career-Enhancing Things You Can Do at www.idgbooks.com

1. Nab source code for your own programming projects.

2. Download software.

3. Read Web exclusives: special articles and book excerpts by IDG Books Worldwide authors.

4. Take advantage of resources to help you advance your career as a Novell or Microsoft professional.

5. Buy IDG Books Worldwide titles or find a convenient bookstore that carries them.

6. Register your book and win a prize.

7. Chat live online with authors.

8. Sign up for regular e-mail updates about our latest books.

9. Suggest a book you'd like to read or write.

10. Give us your 2¢ about our books and about our Web site.

CD-ROM INSTALLATION INSTRUCTIONS

The CD-ROM includes the interactive *One Step at a Time On-Demand* software. This software coaches you through the exercises in the book while you work on a computer at your own pace.

INSTALLING THE ONE STEP AT A TIME ON-DEMAND INTERACTIVE SOFTWARE

The *One Step at a Time On-Demand* software can be installed on Windows 95 and Windows NT 4.0. To install the interactive software on your computer, follow these steps:

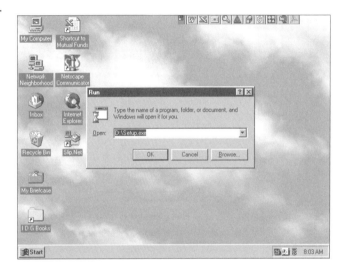

❶ Launch Windows (if you haven't already).

❷ Place the *Access 97 One Step at a Time* CD-ROM in your CD-ROM drive.

❸ Click the Start menu.

❹ Select Run. The Run dialog box appears.

❺ Type **D:\Setup.exe** (where D is your CD-ROM drive) in the Run dialog box.

❻ Click OK to run the setup procedure. The On-Demand Installation dialog box appears.

❼ Click Continue. The On-Demand Installation Options dialog box appears.

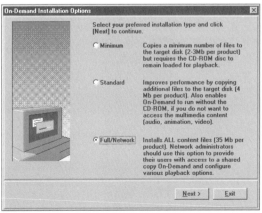

❽ Click the Full/Network radio button (if this option is not already selected).

NOTE

Full/Network installation requires approximately 150MB of hard disk space. If you don't have enough hard disk space, click the Standard radio button to choose Standard installation. If you choose standard installation, you should always insert the CD-ROM when you start the software to hear sound.

9 Click Next. The Determine Installation Drive and Directory dialog box appears.

10 Choose the default drive and directory that appears, or click Change to choose a different drive and directory.

11 Click Next. The Product Selection dialog box appears, which enables you to verify the software you want to install.

12 Click Finish to complete the installation. The On-Demand Installation dialog box displays the progress of the installation. After the installation, the Multiuser Pack Registration dialog box appears.

13 Enter information in the Multiuser Pack Registration dialog box.

14 Click OK. The On-Demand Installation dialog box appears.

15 Click OK to confirm the installation has been successfully completed.

Please see Appendix A, "What's on the CD-ROM," for information about running the *One Step at a Time On-Demand* interactive software.

If you run the One Step at a Time On-Demand *software in Windows 98, we recommend that you don't work in Teacher or Concurrent modes unless you turn off the Active Desktop feature. However, Teacher mode or Concurrent mode may not work properly at all in Windows 98. At the time of the writing of this book, the final release of Windows 98 wasn't available, so we couldn't test all the topics in Teacher mode or Concurrent mode.*

COPYING THE PRACTICE DATABASE

To copy the practice files, you'll create a new folder and copy the practice files into it:

1 Put the practice CD-ROM into your CD-ROM drive (and ignore it for the moment).

2 Double-click the My Computer icon on your desktop.

3 In the My Computer window, double-click your hard drive icon (usually the C drive).

4 In the list of folders, double-click Windows.

5 In the list of folders in the Windows window, double-click Favorites.

6 Select File ➢ New ➢ Folder.

7 Type **Access One Step at a Time** and press Enter.

A new folder is created in your Favorites folder; when you want to quickly navigate the new folder in the future, you'll click the Look In Favorites button on the toolbar of any Open dialog box.

8 Double-click the new Access One Step at a Time folder.

The Access One Step at a Time folder will be empty; you'll copy your practice files into it in the next steps.

9 Double-click the My Computer icon on your desktop.

A second window opens; there should be a My Computer window and an Access One Step at a Time window open. You can drag their title bars to line them up side by side.

10 In the My Computer window, double-click your CD-ROM drive icon.

TIP You can also select the CD-ROM drive from the drop-down list in the toolbar.

⑪ In the CD-ROM drive window, double-click the Exercise folder.

⑫ Choose Edit ➤ Select All or press Ctrl+A to select all the files in the CD-ROM drive window.

⑬ Drag any file in the selected group to move the whole group into the Access One Step at a Time window; then drop them (release the mouse button).

The files are copied into the Access One Step at a Time folder.

⑭ With all the files still selected in the Access One Step at a Time folder, select Properties from the File menu and click the Read-only attribute check box so it is no longer checked.

⑮ Click OK to close the dialog box.

⑯ Close both windows.

⑰ Remove your CD-ROM and replace it in the envelope in the book.